T0330584

Routledge Revivals

Capitalism and Public Policy in the UK

First published in 1985, *Capitalism and Public Policy in the UK* provides a comprehensive account of the development, contemporary character and impact of public policy in the UK. It relates public policy to the distinctive features of capitalism, class relations and the state. The first chapter is used to outline the theoretical framework adopted throughout the book. This sees public policy as strongly influenced by the requirements of the capitalist mode of production, the balance of class forces, historical influences, gender divisions and international relations. Each of the subsequent chapters focuses on a particular area of policy. The relevant theoretical concepts are first introduced followed by an historical account of the development of policy with particular emphasis on the post-1945 period. Where appropriate the impact of a particular area of policy on inequalities of class, gender, race and age is examined. Finally, the impact of each area of policy and the state to the process of economic change, to class relations and to other social divisions. It will be of interest to all those studying the state, public policy and political economy generally.

Capitalism and Public Policy in the UK

Tom Burden and Mike Campbell

First published in 1985
By Croom Helm Ltd

This edition first published in 2023 by Routledge
4 Park Square, Milton Park, Abingdon, Oxon, OX14 4RN
and by Routledge
605 Third Avenue, New York, NY 10017

Routledge is an imprint of the Taylor & Francis Group, an informa business

Publisher's Note
The publisher has gone to great lengths to ensure the quality of this reprint but points out that some imperfections in the original copies may be apparent.

Disclaimer
The publisher has made every effort to trace copyright holders and welcomes correspondence from those they have been unable to contact.

A Library of Congress record exists under ISBN: 0709906854

ISBN: 978-1-032-54057-3 (hbk)
ISBN: 978-1-003-41530-5 (ebk)
ISBN: 978-1-032-54129-7 (pbk)

Book DOI 10.4324/9781003415305

Capitalism and Public Policy in the UK

Tom Burden and Mike Campbell

CROOM HELM
London • Sydney • Dover, New Hampshire

© 1985 Tom Burden and Mike Campbell
Croom Helm Ltd, Provident House, Burrell Row,
Beckenham, Kent BR3 1AT
Croom Helm Australia Pty Ltd, Suite 4, 6th Floor,
64–76 Kippax Street, Surry Hills, NSW 2010, Australia

British Library Cataloguing in Publication Data

Burden, Tom
  Capitalism and public policy in the UK.
  1. Capitalism 2. Great Britain — Economic
  conditions — 1945– .
  I. Title II. Campbell, Mike
  330.12′2′0941   HC256.6

  ISBN 0-7099-0685-4
  ISBN 0-7099-0686-2 Pbk

Croom Helm Ltd, Washington Street,
Dover, New Hampshire 03820, USA

Library of Congress Cataloging in Publication Data

Burden, Tom.
  Capitalism and public policy in the UK.

  Includes index.
  1. Communism — Great Britain. 2. Great Britain —
  Economic policy. Capitalism — Great Britain.
  I. Campbell, Mike. II. Title.
  HX244.B87 1985   320.5′32   85-9995
  ISBN 0-7099-0685-4
  ISBN 0-7099-0686-2 Pbk

Phototypeset by Sunrise Setting, Torquay, Devon
Printed and bound in Great Britain by
Biddles Ltd, Guildford and King's Lynn

CONTENTS

PREFACE

This book aims to provide an analysis of the nature, development and impact of public policy in the UK. The range of policies dealt with covers those directed towards the economy, industry, labour, incomes, housing, health and welfare, education and science, law and order, and foreign relations. Throughout, a Marxist framework is employed, relating policy to the changing structure and organisation of capital, labour and the state. As such, the approach is one of 'political economy' which breaks down the barriers to understanding posed by employing orthodox academic disciplines. The book also attempts to overcome the divide between highly abstract analyses of the state, on the one hand, and a purely descriptive approach to policies, on the other.

The book does not assume a substantial prior knowledge either of Marxism, or the policy areas discussed, or orthodox academic disciplines. The book's layout and approach is designed to assist the reader in organising his/her own understanding of the issues raised. The book can be read sequentially, or individual chapters can be read independently, or indeed themes can be explored by following the advice given in the last section of Chapter 1. In order to save space footnotes have not been used, but at the end of each chapter there is a short guide to further reading. This includes both general references and other references classified according to the chapter subsections to which they are relevant. A substantial bibliography (over 500 entries) keyed to the Contents may, however, be obtained on application to the authors.

We hope the book will prove useful to students studying the state, political economy and government policy, in politics, economics, sociology, social policy and public policy courses. It will also be useful to academics interested in policy, the state, political economy and British capitalism generally. Indeed, we hope that anyone who is interested in the role of the state and government policy, including those actively involved in politics, will find it of value.

The process of joint authorship, like all collective endeavours, has proved both difficult and rewarding. Future literary archaeologists may wish to know that the first drafts of Chapters 2, 3 and 4 were written by Campbell and the rest by Burden. These drafts were then jointly rewritten. Thanks are due to Jim Butterfield, Mary Heycock, Jim Morgan, Helen Pickering, Paul Sutton and Maria Tighe, who read and commented on various chapters. However, given the scope of the book, errors and omissions no doubt remain. Finally, our thanks to Rosa Hall, Jean Harmer, Anne Haworth and Sue Widdowson who deciphered and typed the manuscript, often under pressure of time and at a rate of pay regrettably typical of that provided for female wage labour.

Tom Burden
Mike Campbell

1 MARXISM AND PUBLIC POLICY

1.1 The Needs of Capital: Accumulation, Legitimation and Security

The aims of this book are fourfold: first, to examine the historical development and the present character of both public policy and the state in the UK; second, to pursue these objectives using a Marxist approach which links public policy and the nature of the state to the process of capital accumulation and to class relations; third, to examine the determinants of policy and policy changes; and fourth, to examine the impact of public policy on social inequality and on the operation of the capitalist system. The central organising concepts of the book are capitalism, the state and public policy. *Capitalism*, here as elsewhere, is used in two senses. It is used in a restricted sense to refer solely to a theoretical model of the '*capitalist mode of production*' (*CMP*), which is characterised by the private ownership of capital and by wage labour. The term capitalism is also used more loosely to refer to actual capitalist societies, as in 'British capitalism'. The *state* is used here to refer to the whole range of institutions and activities in the public or state sector. The state sector needs to be distinguished from privately owned economic enterprises, family and kinship institutions, and political parties, which make up *civil society*. *Public policy* refers collectively to all the different areas of activity undertaken by the state, such as forms of intervention affecting the economy, social services, law and order and foreign policy.

The starting point used in our understanding of public policy is the concept of the '*needs of capital*'. This term describes those essential requirements which have to be met in order for capitalism to continue. When these needs are specified, it is possible to identify the areas of state policy primarily directed towards meeting them. This approach is functionalist in so far as it identifies essential functions that *have* to be performed. In this approach, *accumulation* and *legitimation* are major requirements and thus are foci of policy. Accumulation involves *production* and *reproduction*, each of which is needed to ensure that the CMP generates sufficient profit, while legitimation refers to the requirement for sufficient consent to the existing order to allow it to continue. To these can be added the

Table 1.1: State Intervention and the 'Needs of Capital'

Needs of capital			*What intervention seeks to ensure*
Accumulation	Production	Capital in general	Efficiency of capital in general
		Individual capitals	Accumulation in particular firms or industries
		Labour efficiency	The productive capacity of labour power
	Reproduction	Labour reproduction	The day-to-day ability to provide labour power
		Generational reproduction	The supply of new labour power from rearing children
	Legitimation	Internal security	Ideological acceptance of the existing order
	Security		Minimisation of internal threats to person and property
		External security	Minimisation of external threats to person and property

maintenance of the physical *security* of persons and property within the CMP from internal and external threat.

Since accumulation, legitimation and security are preconditions for the survival of capitalism, they form a major focus for public policy. Table 1.1 summarises schematically the relations between state intervention and the 'needs of capital' in each of these spheres. However, a major weakness of a purely functionalist or 'capital logic' approach to public policy is that it fails to offer historical explanations of the nature of the policies which meet these functions, and moreover explains them as an automatic response to the needs themselves. In addition, such accounts fail to recognise that not all policies are equally 'functional' for capital. These weaknesses are avoided here by the use of a historical approach, and by concrete analysis of the determination and impact of a range of policies. Indeed the analytical framework used recognises the following complexities of 'actual existing' capitalism: class conflict, intra-class divisions within both capital and wage labour; the complex and uneven nature of historical development; and the existence of a degree of political autonomy of the state.

The rest of the chapter is organised as follows. In section 1.2, an outline of the simple Marxist model of the CMP and its treatment of the economy, ideology, the state and class relations is given. In section 1.3, this model is elaborated by the addition of three complicating factors: historical influences, gender and the international dimension. Finally, in sections 1.4 and 1.5 the overall organisation of the book, and how this relates to the theoretical structure, is explained.

1.2 The Marxist Model: Even Development

The term capitalist mode of production (CMP) refers to a simplified theoretical model, not an actual capitalist society. The main purpose of this model is to identify the fundamental linkages and processes that operate in this mode of production, and to provide a set of theoretical concepts and a broad methodology for the analysis of capitalist society. This basic model is simplified by three restrictive devices. (1) History is ignored, in particular the fact that the CMP develops within an already existing mode of production which, in reality, will influence its development. (2) The model is largely 'sex-blind', in that it does not systematically treat the issue of gender. (3)

The model deals with a single capitalist society so that the influence of the international system is not incorporated. The simple model allows a depiction of the range of processes and structures that are intrinsic to the CMP when it develops in a 'pure' form, in which all tendencies can operate without encountering significant barriers to their development.

The Marxist method of analysis is known as *historical materialism*. It is based on the view that the most significant feature of any society is its *mode of production*. The mode of production thus 'determines' the other features of society, in that it is the predominant influence on their development. The simple Marxist model rests on the architectural metaphor of an economic foundation or *base*, on which the other features of society, ideology, the state and class relations, are erected as a *superstructure*. Any mode of production possesses a distinctive combination of two elements: the *forces of production* and the *relations of production*. The forces of production are the resources available for productive work, including capital equipment, technical knowledge, and the size and skill of the labour force. The relations of production are the distinctive forms of ownership and control of productive resources, including both capital equipment and labour.

The relations of production in the CMP involve the ownership of the *means of production* by a *capitalist class* and the existence of a *working class*, the members of which do not own the means of production and have to sell their *labour power* to the capitalist class in order to obtain an income. In the CMP, members of the capitalist class expend money both on means of production (constant capital), which may be fixed (machinery, tools, equipment and so on) or circulating (raw materials, power and so on), and on *labour power* (variable capital). They are able to gain possession of the value of output produced by the labour of workers (*surplus value*), because they can employ them at wages below the value of their output. Those members of the working class available for work who are unable to find employment constitute an *'industrial reserve army'*, which exerts a constant downward pressure on wages by affording a supply of labour for the capitalist class and competition for existing jobs.

Wage labour has a number of distinctive features. It involves submission to the authority of the capitalist at work in a situation where raw materials, tools, machinery and the finished product are all owned by the capitalist, and where control of the *labour process* is in his hands. Workers compete for jobs, and wages are forced down through the competitive process to the lowest level necessary to achieve the *reproduction* of workers' capacity to provide labour power. It is essential to capitalism that the labour force receives sufficient wages to maintain its working capacity and to allow the upbringing of children, who will in turn become part of the labour force. In the CMP, these processes of *labour reproduction* and *generational reproduction* normally occur within the family-household.

The basic dynamic process in the CMP is the *accumulation of capital*. The CMP is characterised by *competition* between individual firms in the search for the maximum extraction of surplus value and hence *profit*. Prices of commodities, however, are forced down through the competitive process and capitalists are forced continually to seek lower costs of production in order to survive. The process of competition between firms and the movement of capital to those lines and locations of production offering the best prospects for profits leads to a tendency for the rate of profit to be equalised throughout the CMP through *the law of value*. The need for firms to reduce costs creates pressure for advances in science and technology, and for their incorporation in the labour process. Competition also forces capitalists to minimise wage costs per unit of output by intensifying the exploitation of labour.

The competitive process leads to the *concentration and centralisation of capital*, as firms are destroyed or taken over by their competitors and industries become dominated by a few large firms. The continual restructuring of production to increase productivity, and thus surplus-value extraction, tends to reduce the numbers of workers employed, and to increase the size of the industrial reserve army, unless markets are expanding fast enough to offset this tendency. Paradoxically, the continual substitution of means of production for labour power, which is designed to *increase* profitability, produces a *tendency for the rate of profit to fall*. This arises because labour power is the only source of surplus value, and hence of profit, and thus a reduced reliance on it reduces the rate of profit under certain conditions. The tendency of the rate of profit to fall exerts pressure on the capitalist class to seek a higher rate in other sectors or nations.

Accumulation, however, does not proceed without interruption. An inherent feature of the CMP is the tendency towards periodic *crises* brought about by a fall in the rate of profit, leading to reductions in investment, employment and output, an acceleration in the destruction of inefficient firms, and downward pressure on wages caused by increased unemployment. The destruction of these unprofitable firms and the downward pressure on wages lead, in turn, to a rise in the rate of profit. In this way economic crises create conditions for a new wave of accumulation.

In the basic model of the CMP, a *dominant ideology* develops to reinforce the economic dominance of capital over labour. Some of the surplus generated in the process of production is used to maintain an intellectual stratum ideologically attached to the capitalist class, which will articulate and disseminate an ideology which justifies the economic and political dominance of the capitalist class. The development of an ideology legitimating the authority and economic dominance of the capitalist class is the basis both for unity within it and a means of ensuring the acquiescence and consent of the working class, who develop a *'false consciousness'* which depicts its own position as favourable or natural and inevitable.

The basic model of the CMP employs an *'instrumentalist'* conception of the state in which it acts as the instrument of the capitalist class whose economic and ideological dominance is augmented by state power to ensure that public policy meets the 'needs of capital'. Public policy towards production involves the maintenance of a legal system through which business contracts necessary for complex patterns of exchange and payment take place. The state will also regulate the currency. Labour and generational reproduction may be aided by the maintenance of a legal basis for the family-household. The state also provides coercive agencies to maintain security in the face of possible individual and collective threats to persons and their property. External security is also maintained through the provision of armed forces.

As the CMP develops, the nature of class relations changes. The working class continues to grow in size as the process of *proletarianisation* takes place, forcing an ever-increasing number to rely on wage labour. The increase in the wealth of the capitalist class and the destruction of small enterprise leads to *class polarisation* between the capitalist and working classes. The search for production at the lowest cost produces a spatial concentration of enterprises based on the cost advantages of particular locations. In turn, the consequent spatial concentration of housing and population produces the *industrial city*, which is the characteristic form of settlement of the CMP. The operations of the urban land market and the high level of resources available to the capitalist class for consumption result in a form of spatial segregation between the housing of capitalists and workers. The growth in the size of firms and their spatial concentration place large numbers of workers in similar conditions, and together with the continuous pressure to minimise wage levels and intensify the labour process, creates the conditions for the emergence of trade unions, as workers seek to better their pay and conditions. The growth of trade union organisation and action within the workplace leads to a growth in intercommunication and co-ordinated action between members of the working class in different communities, occupations, firms and industries. The *class struggle* thus increases in intensity and scope.

These changes in class structure are accompanied by changes in ideology. As conflict between the working class and the capitalist class develops, so too does a counter ideology. At first this attempts to legitimate the demand for better pay and conditions. As the CMP develops further, these develop into political demands. *Democratisation* occurs as access to political participation is widened as a response to the demands of the working class.

The structure and role of the state changes under these conditions, as the changing balance of class forces challenges the hitherto total dominance of capital in determining state policy. The concentration of industry, the increased utilisation of science and technology, and the existence of periodic crises provide opportunities for the state to intervene on behalf of capital. There is a growth of state intervention to improve working-class living standards, due to the growing political influence of the working class. The state also takes on a range of ideological functions as the challenge to the capitalist class develops. Social control is increasingly formalised, and the repressive apparatus and the legal framework are expanded in order to extend control of disorderly behaviour which threatens persons and property. Thus the dynamics of the accumulation process and the changes in class structure and relations lead to growing state intervention as capitalism continues to develop.

The outline of the basic Marxist model of the dynamics of the CMP given above, however, can only be a starting point for analysis, because of its abstract simplicity. Capitalism is not governed by iron laws which operate with uniformity and precision, but by developmental tendencies which encounter various barriers to their full realisation. A more complex depiction of capitalism needs to include the influence of history, gender divisions and international relations. The ways in which these factors modify the intrinsic developmental tendencies provide the key to understanding the specific character of any given capitalist society, in particular the unevenness and complexity of its economic structure, the distinctive nature of ideology, the particular structure and role of the state, and the complex form taken by divisions within, and relations between, classes.

1.3 Uneven Development: History, Gender and the International Environment

The joint effect of these complicating processes is a more complex and uneven pattern of capitalist development. Table 1.2 illustrates the actual complexity of the economy, ideology, the state and class relations (row headings) produced by the impact of historical factors, gender divisions and international influences (column headings). The complexity produced by uneven development makes the task of the state in maintaining capitalism more complex, as can be seen in the final column. These 'key problems' constitute what are sometimes referred to as contradictions, that is, they refer to problems generated by the operation of capitalism that cannot be completely or finally resolved within the existing mode of production.

The influence of *historical factors* is such that any capitalist society will contain elements which developed in the previous mode of production. The CMP does not in reality construct an entire society anew. Accumulation may be affected by the survival of elements of economic organisation pre-dating capitalism. Some sectors of the economy may develop much earlier than others, and this may establish a leading position for them in the economy as a whole. A distinctive spatial and occupational distribution of economic activity may result. Development in other sectors may be retarded as a result of this uneven development. The dominant ideology may incorporate aspects of a previous mode of legitimation. In some peripheral regions and in various professional organisations, capitalist values may not fully penetrate. Parts of the state apparatus may incorporate the practices and ethos of a previous ruling class. The class structure itself may contain significant residual classes from a previous mode of production that have not been displaced, such as a landed aristocracy or a peasantry. Uneven economic development will also divide both the capitalist and the working classes into

Table 1.2: Uneven Development in Actually Existing Capitalism

	Historical factors	*Gender divisions*	*International environment*	*Key problems for the state (i.e. contradictions)*
Economy	Survival of pre-capitalist forms of organisation Uneven economic development	Sexual division of labour Women's disproportionate membership of the reserve army of labour Women's role in labour and generational reproduction	Economic interchanges involving trade and investment International division of labour Barriers to development caused by foreign investment Labour migration	To overcome the negative impact of uneven economic development To maintain mobility of labour and generational reproduction
Ideology	Survival of pre-bourgeois values and culture Incomplete penetration of capitalist values in peripheral regions	Sexism Domesticity Familialism	Nationalism Global ideological struggle	To construct hegemony To combine ideological elements into a coherent whole
State	Survival of archaic parts of the state apparatus Existence of departmental traditions	Patriarchy Maintenance of women's dependence on men Reinforcement of women's domestic role and unequal economic participation	Political interpenetration — colonialism, imperialism and militarism Subjection to foreign political influence Involvement in supra-state bodies	To meet various threats to security To construct a stable ruling bloc To respond to the balance of class forces To maintain the dominance of capitalist class in state
Class structure	Existence of residual classes, such as peasantry and aristocracy Existence of fractions in capitalist and working class	Sexual divisions within classes Existence of women's movement	Ethnic divisions Internationalisation of class structure Class dominance shifted by the outcome of international economic and political rivalries	To maintain divisions in the working class To maintain the unity of the capitalist class

fractions, for example, based on variations in the level of development of productive forces, the size of typical enterprises in an industry, or in regional development.

Gender differences form the second complicating factor. Their origins are partly historical, but the forms they take are also influenced by the nature of capitalist development in any given society. Their significance for the process of accumulation is substantial. The participation of men and women in wage labour is likely to differ, due to barriers to the proletarianisation of women, thus giving rise to a sexual division of labour. Capitalists, and the top levels of management who perform the functions of capital, are normally male, giving a sexual division of ownership. Women usually form a major element in the reserve army of labour. They are also likely to undertake most of the unpaid labour required for labour and generational reproduction. Gender differences are often reflected ideologically in sexism, in which the subordination of women is justified. Women's key role in the family-household may be reinforced by ideological support for domesticity and familialism. Leading positions in the state are likely to be held by men and state policy will reinforce the unequal position of women. Gender differences will also create divisions within classes and provide the conditions for movements based on gender.

The third complicating factor is the *international environment*. Any given capitalist state must now develop in an international system containing both capitalist and socialist states at varying levels of development. This system has a substantial impact. Accumulation will be affected by the pattern of international trade and investment in which the economy is involved. The development of a world economy may also influence domestic economies through the development of an international division of labour. Relations with other states create an important element in dominant ideologies usually in the form of nationalism. In addition, participation in the class struggle on a global scale as in the East-West conflict may also be a basis for ideological mobilisation. The nature of the state is influenced by the existence of other states. Political power or influence may be wielded by one state in the territory of another. State power may be constrained by involvement in supra-state bodies. The state apparatus may be destroyed or strengthened through war. International factors also affect the class structure through the international division of labour, which influences wage levels and the work available in a given state. In addition, labour migration may lead to the existence of ethnic minorities, which can create further divisions in the working class. The degree of dominance of the capitalist class can be affected by the outcome of international economic competition or international political rivalry and conflict.

1.4 Capitalism and Public Policy

We have seen complexities introduced into the analysis of the economy, ideology, the state and the class structure by the influence of historical factors, gender and the international system. In place of the simple conceptions of the basic model (Table 1.1), a highly complex pattern exists (Table 1.2). Moreover the simple relation in the basic model between the mode of production and ideology, the state and class structure is also modified to allow for a substantial degree of reciprocal influence.

While the maintenance of capitalism continues to require the successful performance of the functions of accumulation, legitimation and security, this can now be seen as more problematic and more complex. For example, the uneven development of different sectors of the economy and the possible inadequacy of the arrangements made for labour and generational reproduction threaten accumulation. Legitimation is made more difficult by the complex array of ideological elements that have to be combined somehow into an effective legitimating ideology. This process involves the construction and reconstruction of *hegemony*, in circumstances in which significant ideological shifts can come about from a variety of sources. The achievement of security both internally and externally becomes more difficult, because the sources of threat and potential threat are more widespread. In addition, the state is confronted with an array of complex policy problems in attempting to deal with various threats to accumulation and legitimation which cannot be left to solve themselves. It has to do this in circumstances in which the state apparatus may be inadequately equipped and internally divided, due to the complexities produced by uneven development. In this complex model, the actions of the state are less clearly 'determined' by the 'needs of capital' since these are more difficult to specify, and because the complexity of the possible balance of class forces may allow a range of policies to be pursued. The state thus exhibits a higher degree of *relative autonomy*. The class structure introduces further complications. As well as sexual and ethnic

Table 1.3: Accumulation, legitimation and security, and the structure of the book

Chapter	Global capital	Accumulation Production Selected capital	Labour effiency
2. Economic policy	Stabilises overall demand		Reduces downward wage pressure
3. Industrial policy	Provides energy and raw materials	Subsidises some capital. Reproduces spatial variation	Reduces local labour shortages
4. Labour policy	Reduces labour costs. Allows labour to take part in planning		Improves mobility and training
5. Income support policy	Diverts surplus from capital		Reinforces labour incentives
6. Housing policy	Capital expenditure diverts surplus	Stimulates construction industry	Reduces disease due to bad housing
7. Health and welfare policies	Capital expenditure diverts surplus	Stimulates supply of health facilities and products	Increases fitness and decreases interruptions of working capacity
8. Cultural policy: education, science, and the media	Capital expenditure diverts surplus	Stimulates supply	Provides work-related skills
9. Law and order policy	Protects capital. Secures contracts	Stimulates supply	Regulates industrial conflict
10. Foreign and defence policy	Regulates foreign trade and investment opportunities	Stimulates supply	Immigration as source of cheap labour

Accumulation Reproduction		Legitimation	Security	
Labour reproduction	General reproduction	Legitimation	Internal security	External security
Provides resources for improved wage levels		Reduces un-employment Raises living standards		Maintains over-all economic capacity
		Smoothes rapid change		Maintains strategic industrial base
	Provides 'family wage'	Establishes employee rights Reduces severity of labour conflict	Reduces violent industrial conflict	
Reduces fluctu-ations in family income and pro-vides minimum income level	Provides minimum in-come for non-workers	Maintains surplus population	Provides sub-sistence for non-workers	
Provides con-ditions for main-tenance of working capacity	Provides shelter for non-workers	Reduces homelessness		
Improves health of work force	Improves health Expands dependent population	Demonstrates state concern	Regulates non-political forms of deviance	Maintains fitness for military service
	Socialises process of child-rearing	Habituates to authority Reproduces culture	Regulates behaviour of young	Maintains national and patriotic sentiments
Regulates family	Defines 'liable relatives' to look after dependants	Provides equal rights Enforces state authority	Protects persons and property Establishes public order	
		Provides basis for national identity	Generates rationale for regulation of political deviance	Protects from foreign threat and enforces interests overseas

Note: Reading across the rows shows some of the implications for the capitalist system of the area of policy dealt with in a given chapter. Reading down the columns shows the effects of the policies discussed in various chapters on a particular area crucial to the working of the capitalist system. These effects can be positive or negative. This table is *illustrative* only.

divisions, and the existence of intermediate and residual classes, both the working class and the capitalist class are divided into fractions. This complex class structure influences the exercise of power in the state. In democratic nations, a *ruling bloc* must be constructed in which the dominant fraction of the capitalist class can play a leading role. In addition, a sufficient degree of unity must be maintained within the capitalist class to ensure its support. The working class must either be excluded from power, neutralised ideologically, divided, or allowed to participate only on terms that do not threaten the existence or further development of capitalism.

However, the extent to which policy in general meets the needs of the capitalist class must not be prejudged. The degree of dominance of the capitalist class is never total and varies from one society and from one period to another as a result of different patterns of development and of variations in the balance of class forces. The capitalist class itself may be divided about the degree to which policy should reflect the logic of capital alone. Particular policies may confer substantial benefits on the working class and sections of it. Other policies, designed to aid capital, may also represent gains for the working class. Policies also frequently fail to have the effects sought by those who introduce them. The implications for public policy of this complex and uneven nature of actual capitalist development will be taken up in the following chapters.

1.5 The Plan of the Book — How to Read It

The remainder of the book consists of nine chapters, each dealing with a major area of policy. Those covered include the major areas of state policy in the contemporary UK, and their contribution to accumulation, legitimation and security is a key theme of the book. The order of the chapters is determined by the principal direction of the policy area with which each chapter deals. Chapters 2–7 thus deal with policies *principally* directed towards accumulation. Chapters 2–4 deal with production and Chapters 5–7 deal with reproduction. Chapter 8 deals with legitimation, and Chapters 9 and 10 deal with internal and external security respectively. Table 1.3 shows the overall structure of the book and gives examples (reading across the rows) of the ways in which the different policy areas affect accumulation, legitimation and security. Reading down the columns illustrates the impact of particular 'functions' on various policy areas.

Table 1.4: The Location of Various Themes in Different Chapters

Theme	Chapter								
	2	3	4	5	6	7	8	9	10
Theoretical issues	2.1	3.1 3.2	4.1 4.2 (4.3.6)	5.1 (5.3)	6.1 (6.3)	7.1	8.1	9.1 (9.2.1) (9.2.2)	10.1 (10.3.1) (10.3.2)
Historical development until the Second World War	2.2.1 2.2.2	3.3.1 3.3.2	4.3.1	5.2.1 5.2.2 (5.2.3)	6.2.1	7.2.1 to 7.2.4	8.2.1 (8.3.1) (8.4.1)	(9.2) 9.3 (9.4.1) (9.5.1) (9.6.3)	10.2
Post-War Policy	2.2.3 2.2.4 2.2.5 2.2.7	3.3.3 to 3.3.7	4.3.2 to 4.3.6	(5.2.3) 5.2.4	6.2.2 6.3	7.3	8.2.2 8.2.3 (8.3.1) (8.4.1) (8.4.2)	(9.4.1) (9.5.1) 9.5.2 9.6.2 (9.6.3) 9.7	10.3 10.4
Impact on Inequality (Class, Sex, Race, Age)	(2.2.3) (2.2.8)		4.4	5.4.1 5.4.2	6.4	7.4	8.2.5	9.6.1	
Impact on Capitalism	2.2.6 2.2.8 2.3	3.4	4.5	5.5	6.5	7.5	8.2.6 8.3.2 8.4.3 8.5	9.8	10.5

Notes:　Entries in brackets indicate that only part of the section deals with the designated theme.

Readers wishing to search for particular issues should also consult the detailed table of contents and the index.

The format of the chapters is as far as possible based on a common plan. Every chapter begins with a discussion of theoretical issues by expanding on those elements of the theoretical framework introduced in this chapter which are most relevant to the area of policy under discussion. Every chapter contains a historical account of the development of policy designed to illustrate how key features of policy have arisen. Every chapter also deals in more detail with contemporary policy and its development in the post-war period. Several chapters deal with the impact of policy, either on inequality generally, or on particular groups. Every chapter ends with an analysis of the impact of policy on accumulation, legitimation and security.

This common format enables the book to be used in a variety of ways. As well as being read straight through, the book can be employed to follow particular themes of interest to the reader such as (a) theoretical issues relevant to the study of policy; (b) the historical development of policy; (c) post-war policy; (d) the impact of policy on inequalities; (e) the impact of policy on capitalism in the UK. The sections that deal with these themes are given in Table 1.4.

Further Reading

General

Borstein, S., Held, D. and Krieger, J. (1984) *The State in Capitalist Europe*, George Allen and Unwin

Bottomore, T. (ed.) (1985) *A Dictionary of Marxist Thought*, Basil Blackwell

Brewer, A. (1984) *A Guide to Marx's Capital*, Cambridge University Press

Campbell, M. (1981) *Capitalism in the UK: A Perspective from Marxist Political Economy*, Croom Helm

Coates, D. (1984) *The Context of British Politics*, Hutchinson

Cornforth, M. (1968) *Dialectical Materialism*, Vols. 1 and 2, Lawrence and Wishart

Fine, B. (1984) *Reading Marx's Capital*, Macmillan

Held, D. *et al.*, (eds) (1983) *States and Societies*, Martin Robertson

Jessop, B. (1982) *The Capitalist State*, Martin Robertson

Miliband, R. (1984) *Capitalist Democracy in Britain*, Oxford University Press

Miliband, R. (1977) *Marxism and Politics*, Oxford University Press

McLellan, D. (ed.) (1983) *Marx: The First 100 Years*, Fontana

McLennan, G., Held, D. and Hall, S. (eds) (1984) *State and Society in Contemporary Britain*, Polity Press

Therborn, G. (1980) *What Does the Ruling Class Do When It Rules?*, Verso

Wright, E. O. (1979) *Class, Crisis and the State*, Verso

Readers who wish to follow the developing literature on the state and public policy are advised to consult regularly the following publications: *Capital and Class* (quarterly); *Critical Social Policy* (quarterly); *Labour Research* (monthly); *Marxism Today* (monthly); *New Left Review* (two-monthly); *New Socialist* (monthly); *Socialist Register* (annually).

2 ECONOMIC POLICY

2.1 The Marxist Approach to Economic Policy

This chapter is concerned with the role played by the state in influencing the behaviour and performance of the national economy as a whole. It gives an account of the changing nature of state economic policies and their determinants, as well as an assessment of them. Section 2.1 provides a theoretical examination of the role of the state in economic policy. This is followed in section 2.2 by an analysis of economic policy in the UK from the nineteenth century to date, focusing particularly on the period after 1945. Finally, section 2.3 draws together the major themes of the chapter.

2.1.1 Economic Policy and the Needs of Capital

In the basic model of the CMP, there is a superstructure of institutions of which the state is a part. Thus it is argued that the state reflects the interests of those who own the means of production and so regulates the system on behalf of the capitalist class. State intervention arises both because the state is able to act as the ideal 'collective capitalist', seeing the needs of capital as a whole, resolving antagonisms between individual capitals or fractions of capital, and because, as capitalism develops, its laws of motion create barriers to profitable accumulation and realisation. These include the tendency for the rate of profit to fall, the size of the industrial reserve army, the uneven nature of economic development sectorally, spatially and temporally, and increasing problems of realising the accumulated surplus value. This view of state economic policy sees the origins, developments and limits of state economic policy arising from the needs of capital.

2.1.2 Economic Policy and the Class Struggle

A necessary consequence of the existence of capital is, however, the existence of labour. The relations between these classes are necessarily antagonistic and give rise to struggles. Hence the state acts in the context of such struggles and thus changes in economic policy may arise as a result of the changing balance of class forces. Capital has 'needs', but labour has 'demands'. The resolution of these often competing forces will influence economic policy and the extent to which it benefits capital or labour. The nature of this 'resolution' will depend not only on the balance of class forces, but also on the prevailing economic material conditions. Although economic policy may, at certain times, benefit labour, how temporary such situations are depends on the extent to which accumulation is profitable enough to bear them. State economic policy, though not determined by capital, is structurally constrained by its needs, particularly in periods of economic decline and crises, when profitability is most threatened. The fundamental requirement of the CMP remains profitable capital accumulation.

2.1.3 Fractions, State Autonomy and Limits

An adequate theory and concrete account of economic policy requires an understanding of some further complexities in 'actually existing' capitalism in the UK. Divisions exist within classes in contemporary capitalism. For example, there may be differences of interest between financial and industrial capital or between domestic and international capital. There may too be differences of interest between men and women, between public and private-sector workers, and between the unemployed and the employed. The strategy the state adopts to reconcile the conflicting interests of classes and their fractions is also of importance. Policies may aim to diminish the social conflict and tension that arises in a capitalist economy, particularly in periods of economic decline and crises. The state must manage not only the accumulation process, but also its legitimation. Concessions may therefore be given in order to legitimate the overall strategy of the state. It may adopt a policy designed to discipline labour and weaken its organisation, as well as encourage and reinforce the ideology and values of capitalism. The state therefore has some autonomy and the strategy it adopts depends not only on material conditions and the balance of class forces, but also on the ideological complexion of government.

There are also limits to the capacity of the state and its economic policies to 'solve' economic problems. There are three aspects to these limits, in addition to the possible opposition of labour already identified. First, within the state apparatus itself there may be opposition to certain economic policies, for example, from the civil service, a 'spending' department, the Treasury, or from one of the ministries. There is a struggle *within* the state over economic policy. Second, the policy process is important. It cannot be assumed that capital's needs are unambiguously expressed and articulated by its political representatives, nor that they can easily be translated into state action. Third, there are economic limits. These may be caused by international financial pressures or by the impact of the means used to finance expenditure on the accumulation process. Thus the analysis of economic policy must take account of the material economic pressures and conditions of the period; the balance of class and political forces; the ideological pressures; the relations between different fractions of classes; and the ability of the state to implement particular policies, given these economic, political and ideological conditions.

2.2 Economic Policy in the UK

2.2.1 The Age of Laissez-Faire

In the nineteenth century, economic policy was based on the principles of *laissez-faire*. There was a strong presumption against government action with an emphasis on the maintenance of unregulated markets in output, labour, capital and international trade, with as little public enterprise and overall government intervention in economic matters as possible. This was as close to the pure or simple model of the CMP, in the economic sphere, as is possible in reality and reflected the dominance of UK industrial capitalism in the world economy. Capital accumulation was rapid, international competition was virtually non-existent, and pressure from the working class was limited. The limited role of the state in economic policy is well illustrated by the pattern of public spending in the nineteenth century. Between 1820 and 1870, public spending increased in money terms from £57 million to £69 million, virtually all of which increase (of less than 0.3 per cent per year) was due to expenditure on the Crimean War. This was less than the rates of increase in national income and population. The aim was to ensure a balanced budget, with the utmost frugality in spending and taxation. However, as economic conditions began to deteriorate towards the end of the nineteenth century, increasing doubts arose about non-intervention in the economic sphere. The 'Great Depression' caused domestic realisation problems and unrest in sections of the working class, and posed threats to civil order. Moreover, the UK's declining competitiveness led to increasing import penetration and loss of export markets. However, no major changes in economic policy occurred, with the exception of a more protectionist stance on trade.

The high levels of unemployment that were experienced did not lead to major economic policy initiatives, as unemployment was seen, to the extent it was a problem at all, as a social problem to be dealt with through, for example, unemployment insurance and labour exchanges. Indeed in the late nineteenth century, unemployment was highest amongst casual workers, notably in the ports. It was the threat of civil unrest posed by their 'degenerate' behaviour, their 'pauperism', their poor physical shape to fight in wars, as well as the fear that the respectable unemployed might be 'contaminated' by them which prompted such policy action.

2.2.2 Economic Policy between the Wars: Depression and Recovery?

The First World War led to considerable changes in British capitalism. The pace of scientific and technical advance increased and extensive changes took place in the labour process with the introduction of work-study and assembly-line methods. In the latter part of the war, economic intervention grew through control over strategically important industries and attempts were made to increase the co-operation of the industrial working class through the involvement of trade union leaders in collective bargaining at national level. There were also increases in public expenditure necessitated by the war and financed mainly by borrowing. The major long-term impact of the war on the economy came from the loss of export markets as a result of the stimulus to industrial development that occurred in some of Britain's traditional trading partners, because of wartime non-availability of British goods, due to the German maritime blockade and the diversion, within the UK, of industry to military production. In addition, the reparations imposed on Germany and the changing patterns of international competitiveness and trade helped to destabilise the international financial system.

The major economic policy shift in the 1920s was the return to the gold standard in 1925, where the price of sterling as a currency on exchange markets was fixed in terms of gold at pre-war parity of \$4.86 to £1. This decision was to dictate economic policy in the 1920s, for, in order to restore the conditions necessary for it, a contractionary monetary policy was required. To be competitive at this new higher exchange rate, UK prices (which had risen during the war) had to be reduced, which in turn required deflation of the economy through severe credit restrictions, meaning high interest rates, which would also attract foreign deposits and thus maintain the high exchange rate. This deflation caused unemployment to rise, wages to fall, and reduced the market for industrial output. The high exchange rate also reduced the international competitiveness of manufacturing industry. Thus the maintenance of a high exchange rate was given priority over domestic manufacturing. Public spending, including public-sector workers' wages, was also cut to reduce government borrowing, in an attempt to remain on the gold standard. Despite the severe economic implications for the domestic economy, the international financial interests of the city were paramount. The city wanted an end to uncertainty and currency fluctuations on the foreign exchange markets, and the removal of restrictions on foreign lending. The structural problem of deteriorating competitiveness, worsened by the return to the gold standard, was not addressed, except through the disciplining of labour as a result of the higher unemployment and wage cuts.

However, in 1931 the new National government abandoned the gold standard and free trade. The pound depreciated on the exchange markets and a general protective tariff was introduced on the import of all manufactured goods. This meant that monetary policy could now be insulated from external pressures and a 'cheap-money' policy of low interest rates was introduced, in which the bank rate averaged only around 2 per cent throughout the 1930s. However, this was the only real expansionary policy pursued in the decade, for the 'need' to balance the budget remained even in the severe depression of 1930–3. Indeed the cheap-money policy itself can be seen less as a strategy for economic recovery and more to ease the interest-payment burden of budget deficits. Rising unemployment in the late 1920s and 1930s did lead to government action, because of its effect on public spending. After 1920 unemployment insurance covered most manual workers, and the exchequer's net contribution to it went into deficit when unemployment rose above 5.5 per cent. However, policies were not directed at reducing unemployment *per se*.

What effects did the policy shift from the gold standard, free trade and tight money have on capital accumulation, competitiveness and on the working class? Investment in manufacturing actually declined compared to before the 1914–18 war. The volume of exports never reached more than 81 per cent of their 1913 level between the wars, despite the growth of world trade in the 1930s. By 1938 they were only 57 per cent of their 1913 level. Imports meanwhile reached 114 per cent of their 1913 level in 1938. As far as the working class is concerned, real wages for those in employment rose by rather less than 1 per cent per year between 1920 and 1938, due mainly to falling prices, whilst the unemployment rate never fell below 10 per cent between 1923 and 1939, and reached over 22 per cent in 1932. The overall government approach to economic policy in the period was that of a financial policy, with the importance of 'sound finance' and a balanced budget being paramount, with no attempt to manage the economy as a whole.

2.2.3 Keynesianism, Consensus and the Long Boom

In the Second World War, important changes took place in British capitalism. Accelerated scientific and technological change occurred, especially in aeronautics and electronics, whilst the trade unions became involved in the extensive system of industrial and national planning that was established. The war also led to the establishment of Keynesian demand regulation, which was to develop during the period of the long boom, and to major changes in the capitalist world system and the position of the UK within it (see section 10.3). The strength of the British economy was undermined by the dependence of Britain on the US, exemplified by the 'lend-lease' system, the near-exhaustion of official gold reserves and the liquidation of British holdings of foreign assets to pay for wartime imports, and the slowdown in the replacement of the capital stock in major industries such as railways, mining and construction.

However, the 1950s and 1960s exhibited the most rapid and sustained development of production in the history of the UK and of the world. In the UK, economic growth averaged 2.8 per cent per year between 1951 and 1973, the number of unemployed remained well below 1 million until 1971, cyclical fluctuations in economic activity were heavily damped compared to before the war, and world trade grew by 8.6 per cent per year, on average, between 1950 and 1970, compared to 1.1 per cent between 1913 and 1950. This 'long boom' is unique in the history of UK capitalist development. The approach to economic policy that characterised the period was radically different from that followed in previous periods. Many factors contributed to this change. The experience of coalition government during the war and its 1944 White Paper on employment policy, which accepted the aim of, and responsibility for, 'full employment', played a role in developing a more consensual approach to policy matters. This was necessitated by the need to unite the country at war and offer a more secure and prosperous economic future for those participating in it. Moreover the need for wartime planning of production, labour resources and allocation of goods involved workers, strengthened workers' organisations, and altered the views of the participants about the role of government. The landslide Labour victory in the 1945 election further ensured that the demands of labour had to be accommodated. Overall, then, the balance of class forces had shifted from the pre-war situation. Keynesianism offered a means for the state to respond to labour's demands, yet control them at the same time, so as not to disrupt accumulation. For Keynesians, fluctuations in economic activity (the pace of accumulation) were due to deficiencies of total aggregate demand, giving insufficient spending power to purchase the full employment level of output. Hence, governments could manipulate spending and revenue plans through 'fiscal' policy to regulate total demand in the economy and create full employment. Such an approach to economic policy has the capacity to reduce class conflict by expanding markets to ensure more favourable conditions for realising surplus value, potentially allowing all classes to increase their incomes and ensuring high levels of employment. This is indeed a secure basis for class collaboration, provided capital accepts a commitment to full employment, rising living standards and government regulation of the macroeconomy; and provided labour confines its demands to the narrow limits of increased living standards and jobs; and of course, provided the policies do actually 'work'. Keynesianism thus became the consensus ideology that was required by the state to adjust to the new balance of class forces in the UK after the war. The threats to capital in this approach were seen as minimal. It did not involve direction or intervention at the level of the enterprise nor supplanting market forces at the micro level. The aim was to socialise demand, not production, and indeed Keynesianism ideologically weakened the case for public ownership and planning, by demonstrating that full employment and economic stability was possible without 'socialism'.

How far do the economic policies pursued during the long boom reflect the Keynesian approach? In 1945 the new Labour government, the first ever to have a parliamentary majority, inherited a legacy of considerable state powers in the planning of the economy. However, after the 1945–7 period, the planning system was dismantled and replaced by demand management policies. The retreat from planning, though partly a result of political opposition from capital, was largely a result of the government's lack of commitment to, knowledge of, and interest in, socialist economic planning. The Labour Party was not in essence a socialist party committed to socialisation of the economy, but rather a party of social reform committed to defending the interests of working people in a basically capitalist economy. Indeed the government between 1947 and 1949 pursued a deflationary budgetary strategy running budget surpluses. It also encouraged voluntary pay restraint and devalued the pound by 30 per cent. This was hardly Keynesian reflation, and even the cheap money policy that was followed was largely to reduce the cost of government borrowing and the interest burden of the debt, rather than to stimulate demand.

The 1950s saw Conservative governments continue the trend to deregulation and liberalisation, the restoration of economic power to capital and to the market, but they remained committed to consensual macroeconomic policy in principle. Ideologically, however, they preferred to manipulate demand through monetary rather than fiscal policy, as the latter could involve increased taxes or increased spending and expansion in the public sector, whereas the former would operate indirectly through markets and have a more direct effect on the private sector. It became clear, however, that any attempt to stimulate the economy rapidly by increasing demand through economic policies led to balance of payments deficits as imports increased, and this led to the 'stop-go' cycles wherein each expansionary phase was followed by a contractionary one to correct the balance of payments deficit incurred. Since Keynesianism concentrated on demand, supply was left to capital and market forces, which failed to improve competitiveness, and so the domestic economy was sacrificed through deflation to the so-called 'constraint' of the balance of payments. Limited attempts were latterly made in the early 1960s at indicative planning with the setting up of the National Economic Development Office and Council (NEDO and NEDC), but the means to achieve the modernisation of UK industry were not provided, even when the 1964–70 Labour government extended and co-ordinated it into a 'National Plan' and set up the Department of Economic Affairs (DEA) in 1965. No mechanisms were set up to implement the plans, since this would have meant detailed industrial and enterprise interventions, which would have reduced the control of capital. Thus the balance of payments problem continued to constrain both economic policy and rapid capital accumulation. Despite a £400 million deficit on current

account and a long-term capital outflow of more than £350 million in
1964, the government continued to adhere to the existing fixed
exchange rate and did not devalue the pound, preferring
deflationary policies. Eventually, in November 1967, the pound was
devalued by over 14 per cent and public spending cuts and tax
increases were instituted. A budget surplus was achieved in 1969.
Resistance to devaluing the pound was due to its rule as an international reserve currency. It came from overseas holders, who did not
want the value of their holdings reduced, and the city, whose international banking role was threatened. The Labour government left
office in 1970 with unemployment having risen by 140,000 to
500,000, with inflation doubled at 6 per cent, but the balance of
payments was in a large surplus.

The 1970–4 Conservative government briefly put Keynesianism
'in reverse' in a more systematic manner than previous governments
and pursued a tight budgetary policy. This had a contractionary
effect on output and investment, and unemployment rose quickly to
over 1 million in 1971 for the first time since 1945. The aim was to
improve conditions for producing surplus value (rather than
realising it) by disciplining workers through high unemployment and
freeing market forces. Given the balance of class forces and the
opposition and determination of the labour movement, the
government was forced to retreat on its economic strategy of
deflation and discipline. Large sections of capital, too, argued for a
more expansionist policy, as several major companies went out of
business and the prospects for increased profitability through realisation were limited.

From 1972, the government pursued a more expansionist policy.
Monetary policy was relaxed, taxes were reduced and public expenditure plans were expanded. This major Keynesian expansion failed,
partly because of the remaining low profitability in manufacturing
industry and the continuing strength of union organisation; partly
because the credit explosion led not to a major increase in manufacturing investment (lack of finance was not the problem, it was low
profitability), but to major increases in investment in property and
overseas; partly because of the oil-price rise of 400 per cent in 1973/4,
which radically altered conditions for the production of surplus value
and adversely affected the balance of payments, leading to yet
another deflationary set of policies; and partly because membership
of the EEC from 1973 increased competitive pressures and the flow
of funds overseas. One important final feature of the entire period is

the various attempts to introduce policies to control the growth of wages or 'incomes' policies. These are dealt with in Chapter 4, especially section 4.3. At the end of 1974 the position of capital had indeed worsened from that of 1970. The rate of profit was lower (5.4 per cent compared to 9.6 per cent), inflation was higher, its share of world manufacturing exports was less and accumulation in manufacturing was running at half the rate for the rest of the EEC. Moreover, workers' real take-home pay had increased during the period and major industrial struggles had been won, leaving the labour movement in a strong position.

2.2.4 *Keynesianism, the Long Boom and British Capitalism*

We now turn to an analysis of the causes of the long boom, the extent to which it was fuelled by Keynesian policies, and its effects on accumulation. Although the UK participated in the long boom, UK capital still performed less well than its major international competitors. For example, whilst the UK experienced an annual average growth in GDP of 2.8 per cent over the period 1951–73, France experienced 5.1 per cent, West Germany 5.9 per cent, Italy 5.2 per cent and the Netherlands 5.0 per cent. On a world scale, the necessary political and economic condition of international stability was established under the hegemony of the USA, the most notable achievement of which was the Bretton Woods agreement in 1944 stabilising the world monetary system, fixing the exchange rates and setting up the IMF. World trade grew dramatically as a result of such monetary stability, trade freeing and the reduction of protectionism overseas through the new international agencies of the IMF, GATT and the trading blocs of EEC and EFTA. New foreign markets thus became available, overcoming the limits imposed on accumulation by domestic markets. New investment opportunities arose associated with major product and process innovations, perhaps arising from a new set of triggers producing a 'long wave' of expansion. Moreover, the Second World War provided massive scope for transferring production to new consumer products, as well as technical spin-offs from military research and development. The availability of adequate labour reserves was also vital (see section 4.4). Large increases in the amount of machinery per worker meant that increases in the demand for labour were generally less than the growth of means of production, but nevertheless major labour reserves were needed for such a rapid and sustained period of accumulation. This was tapped through investment overseas in countries not yet industrialised, and domestically from the transfer of workers from the agricultural sector, from immigration, from married women who had previously not worked, and from demobilisation after the war. The labour supply had to be co-operative and quiescent, as there was no high unemployment to discipline their wage demands and their productivity.

Obviously many of these conditions benefited the UK, but some were less favourable for domestic capital accumulation in the UK. First, the freeing of capital flows as a result of the convertability of currencies and reduction of exchange controls further encouraged the overseas expansion of UK capital. Second, the UK's protected imperial markets were opened up by the freer trade to competitors, thus directly competing with UK exports. Third, the UK market became less protected and this increased competition in the UK domestic market. Finally, with regard to labour reserves, the shift from agriculture to industry was largely completed in the UK, and moreover the working class in the UK was better organised with a long history of defensive struggles, embracing a larger proportion of the workforce and with stronger shop-floor organisation than in any other capitalist economy. These are amongst the major reasons why the long boom was weaker in the UK than in most advanced capitalist economies.

Keynesian policies did contribute to the long boom in the UK, though they were a necessary, but not sufficient condition for it. Whilst the abandonment of a balanced budget as a primary aim of economic policy allowed greater discretion in managing the level of demand, it failed to address the major structural problems of the economy. Moreover, the actual budgetary stance taken by governments in the period was generally not reflationary, and policies were usually to dampen demand and constrain accumulation and employment growth. The growth of public spending that occurred during the period was in fact almost entirely financed by increased tax revenue, thus the net effect on demand was limited. Critically, profitability declined over the period from 18.8 per cent in 1955 to 9.9 per cent in 1973, productivity rose less quickly than amongst major rivals, and the share of world manufactured exports collapsed from 26 per cent to 9 per cent between 1950 and 1975, whilst the degree of import penetration into the domestic manufacturing market trebled from 6 per cent to 18 per cent between 1955 and 1973. Thus the long boom reinforced and sharpened the pattern of uneven development between the weaker and stronger capitalist economies, whilst

Keynesian macroeconomic policy contributed at the margin to the stabilisation of these economies by some fine tuning of demand.

The long boom and Keynesian economic policy did, however, substantially strengthen workers' organisations in terms of numbers, strength, organisation and political power. The balance of class power had shifted under 25 years of virtually continuous full employment. Rising living standards and expanding public services had provided major 'concessions' to labour. Indeed, the era came to an end with the three-day week and the defeat of the Heath government in a 'who rules' election prior to a proposed national miners' strike.

This shift in class relations coincided with major changes in the participation of women in waged work. The effects on women were, however, rather more contradictory, for though they benefited significantly from the increase in the numbers of available jobs, there was no real challenge to the domestic division of labour. Most of the women who were drawn into waged work were married women. The proportion of married women in waged work increased from 10 per cent in 1931, to 21 per cent in 1951, to 47 per cent in 1972. Most of the work was part-time, as this was the only way in which waged work could be combined with domestic responsibilities of housework and child-rearing. Alternatively, women would work prior to childbirth and after the children grew up. In either case, women generally continued their unwaged domestic labour as well as their newly found paid labour. Women as wage labour were therefore still viewed as a secondary, temporary reserve of labour to be tapped as needed by the accumulation process, and whose primary responsibilities were in the home and in the production and reproduction of labour power. The dilemma for the state, then, between the traditional role of women and the need for additional wage labour was solved by women doing two sets of jobs, one paid and one unpaid.

2.2.5 The Breakdown of Keynesianism and the End of the Long Boom: 1974–9

This section will first outline the major economic policies enacted in this period; second, it will give an account of the breakdown of the long boom; third, it will explain the abandonment of Keynesian economic policy; and finally, it will indicate the position that capital and labour were in at the end of this period.

The economic policies of the 1974–9 Labour government were dominated by the collapse of the pound, public spending cuts, monetary control, and incomes policy. The rise in oil prices in

1973/4, and its effect on inflation and industrial costs, as well as the rapid growth of wages under the 'social contract' mark 1, industrial militancy and rising prices due to oil prices, further exacerbated the continuing declining competitiveness of UK capital by worsening conditions for both the production and realisation of surplus value. The pound began to fall heavily in 1976 (it had already fallen considerably since 'floating' in 1971), largely as a result of holders of sterling (international bankers) losing further confidence in the prospects for accumulation in the UK (and thus moving out of sterling into other currencies), as a result of continuing declining competitiveness, declining investment, stagnant output, rapid inflation and some concern that the government might stick to its radical manifesto. A $5 billion loan was negotiated with the IMF on condition of public spending cuts and tighter monetary control. The government had already achieved in 1975/6 voluntary agreement with the TUC on a £6 limit on wage increases, after the wages explosion of mark 1 of the social contract. This succeeded in reducing wage inflation, but caused real wages to fall for the great majority of workers: 8 per cent on average. Policies in succeeding years to limit wage increases to £4 or 5 per cent and then 10 per cent, followed by an attempt to impose a 5 per cent phase 4 increase in 1978/9, against both Labour Party conference decisions and the views of many unions, led to the 'winter of discontent' and major strikes. These policies were a direct attempt to speed up accumulation and reduce real wages, or at least prevent them from rising as fast as productivity. They involved an attempt to shift the balance of economic power back towards capital.

The other part of the economic strategy was public spending cuts and tighter monetary policy. At the heart of the control of public spending is the use of 'cash limits', i.e. control of the amount of spending the government is prepared to finance, introduced in 1975. State expenditure had been growing rapidly in the early 1970s, by nearly 7 per cent per year in real terms, and the public-sector borrowing requirement (PSBR), which had been negative in 1970, had by 1976 reached 10 per cent of GDP. Following the financial crises of 1976, cuts of £3 billion in the PSBR were announced for 1977/8 and 1978/9, and fiscal instruments were now to be used to keep the monetary targets that would be announced each year. In 1976, the chancellor announced a monetary target of 9–13 per cent for the growth in money supply for 1976/7. Money-supply targets have remained the central element in monetary policy, and indeed macroeconomic policy, ever since. The cash limits, which are a function of the desired PSBR and money-supply growth, mean also that if the costs of provision rise faster than estimated, then either real levels of provision, or wage increases, or jobs, have to be cut. Much of the increase in state spending had not, however, been in volume terms, but was due to the relative price effect of provision in the public sector, due to the labour-intensive nature of public services and hence the growth in its employment, the growth in transfer payments due to demographic trends and increasing unemployment, and because of the burden of debt interest payments resulting from deficits combined with high interest rates. Debt servicing costs had risen to nearly 13 per cent of total central government expenditure by 1981.

Public spending cuts benefit capital in a number of ways. The main benefit arises if public spending 'crowds out' the private sector. This could not happen directly, unless all resources were fully utilised. However, indirect 'financial' crowding out can occur. Government borrowing reduces private-sector expenditure, including investment, by depriving firms of money capital, because at any one point in time there is only a given volume of savings/credit (money capital). The larger the PSBR, the larger share of this that is needed by government to finance expenditure, unless it creates money. Moreover, reducing government borrowing should lower interest rates, and thus the price of credit, as well as potentially reducing inflation by reducing the money supply and opening the option of reducing taxes. However, conditions for realisation decline as government spending on private-sector output declines, and incomes and employment fall. Moreover, for financial capital a low PSBR means reduced investment possibilities from government bond sales, which are especially lucrative when the rate of profit is low.

The long boom came to an end for several reasons. World economic conditions deteriorated, largely as a result of the barriers that had developed precisely as a consequence of the long boom. Labour supplies in many advanced capitalist economies had been virtually exhausted; many of the sources of rapid productivity growth and opportunities in overseas markets had diminished; international competition had increased and the uneven growth associated with it increased international monetary instability. Commodity prices had risen considerably; political forces hostile to capital were gaining ground in different parts of the world; and finally, partly as a result of these changes, and partly due to virtually full employment, the balance of class forces moved against capital.

However, there were certain particular features of the situation in the UK. The labour movement entered the period growing, confident and powerful. The labour movement has traditionally been strong defensively and the boom had stimulated full employment and wage militancy, which ate further into profitability. Economic decline became absolute. Public spending also was reduced (as a result of very low profits, which ultimately have to finance it), and deflationary monetary policies were pursued. Keynesianism worked in reverse. Moreover, the collapse of the world capitalist economy affected the UK more than most economies, because of its high level of both trade and capital flows. The freeing of these flows (through GATT, membership of the EEC and government policies) meant that weak economies like the UK suffered most. The UK had not adopted an effective strategy for the modernisation of industry – this had been resisted by both capital and labour. In addition, UK capital has always been highly internationally orientated, and so there has been conflict between the development of a productive domestic base, which generally has offered low profits and slow accumulation, and profitable accumulation overseas through both direct and portfolio investment. There are some conflicts here between domestic and international capital and between industrial and financial capital.

Largely, then, because of the contradictions of the long boom, and the particular place of the UK within the world capitalist economic order, the long boom came to an end. The roots of this collapse for the UK lay in the 1950s and 1960s, when the long boom temporarily concealed the fundamental structural problem of deteriorating competitiveness. Throughout this period productivity growth was slow; investment was low – even as a proportion of profits; exports focused on the protected sterling area; the pound and balance of payments were protected by deflation, which further inhibited investment; state expenditure rose as a result of the demands put upon it by both capital and labour, and yet capital was not profitable enough to finance it; and throughout it all the labour movement grew in strength.

2.2.6 *The Limits of Keynesianism*

Keynesian economic policy seeks to manage the level of demand, i.e. the *realisation* of surplus value. However, its effects on the *production* of surplus value may be damaging, for as employment, wages, taxation and public spending rise, conditions for the profitable production of surplus value are likely to deteriorate. There are contradictions between the two sets of conditions. The ability to generate profit depends on both production and realisation of surplus value, and the control of demand will not therefore control accumulation, which is a unity of both 'spheres'. Conditions that improve the production of surplus value worsen them for realising it and vice versa. Wages may be taken as an example. They must not increase so quickly that conditions for the production of surplus value decline, but not so slowly as to affect realisation. At the level of the firm, wage increases are unambiguously bad as conditions for production of surplus value, *ceteris paribus*, deteriorate. Attempts to reduce wage costs, however, in aggregate worsen realisation problems. Thus the state can attempt to regulate one or the other, but not both simultaneously.

Moreover, there is another contradiction between the political objective of short-term social cohesion and the prospects for longer-run growth, because the basis for continual accumulation is restricted by the attempt to resolve conflict, while economic crises generate legitimation crises because labour's demands can no longer be met. However, Keynesianism may also generate a fiscal crisis, causing the restriction of public spending, both because expenditure was outrunning revenue by large and increasing amounts and because much state spending is unproductive and acts as a long-run barrier to accumulation.

There are two further limitations of Keynesian economic policy. First, such policies cannot alter the growth rate in the long run, for they do not seek to expand the productive capacity of the economy. Output can only be increased by demand measures, if the supply potential of the economy is not reached. Thus Keynesianism is essentially a short-run strategy, which is unable to affect growth of the labour and capital stocks on the supply side of the economy, which it leaves to private markets. Secondly, Keynesianism aims to manage economic crises and reduce the fluctuations in output, employment and income that are an inherent feature of capitalist economies. Yet these crises perform important roles in the capital accumulation process, for example in restructuring capital, increasing productivity, eliminating inefficient capital and disciplining labour. In this sense, it reduces the efficiency of the system and the long-term growth of profitable accumulation.

What was the position of capital and labour at the end of the 1970s? The UK economy suffered disproportionately from the collapse of the long boom. Between 1973 and 1979, the economy grew by only 0.8 per cent per year, considerably less than its major competitors. Import penetration of manufactured goods increased from 18 per cent to 25 per cent over the same period, although the balance of payments was temporarily protected by the existence of North Sea oil. Productivity increased by only 5 per cent over all between 1973 and 1978, whilst it increased by between 14 per cent and 29 per cent in the rest of the OECD, and manufacturing investment remained at the same level as 1974. The world economy had dramatically slowed down, offering few export markets in stiff competitive conditions. Furthermore, labour had not been shackled in the interests of capital, for although unemployment reached its highest level since 1932 (over 1.5 million unemployed), real wages had increased by only 2 per cent over the entire period and public services had been reduced, trade union membership had increased by 1.5 million in six years. Despite the attempts to reduce wages, the profit rate fell between 1974 and 1979 from 5.4 per cent to 4.8 per cent.

The era closed as it had begun, in the sense that the balance of class forces had not been altered to benefit capital significantly. A radical restructuring of capital was still required to increase profitability, and the power of the labour movement was still unbroken. The balance of class power was still such that capital could not fully assert its dominance over labour. However, a radical break in economic policy, attempting to restructure capital, labour and the state and alter the existing balance of class forces, was introduced in 1979.

2.2.7 *Thatcherism and the End of Consensus*

This section examines the attempt by the Thatcher government to restore the profitability of UK capital. Its overriding objective is to increase and sustain profitable capital accumulation through improving competitiveness, efficiency and productivity. This requires the restructuring of capital, labour and the state, and the relations between them. This 'supply side' approach to the restoration of the conditions for profitable extraction of surplus value necessitates a free market strategy to shift the balance of class forces by strengthening capital under strict market discipline, weakening labour through market forces, and reducing the economic role of the state, whilst strengthening the state's role in relation to labour. The state increasingly operates to alter the balance of class forces and then maintain the new balance, both materially and ideologically, through mechanisms to increase social control, to reinforce capitalist values and project its own conception of the world as common sense. The free market requires a strong state.

There are several interconnected policies which together make up the strategy of Thatcherism. The principal ones are a tight monetary policy, curbs on public spending, privatisation, and legal constraints on trades unions (see Chapter 4). The purpose of a tight *monetary* policy is to control and hence reduce the growth rate of monetary expansion, and ultimately limit it to the rate of growth of output of the economy. This control is exercised through the medium-term financial strategy (MTFS) which sets annual targets for its growth. Once the volume of money is controlled, it is the market that dictates its price (the interest rate) and its availability (credit). Naturally, holding down the growth of the money supply makes credit more difficult and expensive to obtain, by forcing up market interest rates. The effect is deflationary through reducing the growth of consumer spending and expenditure by capital on means of production and labour power, because increases in the money supply of less than the level of price increases reduces the total real means of payment available to them for purchases. The tighter the policy, the more extensive the unemployment created, the greater the pressures on capitals to compete in declining markets and the greater the liquidity problems and bankruptcies. The effect is to 'crash' the economy, through a type of reverse Keynesianism, but using monetary rather than fiscal means. This improves the 'supply' side of the economy, the conditions for increasing the production of surplus value, in a variety of ways. Competitive pressures drive out the less efficient capitals, thereby raising average productivity and thus rates of surplus value; production shifts to more competitive industries as more capitals go out of business in the least competitive industries. Greater competition also means that managements are pressurised into reorganising working practices through speed-ups and reduced manning levels. At the same time, workers' resistance to such changes are dampened by rising unemployment and a weaker bargaining position. This occurs both through the effects of the 'crash' on the workers, through increased competition for jobs and reduced union membership, and on managements being resistant to wage rises to prevent closure, loss of markets and the loss of further competitiveness. In these ways, the balance of power at the point of production is shifted.

The second element in the strategy is that of curbing *public spending*. Public spending has to be made compatible with the money supply targets. This is because the money supply is linked to the gap between public spending and revenue, i.e. the public-sector borrowing requirement (PSBR). Such borrowing involves the sale of debt to banks; by increasing their assets, this measure increases their capacity to lend and hence increases the money supply. Thus the key element in controlling the money supply is the control of the PSBR, and therefore public spending. Problems for accumulation are posed by rapid public spending growth in a declining economy, most notably its drain on surplus value through taxation and its indirect financial crowding out of private-sector investment through its borrowing. Hence cuts in public spending and PSBR improve conditions for the production of surplus value. They do so for the additional reason that they also effectively operate as a wages policy in the public sector, as any wage increase greater than the 'cash limit' implies cuts in services or jobs. A necessary part of the strategy to curb public spending is an ideological offensive against 'unproductive' or 'wasteful' public spending, and in favour of alternative provision through voluntary organisations, the family or by private capital. However, much public spending benefits capital, as we have seen. Thus public spending is not only reduced, but *restructured* to reflect more accurately the needs of capital and to concentrate more on those activities which are required to provide the framework for, or to sustain, profitable accumulation and which cannot be provided by private capital. Moreover, the social and political impact of a major crash may require increased public spending to control, or even repress, opposition and discontent.

The third major element in the strategy of Thatcherism is *privatisation*, which extends further the rule of the market, private profit and capitalist relations generally. Privatisation involves the transfer of public assets and services to the private sector and takes a variety of forms, including the selling off of nationalised firms, the introduction of private-sector competition, the public issue of shares, and compulsion, or encouragement, for public-sector organisations to tender for contracts. This reduces public spending (for example, in siphoning off demand into the private sector or through intensifying competition), forcing reductions in employment, wages and conditions, and increases in productivity. It also provides profitable opportunities for private capital. Ideologically, it encourages the view that state provision is less efficient and thus less desirable, hence promoting capitalist values. Finally, it weakens public-sector unions in their struggle to maintain services, jobs, wages and conditions. Of course, where the provision of a service or an activity is not profitable or potentially so, it remains within the state sector – unless either voluntary organisations or families can be encouraged to provide it, or it is politically possible simply to abolish its provision.

There are several other elements of the strategy. First, the anti-collectivist, anti-state (and anti-union) ideology must be actively promoted, as it seeks to break the political consensus. Second, subsidies and other forms of financial assistance to industry must be reduced so as to discipline firms into increasing competitiveness, because such assistance keeps less efficient firms and plants in operation, encourages inefficiency, and mitigates the effects of the crash. Third, market discipline is extended wherever possible by removing institutional barriers to market forces, such as planning controls, as in enterprise zones and free ports, or in the freeing of capital and trade movements. This further provides 'freedom' for capital to pursue its most profitable activities and locations. Examples of areas where market forces are not yet 'free' to operate are labour mobility, due to council-house provision; enterprise and initiative, due to personal taxation; the incentive to work, due to social security and unemployment benefits; and competition, due to state monopolies. Action is to be expected here. It is state intervention that has disturbed the 'natural' market order.

There is one final element in the strategy. Opposition to its implementation must be contained and not only at the ideological level. The power of the state must be increased and centralised: increased, in order to impose discipline and authority on those unwilling to accept the free-market logic of the strategy; and centralised, in order to control opposition from elected local authorities antagonistic to the strategy. The former involves strengthening the police and the power of those in authority (on which see Chapter 9), and the latter strictly controlling local council spending and penalising 'overspenders', as well as abolishing the metropolitan county councils – all of which happen to be Labour controlled. This strengthening of state power gives an authoritarian streak to Thatcherism, and reflects a belief in limiting civil liberties, whilst market freedoms are increased.

2.2.8 Thatcherism and the Prospects for British Capitalism

Thatcherism, however, faces certain problems in succeeding in its objective of restoring profitable accumulation. First of all, there are political and social limits to the speed at which such a strategy can proceed. The state must retain some measure of legitimacy, at least in a parliamentary democracy, and hence must slow down or modify policies, if its ideological management is weak. The rapid growth of unemployment, the decline of public services, the stagnation of living standards for many, the bankruptcies and closures may have a destabilising influence and create a threat to internal security through social disorder, resistance and conflict. This not only poses its own problems, but requires public expenditure of the social expenses type (i.e. draining surplus value) to control disorder. Moreover, the growth of unemployment will, all else being equal, cause public spending to increase and the tax base to contract, as spending on unemployment and social security benefits rise and the yield from income taxes falls, thus worsening the PSBR. There are additional problems in the UK, because of the rapidly increasing proportion of the population aged over 65 in the 1980s and 1990s. Health and social security expenditure will have to rise rapidly just to preserve present levels of care, benefits and service.

There are economic problems, too. For profitable accumulation to proceed, surplus value must be produced *and* realised. Thatcherism, whilst improving production conditions, simultaneously worsens realisation conditions. This is because the real incomes of those in employment grow more slowly, as unemployment rises and their purchasing power declines; and as the public-sector expenditure on goods and services purchased from the private sector falls due to public spending cuts. The only way out of this dilemma is by seeking realisation through export growth and investment overseas, while at the same time encouraging foreign investment into the UK to take advantage of the improving production conditions. Policies of free trade and unrestricted capital movements are vital to ensure success for the strategy, though they are constantly threatened by the growth of protectionism, slow world economic recovery and monetarism in other advanced capitalist nations.

There is a second economic problem. Domestic production may suffer, both because of the reduction in industrial capacity as plants close and because of the movement of capital out of the UK. Moreover, tight monetary policies and their concomitant of high real interest rates may attract funds into sterling, thus causing the pound to appreciate, and worsening competitiveness. Finally, some resistance to Thatcherite policies can be expected from within capital itself. Although capital as a whole stands to benefit from the strategy's success, many individual capitals, particularly those domestically based in older industries, will suffer.

Thatcherism offers a largely coherent analysis and strategy to reverse long-term economic decline in the interests of capital. Its success has to be assessed in terms of its effects on the prospects for accumulation, and the variables which affect this. Thus, for example, a rapid growth in unemployment, high company liquidations and a reduction in the share of public expenditure in GDP are signs of the success, not failure, of the strategy. Others 'signs' of success would be increasing rates of productivity growth and investment.

During the period 1979–83, unemployment (registered) increased by 150 per cent from 1.2 million to 3.1 million, whilst real wages grew by around 5 per cent over the whole period. Company liquidations trebled to over 3,000 a year, and industrial output declined by 11 per cent, compared to 4 per cent in the OECD as a whole. Thus the 'crash' undoubtedly occurred, was more severe than elsewhere, disciplined the labour force and rationalised capital. Moreover, monetary control was tight enough to reduce the PSBR from 5.4 per cent of GDP in 1978–9 to 3.4 per cent in 1982–3, and to reduce inflation from 10 per cent to 5 per cent. The strategy has therefore been successful, in its own terms, to some extent, and as a result we would expect a major improvement in competitiveness, indicated by rapid productivity growth, rapidly growing investment and improved manufacturing-trade performance. Productivity has indeed increased since 1980, with a particularly rapid growth of 10 per cent in 1981, but manufacturing investment has declined by 35 per cent and in 1983 the UK had a trade deficit on manufactured goods, for the first time since the industrial revolution, which by 1984 had reached over £4,000 million, despite an overall reduction in the exchange rate of 20 per cent. Investment overseas has speeded up dramatically, partly as a result of exchange-control abolition in 1979, with over £23,000 million leaving the UK over the period. The crux, though, is the effect of the strategy on domestic manufacturing productivity. Increases here are largely due not to the introduction of new machinery and technical progress, but to the destruction of low-productivity firms and plants, labour intensification and plant relocation. How far these gains can be repeated, as they must be to raise productivity and reduce unit costs to the level of international competitors, depends upon whether the labour movement regains strength and cohesion, if and when unemployment begins to fall and the crises turn into growth. The long-term effects of Thatcherism are thus unpredictable. They depend upon whether the balance of class forces has been fundamentally and permanently shifted, or whether the new balance is solely a function of the deepest economic crisis since 1929.

Thatcherism has weakened the labour movement and altered the balance of class forces. The rapid growth of unemployment has reduced bargaining strength, union membership and funds, as well as undermining power at the level of the shop floor and the collective spirit and confidence of workers. Deteriorating working conditions, the continuous threat of job loss, and the legislative attacks on unions further exacerbate their position and exercise social discipline and control. But it has also affected relations between men and women in the labour market, movement and at home. Women's jobs are more easily threatened than men's, not only because many married women work part-time and are less well unionised and lack the same legal rights as full-time workers, but also because of the industrial, occupational and spatial distribution of women's jobs. Women's unemployment is also less visible in the unemployment figures and less expensive to the state, since women are less likely to register as unemployed because many are ineligible for benefit. Furthermore, Thatcherism provides ideological legitimation for women's reduced labour-market participation, urging women to stay at home and care for the family, when jobs are scarce and social services are being eroded (see Chapter 5).

2.3 Economic Policy and British Capitalism

It is clear from our analysis that state economic policy has failed to resolve the underlying economic and political problems of the UK capitalist economy and to sustain rapid profitable capital accumulation. The long-term historical and relative decline has not been reversed (see also Chapter 3), whilst the unique period of stability and expansion of the long boom, owing less to government policy than is often supposed, collapsed under its own contradictions and the dynamics of capitalist development. The structural problems of the UK economy, the chronically slow growth of productivity, and hence declining competitiveness, and the particular balance of class forces and fractions of capital, have not been decisively tackled.

Several key issues have arisen in our analysis of economic policy in
the UK. First, there are major limitations on the ability of the state to
resolve the problems which arise in the accumulation process. This
recognition has led, *inter alia*, to public spending being a crucial
theme in the analysis of economic policy. Second, the role of class
struggle and the changing balance of class forces is of vital importance. Their relative fixity for long periods in the post-1945 era made
progress for capital (or labour) very difficult, whilst the considerable
defensive strength of the working class in the UK, in terms of trade
union membership, structure and organisation, its representation by
a mass political party, and its capacity for industrial action, acted as a
central political constraint in formulating and implementing
economic policy. By the same token, this strength must be reduced if
profitable capital accumulation is to be restored under capitalist
relations of production. Third, the international orientation of
sections of UK capital is important. Large sections of both industrial
and financial capital operate on an international scale with considerable global freedom in their actions. The interests of domestic
capital are poorly represented within the state. Much of UK capital
has a less than total commitment to, or interest in, domestic accumulation, and indeed encourages the pursuit of policies designed to
encourage overseas investment and production and the interests of
financial capital, whilst exacerbating the decline of domestic
manufacturing capacity and competitiveness. Fourth, the ultimately
antagonistic interests of capital and labour surface most clearly in
economic crises. In such periods, the state cannot meet the 'needs' of
both. The temporary consensus over economic policy collapses,
along with the existing balance of forces. Policy becomes increasingly directed by the requirement of capital to resolve the accumulation crisis, though it must be remembered that the state also has a
responsibility to legitimate the existing social order.

It has been the interplay of the accumulation process, profitability, class relations and state economic policy which together have
determined both the UK's long-term decline and its current
economic crises. The state has become increasingly involved in class
relations, as it acts to remove the barriers to rapid accumulation.
Struggles against capital increasingly become struggles within and
against the state. Underlying the entire process, however, are
capitalist relations of production, which remain the ultimate barrier
to sustained human progress.

Further Reading

General

Pollard, S. (1983) *The Development of the British Economy 1914–1980*, Edward Arnold, chs. 1, 5 and 9

Tomlinson, J. (1981) *Problems of British Economic Policy 1870–1945*, Methuen

2.1

Coakley, J. and Harris, H. (1983) *The City of Capital*, Basil Blackwell

Harris, L. (1980) 'The State and the Economy: Some Theoretical Problems', in *Socialist Register*, Merlin

2.2

Armstrong, P., Glyn, A. and Harrison, J. (1984) *Capitalism Since World War II*, Fontana

Coates, D. (1980) *Labour in Power?*, Longman, chs. 1 and 4

Crouch, C. (ed.) (1979) *State and Economy in Contemporary Capitalism*, Croom Helm

Glynn, A. and Harrison, J. (1980) *The British Economic Disaster*, Pluto

McLennan, G., Held, D. and Hall, S. (1984) *State and Society in Contemporary Britain*, Polity Press, chs. 3 and 9

Rowthorn, R. (1982) 'The Past Strikes Back', *Marxism Today*, vol. 26, no. 1 (January)

2.3

Barrett, M. (1980) *Women's Oppression Today*, Verso, ch. 5

See also references for section 2.2 above.

3 INDUSTRIAL POLICY

3.1 The State and Industrial Policy

This chapter considers the determinants of industrial policy, the changes it has undergone and its impact on accumulation. In section 3.1.1, the nature of competition between capitals is examined. In sections 3.1.2–3.1.4, a framework for understanding industrial policy is developed, beginning with the simple model of the CMP, where the 'needs' of capital are the only determinant of industrial policy, then examining in turn the impact of class relations, fractions of capital and labour, the spatial structure of classes and the limits to state intervention. Section 3.2 analyses the strategies and instruments that the state has at its disposal for industrial policy. In section 3.3, the development of industrial policy in the UK is outlined in periods corresponding to particular stages in policy development. Finally, in section 3.4 the overall impact of industrial policy on British capitalism is considered.

3.1.1 Competition between Capitals

Autonomous capitalists produce commodities for sale, and are thus in competition with each other in the search for profit through the extraction of surplus value which, when realised as profit, can either be consumed or accumulated in the purchase of more means of production and labour power. Capitalists, however, are compelled to accumulate because of competitive pressures. They must reduce costs *vis-à-vis* competitors by using more advanced and efficient techniques and means of production and by growth to achieve scale economies. In consequence, the strong and efficient survive, and the weak and inefficient go to the wall. Moreover, competition ensures that the forces of production continually develop and that restructuring of changes in the organisation of production occurs. Competition also generates a tendency towards the equalisation of profit rates across sectors. Consequently disproportions of output and profit-rate variation are temporary. Production is continuously reorganised between sectors, within sectors and within individual firms, as a result of the competitive drive for accumulation.

There are three other characteristics of competition between capitals. First, capitals do not restrict their activities either to individual commodities or to particular nation states. There is a tendency towards diversification and internationalisation of production into sectors and locations which offer (temporarily) higher profit rates. Second, mobility of capital is a vital precondition for competition, for without it profit signals cannot be responded to. Third, competition is a function of the *relative* size and efficiency of capitals, and hence rivalry is ensured.

The full working out of this competitive process requires the development of a credit system. Capitals require borrowing facilities to gather together the sums necessary to purchase means of production and labour power in advance of future profit. Financial institutions are required to mobilise and transform money capital (savings) into productive capital (investment), reduce the cost of circulation of commodities, and accelerate the turnover time of capital. Further accumulation can be quickened by the development of joint-stock corporations, wherein shares in the organisation can be sold to raise capital, in anticipation of a share in expected profits. Competition between capitals also takes place in a spatial context. Capital will seek out those locations which are advantageous in relation to the cost of means of production and labour power, thus temporarily providing excess profit and continuously changing the spatial organisation of production.

3.1.2 Industrial Policy and the Needs of Capital

In the simple model of the CMP, the state reflects the needs of capital and acts automatically on its behalf. Initially, the state provides for the establishment of conditions allowing free, competitive exchange, abolishing restrictions on the mobility of means of production, labour power and money capital, and guaranteeing private property rights. In these ways the conditions are established for competition to operate in the manner outlined in the previous section. However, there are also a variety of preconditions for accumulation which also have to be established by the state, because individual capitals either are unable to provide them or can only do so at enormous expense or which, once produced, are available also to their competitors, for example, sewerage, water and roads. The state, acting as the ideal 'collective capitalist', provides the necessary infrastructure which individual capitals are unable or unwilling to produce.

However, competition between capitals does not operate in the simple way depicted in the previous section. As capitalism develops, various barriers to accumulation arise. First, measures are required to increase the mobility of resources and the quantity and quality of information available to capital, so that adjustment to changing competitive circumstances can be rapid and disproportions avoided. The development of machinery, scale economies, the continuous growth of fixed capital and the cost of major capital projects makes it increasingly difficult for capital to move to sectors with higher profits. Further, technological innovation accelerates the speed at which machinery becomes obsolescent, and state support is required to finance new technology research and development as it becomes beyond the capacity of individual capitals (for example, in aerospace, nuclear weapons and power, and computers). Capitalist economies also experience cyclical declines in profitability, which offer an occasion for further state intervention. Whilst crises do perform important functions for capital in *general*, reducing the size of unprofitable sectors, eliminating excess capacity and hence restructuring production, *individual* less competitive capitals and sectors 'require' state assistance to mitigate or slow down decline.

Growing international competition may further stimulate state activity to protect domestic capital. Although this may meet the needs of capital in a national sense, it is antagonistic to capital in general, particularly to those sections of capital which have internationalised their operations. A further outcome of the process of competition is the generation of *monopoly* through the competitive process. The *concentration* of capital, which proceeds by capitals reducing their costs relative to their rivals, increases the minimum size necessary to compete, thus providing a barrier to new entry. Capital is also *centralised* through mergers and take-overs. The combined effects of concentration and centralisation give rise to the dominance of a small number of large firms. These firms benefit from control over their competitive environment through price fixing and collusion, and greater economic power over their workforce and in relation to the state.

However, the growth of monopoly reduces the free flow of capital, balanced accumulation is made more difficult and the restructuring of production is contained. Dominant capitals can develop strategies (cartels, regulation of prices or output) in their sector to protect themselves from necessary restructuring. In consequence the state, acting in the interests of capital as a whole, intervenes to restore free, competitive exchange by means of anti-trust policies, or public regulation, or ownership of 'natural' monopolies, where the technical requirements of production are such that only one supplier is required. However, such action is contradictory, for such policies must preserve the benefits of 'monopoly capitalism', while resolving its negative effects on accumulation in general.

The search for profit is a global one, and the *internationalisation* of capital proceeds progressively as the forces of production develop. This causes a dislocation between the organisation of capital and the organisation of the nation state and leads to a progressive decline in its ability to foster accumulation and promote restructuring. Hence, there is a tendency for supranational state organisations to develop to provide a better fit between 'international' capital and its functional requirements. The state will also seek; to ensure that the barriers to international economic transactions are progressively reduced; to support the state's own capital in international locations; and, on occasion, to discriminate against foreign capital.

With regard to the financing of accumulation, the development of the forces of production is restrained by the inability of firms to raise capital for major investments. Hence the state encourages the formation of joint-stock corporations through enabling legislation. Furthermore, to ensure that capital can also raise money by borrowing from an efficient financial system, a central bank is required to ensure the free flow of funds and to regulate the circulation of money capital. Money capital *absorbs* rather than generates surplus value, and an inefficient system thus slows down accumulation.

The spatial organisation of production is a matter of concern for capital. In periods of rapid accumulation, pressure on the costs of the means of production and labour power may arise in specific locations, imposing 'external' costs on capital as a whole, but because of the long turnover time of the fixed capital employed, some capitals may be 'pinned down' and slow to adapt to newly emerging locational requirements. Hence the state stimulates the switching of production over space. The needs of capital are also met by uneven spatial development, stemming from the 'new' spatial division of labour, which develops in the later stages of capitalist development. Whereas in earlier periods regional imbalances stemmed essentially from the uneven development and disproportions between different sectors of production, now it increasingly involves firms in decentralising direct production and routine clerical functions, whilst concentrating control, organisational and research functions. This new spatial division of labour is encouraged by the state through regional policies in order to cheapen particular means of production and/or labour power.

In most cases, then, the role of the state is to accelerate the pace of economic change over and above that which would otherwise occur, in order to increase the pace of accumulation because competition fails to do so at a sufficiently rapid rate. However, unless the restructuring that occurs is more rapid than that of overseas capitals, economic decline will set in and accelerate.

3.1.3 Industrial Policy and the Balance of Class Forces

The structural antagonism between classes produces struggles between them, one manifestation of which is a struggle over state industrial policy. The extent of the industrial and political strength of labour will constrain and modify industrial policy so that it may not completely meet the needs of capital. The extent and nature of intervention thus varies with the balance of class forces in a given period, which varies over time. With, for example, sustained and rapid accumulation, unemployment falls, thus increasing the security, confidence and power of labour. Moreover, the influence of labour has increased in the long term with democratisation and the extension of the franchise, the developing industrial organisation of trade unions, the formation of a party representing the interests of labour and the election of its members to Parliament and, on occasions, forming the government. Thus the state has to damp down labour's resistance by concessions or confront the interests of labour by weakening the forces that have generated its increased strength.

Unemployment caused by state restructuring of capital may create major legitimation problems. Hence policies may be modified to moderate their effects through assistance to declining industries or firms, to provide employment and avoid community and industrial disruption. However, the development of capitalism does not *necessarily* shift the balance of class power towards labour. Severe crises weaken labour, and the concentration, centralisation and internationalisation of capital increases the power of individual capitals over labour.

Class struggle is important with regard to spatial policy, where industrial movement in periods of regional or national decline can be seen as a response to the relative strength of organised labour in different locations. Where this is overlaid by threats to national state cohesion, as for example in Northern Ireland and Scotland, the need for intervention is particularly strong. State action to meet the needs of capital, then, is constrained by the balance of class forces, as labour is generally trying to *slow down* the pace of change. The gap between what capital wants and what the state does may be seen to be a function of the balance of class forces.

3.1.4 Industrial Policy and 'Actually Existing Capitalism'

State industrial policy may also reflect the needs of *different fractions of capital*. The profits of financial capital arise from the redistribution of surplus value from industrial capital. Whilst therefore both fractions compete for a share of this surplus, financial capital does provide vital functions for industrial capital. Furthermore, both share a common interest in maximising the surplus generated in the sphere of production for distribution between them. How, then, can there be antagonistic interests between financial and industrial capital?

In the UK, state policy has been particularly influenced by financial capital and does not necessarily or consistently represent the interests of domestic or industrial capital. Financial capital has little interest in the domestic industrial economy, as its profits are not dependent on the UK domestic industrial sector, and as such it has much in common with international sections of industrial capital. In recent years, changing trade and foreign investment patterns, as well as the City's increasing role as a centre for international borrowing and lending of the US dollar, have meant that financial capital is even less dependent on the UK domestic economy than in the past. This lack of integration between financial and industrial capital has had two major effects. Policies are pursued which reflect financial, rather than industrial, interests, for example with regard to exchange and interest rates. The necessary freedom of action in money market activities also prevents certain types of industrial policy from being introduced. Financial capital plays a limited role in financing domestic accumulation and does not accord its viability a high priority. This reduces the strength, unity and determination of capital to push for industrial policies to restructure domestic industry. This is further exacerbated when the party that is supposed to represent politically the interests of capital is in government, since it largely favours financial rather than industrial interests. Indeed the Labour Party, representing and dependent on organised labour, may, in representing *its* voting and class constituency, provide policies more oriented to domestic industry. Within industry itself there are further conflicts which affect the nature of industrial policy. The interest of capitals in declining sectors differ from those of capitals in new and expanding sectors. Similarly, policies that benefit monopolistic sectors may not benefit competitive sectors.

Within labour there are also fractions, and the relative strength of these may change over time, affecting the nature and strength of labour's 'demands' on industrial policy (for example, with regard to manual vs non-manual workers; private vs public; and men vs women). The spatial structure of both labour power and capital creates diverse local class structures, which have become increasingly complex as a result of recent restructuring of both capital and labour. In consequence, there is a spatially differentiated balance of forces.

Finally, there are three further factors which affect the determination of industrial policy. First, strategic considerations of national security as well as major wars generate intervention under the pressure of events, which affects the future course of intervention since capital, labour and the state all learn from previous experiences. Second, there are limits to the extent to which state industrial intervention can be successful. This is because the political representatives of capital may imperfectly articulate or represent their objective needs; because there are structural limits to state intervention involving additional state expenditure; and because of the state's limited control over industrial decisions. Third, the 'economic' problems facing industry may simply be displaced, rather than resolved, when state intervention in industry is designed to deal with legitimation problems.

3.2 State Strategies and Instruments

Capitalism requires a strategy which restructures capital and yet retains social stability. Measures are required to promote greater efficiency and competitiveness, *and* to alleviate the consequent costs, particularly on employment. It must accelerate *and* slow down change at the same time. The balance between these objectives is conditioned by the existing balance of class forces and the extent of the accumulation problems faced. There are essentially two types of strategy available to sustain or restore accumulation, although, given the complexity of the forces determining state industrial policy, neither of these will be found in a *pure* form. A *social market strategy* is one of disengagement, as it reduces intervention towards private capital, particularly if designed to decelerate the pace of change. It seeks to break down barriers to the operation of the competitive process. It provides for restructuring through market rather than state direction. A *direct intervention strategy* provides for restructuring through state incentives, regulation and the modification of market forces. This strategy requires the co-operation of capital and labour, often through corporatist channels.

The instruments that are available to the state in pursuing these strategies can be divided into five: policies on market discipline; competition; financial assistance; regional assistance; and policies on ownership. The relationship between the strategies and instruments is summarised schematically in Table 3.1.

Table 3.1: Industrial Strategies and Instruments

	Market discipline	Competition policy	Financial assistance	Regional assistance	Ownership
Social market strategy	Liberalise	Strengthen	Reduce	Reduce	Privatisation
Direct intervention strategy	Regulate	Ambivalent	Expand	Expand	Nationalisation

The extension or reinstatement of *market discipline* involves the deregulation or liberalisation of markets by reducing controls and incentives that alter decisions from those that would be taken under market and profitability criteria. It thus speeds up the process of economic adjustment. *Competition policy* involves regulating the relations between capitals in such a way as to ensure that competition is 'free' and not limited by the conduct of individual capitals or the structure of the markets within which they operate, so restraining capitals from abusing positions of dominance. These policies aim to ensure that the benefits of the growth of large firms, especially productive efficiency, are not negated by their enhanced power, which would diminish market efficiency. *Financial assistance* to private capital is designed to speed up accumulation by reducing the cost of means of production (and sometimes labour power) through the replacement of older with newer means of production. This assistance may take the form of grants, subsidies, loans at preferential rates or tax relief. It often involves financing changes in production techniques that would not occur under market regulation, because the concentration and centralisation of capital means that competition and crises are not fully effective in stimulating such changes, and because technological developments increase, over time, the size, risk, lead times, and research and development required for major investments. Financial assistance is used to promote the combination of capitals and their restructuring, as well as encouraging capitals or sectors to scrap existing productive capacity to adjust rapidly to a declining market. Financial incentives may also be used under pressure to give temporary assistance to capitals facing liquidity or profitability difficulties, although such assistance is usually provided conditional on the restructuring of production. *Regional assistance* consists of financial aid to capitals in specific spatially defined areas, as well as control over the expansion of capitals in other spatially defined areas. This is particularly required when there is pressure on costs of production in areas experiencing rapid accumulation, whence regional policy helps speed up the adjustment process. Regional policy may also aid legitimation through policies to encourage more rapidly growing sectors of capital to locate in declining areas and to assist capitals in 'need'. Location controls are designed to reduce the pressure on costs in rapid accumulation areas as well as to provide a source for movement into assisted areas and to encourage capitals to move to areas of potentially more rapid accumulation.

Policies on *ownership* may take the form of *nationalisation* or *privatisation*. The interests of capital in general are entirely compatible with the *nationalisation* of particular capitals or sectors. The existence of substantial economies of scale may create 'natural' monopolies, where competition would be inefficient due to wasteful duplication, smaller-scale operation or because a private monopoly would be exploitative of other capitals. If capitals that provide basic infrastructure to capital in general are unprofitable, then nationalisation secures their supplies. Nationalisation may also be used to prevent the financial collapse of a major capital due to its knock-on effects on other capitals as well as its impact on social stability, or to restructure a sector which is inefficient or suffers overcapacity. This is difficult to achieve under market discipline, if the sector is dominated by a few large capitals indulging in collusive practices. If nationalised industries sell their output at a price yielding less than the average profit rate to private capital, then they transfer value *to* private capital, which increases its average profit rate. However, if they sell at a *loss*, then the subsidies require damage capital. This may lead to the application of stricter commercial criteria. Nationalisation of profitable capitals, or putting them directly in competition with private capitals, similarly is not in capital's interest. On privatisation see pp. 35–36.

Thus the state, through its policies, attempts to guarantee a minimum profit: by taking responsibility for unprofitable sectors; by transferring enterprises founded with 'public' money to private capital; by a variety of 'subsidies' to private capital; and by encouraging the restructuring of production.

3.3 Industrial Policy in the UK

3.3.1 Ascent and Descent: 1780–1914

The state played little role in directly fostering or sustaining the industrial revolution. As industry developed *first* in the UK, there was no need to protect uncompetitive industries or nurture new ones, since there was no effective international challenge. State intervention was limited in the period 1780–1870 to liberalising societal institutions in order to create a framework within which industrial development based on the pursuit of private profit could thrive. Archaic legal provisions were abolished, whilst new ones were introduced to protect property rights, such as those to safeguard against the piracy of industrial designs. Tariffs were progressively dismantled, the international trading network extended and imperial relations with the empire defended by directing colonial exports and imports through the UK and militarily defending colonial trade and possessions. The Poor Law (Amendment) Act 1834 drove unemployed labour onto the labour market through the disincentive of the workhouse, replacing wage subsidies and outdoor relief payments (see section 5.2.1), and the 1846 abolition of the corn laws provided for a reallocation of domestic resources from hitherto inefficient and protected agriculture to efficient industry. As productive forces were not yet highly developed, and as the economic and political power of labour was also limited, the demands on the state for direct action were nonexistent. Policies were as near *laissez-faire* as has ever been possible in a modern state. Nevertheless the state did act to sustain accumulation through the introduction of legislation to allow incorporation, and therefore the formation of joint-stock companies, and to provide for limited liability under the Companies Acts of 1844, 1855 and 1856. These allowed new sources of finance for expansion to be tapped.

However, from the 1870s to 1914 the growth of international rivalry especially from Germany and the USA, the increasing scale and technological advance of industry, the growing strength of labour and the Great Depression (1873–96) prompted a more active role for the state to restructure capital. In the Great Depression, declining sections of capital called on the state for assistance, and the expansion of the electorate through the Reform Act 1867 and the first entry of trade unionists into Parliament in 1874 put further pressure on the state. The state was ill adapted, however, to be the agent of industrial reconstruction, given its previous development and structure. Moreover British capital was heavily involved overseas, both through the international operations of the City and through substantial investment abroad. In 1870, the majority of investment was overseas, and between 1911 and 1913 the amount invested abroad was double that invested in the UK. This international orientation, the cushioning of the balance of payments effects of declining competitiveness through the repatriation of profits, and the monopoly in empire markets, ensured that the pressure on capital and the state to modernise was muted. Indeed the overall reaction was defensive. Although the centralisation of capital proceeded often with state support, it focused not on restructuring, but on price-fixing (more than 500 price-fixing agreements existed in 1918) to protect markets and profits, and to keep inefficient capitals in business through mergers or through the development of trusts and cartels, as for example in cement, tobacco and printing. Agriculture, too, became protected as a result of the 1914–18 war, with the state introducing import levies, guaranteeing prices and initiating marketing boards for agricultural produce. So, despite the beginnings of relative decline, the state did not provide assistance for restructuring the UK's industrial base in the period up to the First World War. Taking a controlling interest in an oil company (now BP) to preserve naval oil supplies in case of war, and a loan to Cunard to build two liners were very much exceptions.

3.3.2 *The Inter-war Years*

In the First World War the pressure of events created an increase in the control of capital by the state. Several industries were taken over by the state (for example, flour, milk and iron ore mines), and others had their output requisitioned (for example, coal). There were controls also on industrial production through output quotas and the physical allocation of raw materials. Although these actions were quickly reversed after the war, mostly by 1919, there remained the legacy that state action in relation to industry was possible, legitimate and workable, and that moreover it had been associated with a boom in profits. Developments after 1918 also provided a stimulus, notably the continuing increase in the size of firms with the development of mass-production Fordist techniques, and the severe depression and collapse of accumulation of 1929–33, which also resulted in substantial regional unemployment. Industrial output failed to grow at all between 1913 and 1923, and only grew by 3 per cent between 1924 and 1932, as the traditional staple industries declined because of continuing relative uncompetitiveness, the return to the gold standard in 1925, and the collapse of world trade in the depression. The response of the state was to encourage further defensive cartelisation, building on the existing trade associations and restrictive practices that prevented the necessary restructuring from occurring. An iron and steel cartel was set up in 1932 (production had fallen by 50 per cent between 1929 and 1932), prices were fixed by agreement and production was regulated to preserve profitability and restrict competitive forces. The Mining Industry Act 1926 encouraged colliery amalgamation and the Coal Mines Act 1930 set up a compulsory cartel scheme. In agriculture, guaranteed prices, as well as import duties, through price regulation and support, were introduced in 1931, and a third of all output was bought by state-sponsored marketing boards.

Little restructuring of these traditional industries was stimulated either through liberalisation or state-financed reorganisation. An exception was the cotton industry. Through the Cotton Spinning Act 1936, financed by a compulsory levy, excess capacity was removed, which resulted in scrapping nearly one-third of total capacity. Amalgamation of the railway companies in 1921 was also sponsored by the state, reducing them from nearly one hundred companies to just four. However, new industries were developing, unaided by state sponsorship, providing consumer goods for the domestic market and, although overall this stimulated industrial production to increase by 30 per cent between 1933 and 1937, their locational requirements for profitable production were different from those of the declining industries. Hence unemployment rose dramatically in the early 1930s, reaching well over 50 per cent in some areas. The response was the Special Areas Act 1934, and amendments to it in 1936 and 1937, which provided for the building of industrial and trading estates, cheap loans and subsidised rents, costing the Exchequer £21 million between 1934 and 1938. Loans were also provided to Cunard to help finance the building of two new luxury liners, the *Queen Mary* and *Queen Elizabeth*, to create employment. These measures were totally inadequate and were seen as temporary. The rise of the Labour Party, and the representation of workers in these areas in Parliament, ensured that some action had to be taken. It was rearmament for war, however, rather than regional policy, which stimulated many staple industries.

3.3.3 The Long Boom and Industrial Policy: 1939–65

The problems of overproduction in the inter-war period gave way to the need to *restrict* non-war production during the Second World War. The state played a major role in fixing output quotas and allocating new materials, with the trade associations acting as agents. The state also took control of aircraft production, expanded control of agriculture and vastly increased the output of the state-owned Ordnance Factories. The period of the war was the only time when extensive moves were made to subordinate private capital to politically determined production decisions, although the British state did not possess the necessary institutions and the accumulate expertise in industrial planning. These interventions were rapidly abandoned, in part because the new Labour government adopted Keynesianism rather than interventionist industrial planning as the major instrument of economic regulation, and direct state control of industry was undertaken by nationalisation, rather than industrial planning.

In the years following the Second World War, state *ownership* was extended by the nationalisation of coal, railways, steel, civil aviation, gas and electricity. Although the balance of class forces played a role in ensuring this transfer of ownership, many of these industries were beyond salvage by private capital, being fundamentally unprofitable and requiring large-scale modernisation. Nationalisation was also supported on pragmatic grounds of co-ordination or natural monopoly or to improve industrial relations. The introduction of *initial allowances*, in 1945, provided accelerated depreciation and thus encouraged investment in private industry.

The National Research and Development Corporation (NRDC) was also set up in 1948, to encourage inventions and their application and so stimulate new products and processes. The Distribution of Industry Act 1945 and Town and Country Planning Act 1947 provided for factory building and loans to enterprises in the newly defined 'development areas', as well as the requirement to obtain an 'industrial development certificate' (IDC) from the Board of Trade before undertaking any new industrial development of more than 5,000 sq. ft, in order to control expansion in rapid-growth areas and divert it to the 'development areas'. With regard to agriculture, the Agriculture Act of 1947 developed the protection of agriculture by guaranteeing prices, based on annual reviews with the farmers. Should prices fall below these levels, 'deficiency' payments would be made in lieu by the state.

With the expansion of the economy in the 1950s, there was little financial assistance to stimulate accumulation 'artificially' and little need to strengthen regional policy. And although steel was denationalised in 1953, there were no other changes to state ownership though nationalised industries were required to 'pay their way', taking one year with another, which was generally achieved because of the rapid accumulation of the period. There were, however, important policy developments in the field of *competition*. Hitherto cartels had been encouraged in order to prevent price wars and falling profits in periods of slow accumulation. Now, however, with rapid accumulation and continuing increases in concentration, cartels and monopolies could 'exploit' their positions by raising prices, because of the lack of competition due to high demand. The Monopoly and Restrictive Practices Act 1948 for the first time intro-duced legislation ostensibly to control monopolies and stimulate competition. It defined a monopoly as existing when at least one-third of a market was controlled by one firm, and empowered the government of the day to refer it to a newly established Monopolies Commission in order to report on it to see if it was undertaking undesirable practices. If so, the firm would be ordered to stop, although there was no way of knowing whether such an agreement was honoured. A case-by-case approach was adopted with no general presumption against monopolies and no attempt to change the structure of markets, but merely the conduct of monopolists in them. This was followed by the Restrictive Trade Practices Act 1956, in an attempt to reverse the pre-war government attitude to collusion and cartels. At this time 75 per cent of manufacturing output was subject to cartel agreements. The Act covered price agreements between firms which were to be registered and presumed against the 'public interest', unless the firm could use one of the 'gateways' of the Act to seek exception. These agreements stifle competitive forces, remove the stimulus to market efficiency and hence slow down technical change and productivity growth. However, the result was to stimulate merger activity, hence increasing concentration further, since price agreements between different parts of the *same* firm are *not* illegal.

The early 1960s saw several policy developments as relative industrial decline continued; concentration and centralisation of capital speeded up (partly due to state policy itself), and the strength of labour continued to develop under conditions of historically, though not relatively, rapid accumulation and high employment. The Resale Prices Act 1964 abolished resale price maintenance, under which retailers had to charge at least a minimum price. This led to further concentration of capital, precisely because of the unleashing of competitive forces. The Monopolies and Mergers Act 1965 for the first time provided for the investigation of mergers. A merger was liable for investigation by the reformed Monopolies and Mergers Commission (MMC) if the government referred it to the commission, and if it gave rise to a new enterprise with more than one-third of the market for a commodity or an asset value of more than £5 million. Additionally, all newspaper acquisitions automatically now had to go to the MMC. Again, the approach involved case-by-case investigation, rather than automatic rules. However, a highly permissive attitude to mergers existed. Of the 500 mergers that fell within the scope of the Act between 1965 and 1970 only thirteen were investigated and four halted. In the same period, only seventeen monopoly references were made.

The deficits of the *nationalised industries* began to increase from the late 1950s, and from 1961 there was increased emphasis on better financial performance and the introduction of more commercial criteria in their operations, notably the introduction of a requirement to earn a particular rate of return, although some allowance was still made for expenditure in the national interest, such as electricity supply to remote rural areas. The financial effects of the cheap provision of basic inputs to private capital was beginning to be felt. *Regional policy* was modified by the introduction of building grants under the Local Employment Act 1960, and for the first time by allowing finance to be provided by the state, irrespective of evidence of availability from other sources. In 1963, automatic standard investment grants on plant and machinery were introduced for the first time, and accelerated depreciation was introduced in an attempt to increase liquidity. Expenditure on regional assistance thus increased from less than £9 million in 1959 to over £40 million in 1965. In 1963 and 1965, controls on location were extended from manufacturing to office development through the Office Development Permit (ODP) system.

Two significant changes in financial assistance developed in this period. First, Investment Allowances, wherein an allowance in excess of the total cost of the investment can be offset against tax, were introduced throughout the UK in 1959; secondly, 'selective' financial assistance was used to provide for restructuring of the cotton industry. The Cotton Industry Act 1959 provided subsidies to scrap old plant, close businesses and requip those that remained. Plant was reduced by a half, concentration increased with six companies taking over more than one hundred others between 1960 and 1966, and employment was reduced by 32 per cent during the period of the scheme's operation (1959–64). The National Economic Development Council (NEDC) and industry-based EDCs were set up in 1963 with tripartite membership, in order to create a joint consensual approach to industrial decline and lack of competitiveness, between government, capital and labour. Its aim was to increase understanding and communication between the three and to defuse conflict, but it had no powers of intervention.

3.3.4 The Quest for Modernisation: 1966–70

The major development during this period of intensified accumulation problems was a more comprehensive and determined attempt to modernise and restructure domestic manufacturing. The Industrial Reorganisation Corporation (IRC) was set up in 1966, in the words of the Act to 'promote industrial efficiency and profitability' by facilitating the development of larger and therefore more productively efficient firms. This was to be achieved by providing loans to newly merged companies as well as to other organisations for restructuring or expansion. It helped foster mergers between GEC and AEI, and BMC and Leyland, as well as restructuring Rolls Royce, Camel Laird and RHP ball-bearings. It also formed International Computers Limited (ICL) from ICT, English Electric Computers and Elliot Automation, in which it purchased shares and to which it provided grants for research and development in order to compete with IBM. However, IRC had to earn a commercial rate of return on its dealings. It had to be satisfied that finance was not available from elsewhere and it had relatively limited sums available. Between 1966 and 1970, it spent £103 million net. Similarly, the Shipbuilding Industry Act 1967 attempted to aid the restructuring of the rapidly declining shipbuilding industry, in order to help it compete internationally. Four unprofitable yards were merged to form Upper Clyde Shipbuilders (UCS) in 1968, and further grants of £20 million were provided for modernisation between 1968 and 1970. More than 30 per cent of all jobs at the yards were lost in the first year after the merger. In 1966, investment grants of 20 per cent were introduced for the first time nationally. These benefited all capitals (unlike investment allowances), irrespective of their profitability, and were thus worth more in periods of declining profitability. Under the Industrial Expansion Act 1968, further loans and grants were made available to projects that otherwise would lack private-sector financial support, where these would promote modernisation. The projects included the building of three new aluminium smelters. In 1968, funds allocated to the NRDC were extended to £50 million. *Regional incentives* to speed up accumulation were also increased under the Industrial Development Act 1966, by expanding the 'development districts' to 'development areas' which covered 40 per cent of the UK land area and by introducing automatic investment grants at the higher level of 40 per cent in these areas. A subsidy on labour costs, the 'regional employment premium', was also introduced in 1967, along with higher levels of assistance still in 'special development areas' (SDAs). In consequence, regional financial assistance increased from £17 million in 1960/1 to over £300 million in 1969/70 (at 1970 prices).

The *nationalised industries*, too, were further encouraged to become more efficient with the introduction in 1967 of 'marginal-cost' pricing criteria, although this still meant that losses had to be financed, as most nationalised industries experienced continuously declining average costs. Within the framework of the 1965 National Plan there was further development of tripartite EDCs, with 37 in existence by 1967, although they still had *no powers* to enforce the necessary changes they identified. *Competition policy* was strengthened by the Restrictive Trade Practices Act 1968, which ensured that 'information' as well as 'price' agreements was now covered. These had been a favourite way of circumventing the 1956 legislation. However, such changes in competition policy had little impact on the growing centralisation and concentration of capital. Indeed other industrial policies speeded it up. By 1968, 50 per cent of manufacturing sales were in industries where five firms accounted for more than 70 per cent of output, and the largest 100 manufacturing firms by 1970 accounted for 46 per cent of total output. Between 1948 and 1972, half of all quoted firms were subject to merger activity.

3.3.5 Disengagement: 1970–2

The election of the Conservative government in 1970 marked a short-lived retreat from the growth of direct state intervention. Ideologically, market forces were preferred to structural reorganisation by the state to stimulate adjustment. The IRC was abolished in 1971 and its investments disposed of. Key sections of the Industrial Expansion Act 1968 on selective financial assistance were repealed. Investment grants were abolished and replaced by initial tax allowances. 'Lame ducks' were no longer to be protected from market forces and six of the EDCs were wound up. Regional financial assistance was also reduced, with the planned phasing out of the Regional Economic Premium (REP) and the abolition of investment grants. These were replaced by tax allowances at a level higher than the national rate, which was worth little as profits were falling. IDC and ODP controls were relaxed. The nationalised industries had some of their 'peripheral' activities sold off. BSC's brickworks, some state-owned public houses, a brewery and Cooks Travel Agency were sold to private capital.

However, the collapse of Upper Clyde Shipbuilders in 1971 led to substantial financial assistance. In the same year, the problems of Rolls Royce's aero-engine division, caused by problems with the RB211 jet engine, where the state had already provided two-thirds (£65 million) of its launching costs, led to its nationalisation. In the Rolls Royce case, its relation to national defence, its export commitments, and especially the penalty clauses on the RB211 contract occasioned its nationalisation. The workforce was cut back by 9,000 jobs. In the UCS case, a sit-in over plans to close two of the yards and retain the other two for sale to new private buyers led to the change in policy. With the onset of a deep economic crisis, with industrial investment stagnant and unemployment reaching one million for the first time since the 1930s, the disengagement experiment was, temporarily, over.

3.3.6 Direct State Intervention: 1972–9

The Industry Act 1972 marked a major change in policy once more to a state-sponsored mode of restructuring of capital. It provided for wide powers of selective, but discretionary, intervention, most notably under sections 7 and 8, making available £1,400 million over five years. It was used to restructure the wool textile industry in 1973 by closing down 10 per cent of all firms in the industry. The powers in the Act, though little used up to 1974, except to attract foreign investment, were widely used in subsequent years. The Act also reintroduced automatic investment grants in the development areas in the form of 'regional' development grants (RDG), over and above automatic accelerated depreciation, and extended them to buildings as well as plant and machinery. The development areas were also extended to cover 65 per cent of the UK's land area and 44 per cent of the population, although the exemption limits for IDCs were raised to increase capital's freedom in the location decision. The parallel Local Employment Act 1972 also provided for the free letting of state-provided factories for a period.

Competition policy was augmented by the Fair Trading Act 1973, which set up the Office of Fair Trading (OFT) to be responsible for referring cases on monopolies and mergers to the MMC. Nationalised industries and commercial services were also brought into the scope of the legislation for the first time, and the monopoly definition was amended from one-third to one-quarter of the market for a commodity. None the less, such changes in policy as this and the 1965 Act failed to slacken the growth in merger activity and growing monopolistic concentration. Between 1963 and 1979, the number of acquisitions varied from 300 to 1,200 and out of nearly 1,800 mergers looked at by the MMC only 18 were halted. The largest one hundred firms amongst those with assets of more than £2 million in 1976 produced 80 per cent of all output. The other main change in industrial policy was the switch from deficiency payments for agricultural price support to the new EEC system, on joining the EEC in 1973, which in itself was a major market-induced attempt to restructure domestic manufacturing by reducing its protection *vis-à-vis* EEC member states. The new support system through the Common Agricultural Policy, instead of providing effective subsidies to farmers for holding prices down, allows prices to be set artificially above world market prices by both levying duties on imports and by the EEC agricultural intervention board purchasing any surplus production at guaranteed intervention prices.

Agriculture remains the only industry to be provided continual financial assistance at considerable levels, reflecting in part the influence of landed elements in the ruling bloc.

The election of a Labour government in 1974 saw a further considerable development in direct state intervention with the unveiling of the 'industrial strategy', which was an attempt to bring together and co-ordinate much of industrial policy through three interrelated elements: the development of planning through the existing NEDC system and new 'planning agreements'; financial assistance available under the 1972 Act; and direct intervention through the new National Enterprise Board (NEB). Some 37 Sector Working Parties (SWPs) were set up and prepared modernisation schemes for sectors comprising around 40 per cent of manufacturing industry. This approach of partnership between government, capital and unions cemented an ideological consensus around notions of the 'national interest' and the 'needs' of industry. However, there were no mechanisms to implement the schemes and they remained more an exercise in incorporation and legitimation, by seeking an alliance between sections of capital and labour, than an effective process of restructuring. A new instrument was introduced in the Industry Act 1975 in the form of the Planning Agreement (PA), which was designed to translate the SWP programmes into action at the firm level. Only two of these were ever made, one with the NCB and one with Chrysler UK, when the board of the latter threatened closure unless they received financial assistance. The £162.5 million provided was tied to a planning agreement. Chrysler later withdrew all car production from the UK, and indeed Europe. The agreements were voluntary and financial assistance was not conditional upon them.

With regard to financial assistance, the Industry Act 1975 removed the requirement in the 1972 Act for the state to establish a lack of private-sector provision before giving financial assistance. That apart, most assistance was provided through the terms of sections 7 and 8 of the 1972 Act. An 'accelerated projects' scheme was introduced in 1975 for one year, in order to bring forward investment plans by providing interest-relief grants. This was replaced in 1976 by a selective investment scheme tied to particular investment projects. These two schemes provided £170 million assistance between 1975 and 1979, with an 'average' state contribution of 10 per cent per project. The Labour government announced thirteen new sectoral schemes to encourage modernisation and rationalisation in the machine tools, footwear and clothing industries, amongst others. This provided £272 million between 1972 and 1980. Assistance was also available for 'rescue' operations (like Chrysler and British Leyland), and together all selective assistance amounted to £700 million per annum by 1979, against £180 million in 1972. In addition, 100 per cent investment allowances were automatically available on plant and machinery, with 50 per cent on buildings. The introduction of the Micro-electronics Industry Support Programme (MISP) and the Micro-electronics Application Programme (MAP) in 1978 and 1979, providing £110 million for the promotion of microelectronics production and applications, further extended state financial assistance.

A new form of more direct state intervention, the NEB, was introduced in the Industry Act 1975. Originally planned as a vehicle to extend and modify state ownership into profitable manufacturing, in practice it provided a new instrument for financing restructuring, with the ideological gloss of introducing some accountability into financial support for capital. The NEB was originally funded to the tune of £700 million, later extended to £1,000 million, with which to purchase *equity* (shares) in private companies and set up its own. The idea was to enlarge the equity and asset base of firms so that they could more easily raise funds, additional to those from the NEB, from private financial capital. There was no intention to purchase equity with the aim of taking over the firm, and all purchases were to be by agreement with the firm concerned. There were no compulsory powers. In addition, the NEB became the holding company for the state's shares in British Leyland, Rolls Royce and other firms. The NEB, though willing to take a longer-run view on investment yields than private financial capital, was required to achieve a rate of return of 15 per cent (at historic cost) on its investments, excluding 'lame ducks' acquired through rescue operations. It thus assessed its investments, and the performance of its subsidiaries in commercial terms. By 1979, although the NEB had 68 companies under its control, 93 per cent of its funds were tied up in six 'rescue' cases, with 87 per cent in British Leyland and Rolls Royce alone. The NEB was to restructure these firms and return them to profitability, where private capital had failed to do so. In so doing, for example, BL shed 32,000 jobs between 1975 and 1979. The cost of restructuring was borne by labour with job losses and intensification of the labour process. Whilst the NEB's original objectives included employment and social ones, these were subordinated to the needs of accumulation. Only 7 per cent of NEB's funds were used for investment in new technology, involving firms like Ferranti and ICL, or for new subsidiaries of its own like Inmos, the microchip manufacturer, which was established in 1978 with £50 million provision from NEB.

In addition to the 'industrial strategy', the period witnessed further developments in industrial policy, most notably with regard to *regional policy* and the nationalised industries. Between 1974 and 1976 regional policy was strengthened, with REP being doubled, IDC controls tightened and more selective assistance available. However, the developing economic and 'expenditure' crises, occasioned by a more interventionist state in a low-growth economy like the UK, led to considerable cutbacks in regional support. Not only were IDCs relaxed, since accumulation, irrespective of location, is better than no accumulation at all, but the abolition of REP was announced and RDGs were in future to be paid in arrears. This regional assistance accounts for a large proportion of total state financial assistance. For example, of the £1,400 million available under the 1972 Act, more than 70 per cent was accounted for by RDG expenditure.

The nationalised industries were faced with further commercial and competitive pressure. Although still shielded by a legal monopoly, external financing limits were set in 1978 with a medium-term financial target of 5 per cent real rate of return on investment programmes. Lending to them was reduced by 50 per cent between 1974 and 1978. Four new public corporations were also formed: British Leyland (BL) British Aerospace (BAe), British National Oil Corporation (BNOC) and British Shipbuilders (BS). BL and BS were nationalised for major restructuring: in the one case, to prevent the collapse of a major exporter with extensive industrial linkages in the UK, and in the other, to prevent a collapse in Labour support. However, BS shed 30,000 jobs in the first two years after nationalisation. BNOC was formed for national strategic reasons, and BAe because of the high cost of aviation projects and its role in supplying defence needs.

Overall, in the period 1972–9 the extent and nature of intervention fluctuated, with total financial assistance peaking at £1,500 million in 1975/6, although public expenditure restraints reduced this to around £780 million by 1979.

3.3.7 A Social Market Strategy: 1979 and onwards

With the election of the Conservative government in 1979, and again in 1983, industrial policy shifted away from state-sponsored restructuring to market discipline, reflecting the political and economic ideology of the government; the failure of the interventionist period, 1972–9, to reverse industrial decline; the deepening 'fiscal' crises of the state; reduced priority to domestic manufacturing; and the growing weakness of the labour movement. Nevertheless such a strategy has proved difficult to pursue consistently and, indeed, substantial state intervention still remains. Unprofitable industries are not supported by financial assistance and many have gone to the wall, including those previously in receipt of state support like the Invergordon Aluminium Smelter and DeLorean cars. Selective financial assistance has all but been eliminated, as it is thought to distort competition by discriminating between different capitals, and no new sectoral assistance schemes have been introduced. The NEB has been forced to sell many of its holdings, for example, in ICL (now taken over by STC), Ferranti, Fairey and Inmos, and its role has been substantially reduced by the transference of BL and Rolls Royce back to the government and its merging with NRDC to form the British Technology Group (BTG) in 1981, thus leaving it to concentrate on high technology.

The *nationalised industries'* External Financial Limits (EFLs) have been tightened, with lending to them reduced from nearly £4,700 million in 1979 to less than £1,000 million in 1984, thus forcing restructuring through increased concentration of output in their most efficient plants in order to raise productivity. Several of their legal monopolies are also being broken, such as those of the Post Office and British Telecom, thus 'liberalising' competition. Others, such as the electricity boards, have been forced to increase their prices to meet new financial targets. The importance of 'social' criteria in their operations has also been reduced — for example, in the case of 'non-economic' bus routes. Profitable sections of the nationalised industries are being privatised with asset sales reaching £3,600 million between 1979 and 1984, and the raising of over £4,000 million on the sale of British Telecom alone in 1984. The Jaguar division of BL has been sold off and the profitable warship yards of BS are also to be sold.

Regional financial assistance has also been reduced to 50 per cent of the 1974–9 average figure with a reduction in spatial coverage (from 44 per cent of the population to 27 per cent) and a cut in the value of RDGs to 15 per cent from 20 per cent. IDCs were abolished in 1982. Further plans are in hand to reduce expenditure even further from 1985, with greater selectivity in grant provision, reduced spatial coverage and reduced rates of grant; £20,000 million has been spent between 1963 and 1983 (at 1982 prices). New developments in regional policy involve the establishment of Enterprise Zones (EZs) and Freeports. Eleven of the former were designated in 1980 and a further fourteen in 1983 and 1984, involving, *inter alia*, no payment of rates for ten years and 100 per cent allowance for capital expenditure on buildings. Thus, an anti-state-intervention ideology is accompanied by a package of fiscal concessions. Six freeports are to be introduced from 1984, where no customs duties are payable, providing the output is exported.

State *expenditure* on industry has itself been restructured, in part towards expenditure on research and development. Although new technology is largely to be imported through foreign direct investment, in order to speed up structural adjustment, expenditure on assistance to high technology has increased by 90 per cent, especially in the field of microelectronics. The major assistance, however, has continued to go to BL, BSC and the NCB. In the case of BL, closure would cost more than the financial assistance and its knock-on effects on the balance of payments and other firms would be considerable. However, the firm is close to profitability and possible privatisation, now that it has been restructured by the state, with a further £1,000 million spent between 1981 and 1983, and with trade union organisation weakened in the process. In the NCB case, the government was forced to retreat on pit closures because of union pressure in 1981 and 1982, and it provided an additional £500 million to the NCB in 1982 in compensation for the non-acceleration of the pit-closure programme. In 1984, similar, but stronger union pressure led to a 12-month national strike over pit closures, but the state has refused to provide further financial assistance to keep 'uneconomic' pits open.

3.4 Industrial Policy and British Capitalism

This section contains a brief analysis of the overall impact of industrial policies on accumulation. A key measure of the changing competitiveness of capital is productivity growth. As can be seen from Table 3.2, productivity growth has been slow throughout *the*

Industrial Policy

Table 3.2: Average Annual Percentage Change in Output per Person in Manufacturing in the UK

1860–70	1870–80	1880–90	1890–1900	1900–13
1.1	1.2	0.5	0.2	0.2
1924–37	1935–49	1950–73	1973–8	1978–82
2.1	1.3	3.1	0.2	1.0

Sources: D.H. Aldcroft and H.W. Richardson, *The British Economy 1870–1939* (Macmillan, 1969); S. Aaronovitch and R. Smith, *The Political Economy of British Capitalism* (McGraw-Hill, 1981); D. Jones, 'Productivity and the Thatcher Experiment', *Socialist Economic Review*, (1983).

UK's industrial development, with the notable exception of the long boom period of 1950–73. Productivity growth has since declined to levels experienced in the late nineteenth and early twentieth centuries, although some progress has been made since 1979 (see Table 3.3). When comparison is made with the UK's major competitors, the productivity picture appears even more problematic. From Table 3.3 it can be seen that in general UK productivity growth has consistently lagged behind major competitors, often considerably so. Indeed, even in the long boom years when UK productivity growth was fast by its own *historical* standards, its *relative* position was deteriorating rapidly.

One aspect of the slow productivity growth is low investment. Indeed, between 1963 and 1969, expenditure on acquiring

Table 3.3: Percentage Average Annual Change in Productivity: the UK and some major competitors

	1870–1913	1918–50	1950–76	1976–9	1979–82
UK	1.1	1.5	2.8	1.2	2.5
USA	2.1	2.5	2.3	2.1	3.0
West Germany	1.9	1.2	5.8	3.7	1.5
France	1.8	1.7	4.9	3.9	2.5
Japan	1.8	1.4	7.5	7.7	1.0

Sources: A. Gamble, *Britain in Decline* (Macmillan, 1981); S. Pollard, *The Development of the British Economy 1914–80* (Edward Arnold, 1981); *National Economic Review,*, November 1984.

Table 3.4: Investment[a] as a Proportion of GDP

	1960	1965	1970	1975	1980
USA	17.2	19.1	17.3	15.3	20.3
Japan	24.1	28.3	35.0	32.1	32.4
France	18.6	21.7	23.4	23.2	23.0
West Germany	24.6	26.7	26.4	23.0	25.0
UK	15.0	17.5	18.7	17.8	14.7

Note: [a]Gross fixed capital formation.
Source: K. Williams, J. Williams and D. Thomas, *Why Are the British Bad at Manufacturing?* (Routledge and Kegan Paul, 1983).

subsidiaries exceeded net investment. Firms were growing more by merger than investment in *new* means of production. Table 3.4 demonstrates that investment as a proportion of GDP was often considerably lower than in major competitors. Indeed, on the basis of *net* fixed capital formation figures between 1955 and 1981, it never exceeded 19 per cent, whereas in *every* single year in France, West Germany and Japan it exceeded 20 per cent. Moreover the *pattern* of investment is important, as between one-third and two-thirds of finance for research and development is provided by the *state*. Half of this is defence-related investment, and has operated as a drain on technical innovation in civil manufacturing. Furthermore, investment *overseas* has been considerable, and has continued to increase, especially in the 1970s and 1980s. It amounted to £860 million in 1971, £4,630 million in 1978 and over £10,000 million by 1981. Latest figures show a total outflow of nearly £20,000 million in 1984. Such overseas investment has been financed by the city capital markets, whose international orientation not only leads to policies on exchange and interest rates against the interests of domestic accumulation, but also to a coincidence of interests with international manufacturing capital (the multinational corporations) in financing investment overseas rather than domestic investment, as profit rates are higher. However, changes in the patterns of trade and in the role of the pound have weakened even these links with the UK economy, as the City is now primarily a banker to the US dollar through the Eurocurrency markets.

The balance of class forces in the UK shifted towards labour in the long boom and this prevented the major restructuring necessary to restore rapid accumulation, because of labour's defensive strength, particularly in the workplace (see Chapter 4). Through other policies, however, the state is currently in the process of reconstituting the balance of forces to those characteristic of the period prior to the long boom, in order to enable it to break labour's resistance, to speed up accumulation and to increase the productivity of any given volume of investment. As the UK is a very open economy its international competitiveness is particularly crucial. Manufacturing now accounts for 75 per cent of all exports (even including North Sea oil) and 65 per cent of imports. Three-quarters of all exports are accounted for by less than 200 firms, and a third of the value of exports involves trade between branches of the same firm. The proportionate size of exports and imports is considerably greater than thirty years ago, ensuring that weak international competitiveness has an even bigger impact on domestic accumulation. Whereas the value of manufactured exports exceeded manufactured imports by 250 per cent in the mid-1950s, the latter for the first time in 1983 exceeded the former, and the UK's share of world trade in manufactures has fallen from 20 per cent in 1955 to 8 per cent in 1984. The transition from protected empire markets has been particularly painful.

As a result, UK industrial output has grown very much more slowly than the UK's major competitors and in recent years has actually declined absolutely, although some recovery is apparent since 1981, as Table 3.5 demonstrates. None the less, at the end of 1984 manufacturing output remained more than 10 per cent below its 1979 level. Profits, the ultimate arbiter of industrial survival, have declined steadily, even through the long boom. Manufacturing profit fell from 21.3 per cent in 1951 to 17.5 per cent in 1960, and from

Table 3.5: Percentage Change in Manufacturing Production, 1951–83

	1951–66	1966–74	1974–9	1979–81	1981–3
France	127	56	10	−8	−1
West Germany	185	43	10	−1	−2
Italy	227	53	10	6	−6
Belgium	61	46	5	−1	3
UK	57	18	−1	−14	2

Source: R. Rowthorn, 'The Past Strikes Back', *Marxism Today* (January 1982); OECD *Indicators of Economic Activity* (OECD, 1984).

9.9 per cent in 1973 to 1.7 per cent in 1981. This has been an especially critical problem in the UK where accumulation for individual capitals proceeds more through retained profits than bank lending or new issues. Industrial policy would seem to have failed to reverse declining competitiveness and faltering accumulation. Whilst the growing role of the state in industrial policy is largely conditioned by the structural 'necessities' of the accumulation process, by economic crises, and by the state of class relations, it is precisely the failure of these interventions in the distinctive conditions provided by British capitalism that has led to attempts to reverse the direction of industrial policy in such a way as to use market forces and the pressures of competitive accumulation in an open international economy, to restructure industry. The only other alternative would be to transform the organisation and relations of production in a socialist direction, but present circumstances do not provide favourable conditions for the pursuit of this option.

Further Reading

General

Aaronovitch, S. and Smith, R. (1981) *The Political Economy of British Capitalism*, McGraw-Hill, chs. 6, 8, 10, 14, 15, 17, 18
Blazyca, G. (1983) *Planning is Good for You*, Pluto

3.1

Grant, W. (1982) *Political Economy of Industrial Policy*, Butterworth
Williams, K., Williams, J. and Thomas, D. (1983) *Why Are the British Bad at Manufacturing?*, Routledge and Kegan Paul

3.3

Coates, D. (1980) *Labour in Power?*, Longman, ch. 3
Dunford, M., Geddes, M. and Perrons, D. (1981) 'Regional Policy and the Crisis in the UK: A Long Run Perspective', *International Journal of Urban and Regional Research*, vol. 5
Gamble, A. (1985) *Britain in Decline*, Macmillan
Grove, J. W. (1962) *Government and Industry in Britain*, Longman
McLennan, G., Held, D. and Hall, S. (1984) *State and Society in Contemporary Britain*, Polity Press, ch. 3
Young, S. and Lowe, A. V. (1974) *Intervention in the Mixed Economy*, Croom Helm

4 LABOUR POLICY

4.1 The Marxist Approach to Labour Policy

This chapter considers the policies pursued by the state in relation to the labour force and examines the way in which these alter the terms of the relationship between capital and labour. This section analyses the general nature of the relation between capital and labour and the state's role in it; section 4.2 examines alternative strategies open to the state in its attempts to secure the continuing domination of labour by capital. Section 4.3 deals with the actual policies that have been pursued by the state. In section 4.4, labour policy concerned with the expansion and contraction of the labour force is examined, and lastly, in section 4.5, the overall impact of labour policies on British capitalism is reviewed.

4.1.1 Capital and Labour: Wage Labour, the Labour Process and Trade Unionism

The relations between capital and labour are governed by the relations of production. In the basic model of the CMP, the means of production are privately owned by the capitalist class and workers must sell their labour power in return for a wage. Labour power is a commodity purchased as a means to the production and realisation of surplus value in the form of profit. The surplus arises because workers can be put to work for more hours, and therefore create more value than is paid in the wage. This occurs because capitalists have control over the labour process. The control and direction of labour in the working day is at their discretion, and the surplus labour time worked forms the source of surplus value.

There is an objective conflict of interest between, and a structural imbalance in, the power of capital and labour. In the labour *contract*, the worker is paid less than the value he/she produces. In the labour *market*, whether or not a worker is employed depends solely on the prospects for profitable accumulation. Yet workers depend for their livelihood solely on whether and at what wage they can sell their labour power. The objective position and power of labour is largely dictated by forces over which it has little control, both in the labour market and in the labour process. In the former, the demand for labour power is determined by the fluctuating pace of accumulation. When the demand for labour power falls, unemployment rises, the size of the industrial reserve army grows and exerts downward pressure on wages. Attempts by capitalists to restore profitability by restructuring production also reduce the number of workers required for any given level of output.

With regard to the labour process, labour is also subordinate. Management, as the representatives of capital, can exercise control and authority through methods like the regulation of effort, speed of work and discipline; through mechanical means, built into the design of machines with which labour works; and through direct personal supervision. The scope for control by capital has increased greatly with the development of new forms of machinery and the mechanisation and automation of production. These have increased the fragmentation and routinisation of work, and the extent of control by management over each stage of the labour process. Moreover objective economic conditions influence the extent of the power of capital over labour. Restructuring the labour process is more prevalent in recession, as changes are easier to instigate, for example, through relocation or reduced manning levels.

Different fractions of capital may adopt different strategies of control and subordination. For example, large capitals who use bureaucratic rules for control find that these can be implemented with greatest acceptability, if they are formulated in consultation with a group who represent workers' interests, like a trade union. Small capitals, on the other hand, may oppose the very existence of such groups and refuse to consult or negotiate with them.

However, the terms of the relationship between capital and labour are not entirely set by capital. Workers can join together to form unions to represent their interests and so bargain collectively from a position of increased strength with their employers. This strength depends crucially on union 'density', the proportion of workers who are members of such a union. This has fluctuated in the present century, rising from 12.7 per cent in 1900 to 45.2 per cent in 1920, falling to 22.6 per cent in 1933 and tending in the main to rise thereafter, reaching a peak of 54 per cent (12 million people) in 1979, although since then it has fallen to just less than 50 per cent in 1983. Moreover, the extent of unionisation, and hence the potential power of labour, varies considerably across different sectors of the economy, between different occupations of worker, between men and women, and between different sizes of firm. The strength of labour also depends on its discipline, organisation, resources, unity and perspective. Union organisations may be oligarchic; the ideological hegemony of capital may persuade union members to limit and curtail the extent and nature of their demands, so ensuring deference and legitimacy to existing power relations; and union demands may be economistic, confined to 'industrial' issues.

There are tendencies to division and sectionalism, which weaken the working class. Unions do not unite all those who sell their labour power on the market and they do not represent the working class as a whole. Instead, workers combine on narrower lines of common interest, forming a series of craft, industrial and general unions wherein workers organise and identify with specific skills, firms, industries or trades. For example, skilled craft unions may act as a sectional interest to preserve 'the aristocracy of labour' and discourage new entrants to their trade. Indeed their power will rest precisely on the inability of employers to replace their members by others from the ranks of the reserve army, whereas unskilled workers have, by definition, no such power. There are other divisions too, for example, between rank-and-file union members and the union's bureaucracy and leaders. Indeed unions may become an agency of control over their own members through the union hierarchy. The unity of a trade union is particularly influenced by the pattern of control, accountability and democracy within it.

A division also exists between that section of the labour force that is normally able to secure full-time and relatively continuous employment, and those groups such as youth, women, blacks and the old who are likely to be insecurely and intermittently employed, and who therefore constitute the main body of the reserve army of labour. Labour policy, therefore, is also involved in dealing with the particular problems that arise as a result of the position occupied by these groups on the margins of the labour force. This aspect of policy is examined separately in section 4.4.

The precise terms in the relation between capital and labour are influenced by a variety of forces. The degree of worker resistance and the level of class struggle are conditioned by prevailing economic conditions; by the ideology of workers and employers; by the divisions within capital and within labour; by the strategies capital uses to exercise control; by the organisational strength of labour. In addition, the state also plays a major role in the relations between capital and labour.

4.1.2 The State and the Relations between Capital and Labour

This section considers the state's objectives and the strategies open to it to secure them. According to the simple model of the CMP, the state can be expected to act on behalf of the capitalist class, partly because those with economic power will possess political power, which will be used when barriers to accumulation arise that have to be overcome. The needs of capital are automatically met and the rhythm of intervention is dictated by the rhythm of accumulation.

However, the existence of functional requirements of capital does not necessarily mean that the state can or will meet them, since both capital and the state are affected by the balance of class forces. Labour makes 'demands' on the state, as it does on capital, and the conflicts between labour and the state, and labour and capital, may give rise to concessions being won, depending on labour's relative power. However, concessions may not necessarily prevent conflict in the longer run, if they further increase the relative power of labour.

The state exhibits relative autonomy in relation to the immediate demands of capital, giving it some political space in the policies it pursues and in the institutions and mechanisms it uses. Moreover, there may be conflict within the state over strategies for the regulation and control of labour. This will be more likely, the more imperfect is the articulation of the needs of capital, the less the divisions within labour, and the greater the need for legitimation and consent. However, objective economic conditions do play a central role in structuring state policy. The worse the condition for profitable accumulation, the greater the 'needs' of capital, and the more coherent their articulation, then the less the strength of labour and the less is the need to buy consent.

4.2 Alternative Strategies in Labour Policy

Alternative strategies are open to the state to ensure the continuing domination of labour by capital. The crucial determinants in the choice of strategy are the balance of class forces and the conditions of accumulation. When labour is relatively strong, the state may have to compromise with labour. When labour is weak, such compromises are not required. When accumulation is rapid, concessions are possible; when it is slow, concessions create further barriers to accumulation. Table 4.1 presents a schematic picture.

Table 4.1:   The State and the Labour/Capital Relation

Accumulation	Relative strength of labour	
conditions	Strong	Weak
Strong	Voluntarism	Voluntarism or confrontation
Weak	Corporatism	Confrontation

When accumulation conditions are strong, the state can adopt a strategy of '*voluntarism*', leaving labour to bargain collectively through its representatives. This is so whether unions are strong *or* weak, for in the former case, concessions can be 'afforded' by capital, whereas in the latter, labour is not strong enough to wring compromises from capital. The labour/capital relation, either way, poses no threats to profitable accumulation. However, in this latter case, because labour is weak, the state may employ a strategy to renegotiate the terms on which collective bargaining is conducted through *confronting* labour. When accumulation conditions are *weak*, unions cannot be granted concessions without posing further problems, so the state may need to intervene to prevent this from occurring, using a strategy of *corporatism*. This involves reducing the autonomy and power of labour organisations by integrating them into political decision-making and/or increasing control over their actions. When accumulation conditions are weak *and* unions are weak, the state can pursue a strategy of confrontation to shift the existing balance between capital and labour in favour of the former. It has no need to offer concessions.

It is important to note that, in reality, the boundaries between different strategies are blurred; that union strength is a product of longer-term forces than current accumulation conditions; that past attempts to use particular strategies may influence current approaches; and that the political and economic philosophy of the party forming the government will affect the strategy chosen. Moreover, the existence of divergent interests between the fractions of capital and labour allow the state to select a *particular* articulation of capital's interests, and the process of intervention itself influences both the balance of forces and the pace of accumulation.

In the *voluntarist* strategy, the state does not interfere with the bargains struck in negotiation between labour and capital and there is no attempt at legal regulation. This approach does *not*, however, mean that the state is neutral. Rather, it implies the political endorsement and legitimation of existing economic relationships.

However, such an approach does recognise the existing power of labour and makes no attempt to interfere with the principle of freedom of association and recognition of unions. This strategy is a 'compromise': capital cannot *impose* its will, and its terms depend on the strength of labour. When labour is relatively weak, a state strategy of non-intervention will benefit labour much less than when it is relatively strong. However, although in collective bargaining unilateral control is ceded and conflict becomes institutionalised into the bargaining process, which becomes a 'contested terrain', nevertheless the *basis* of capital's control is not challenged. This strategy is ineffective when labour is powerful, particularly when accumulation is weak, since it further threatens accumulation.

Corporatism is a strategy that integrates trade unions as representatives of labour, and employers' organisations as representatives of capital, into the policy-making apparatus and policy implementation at the *leadership* level. Moreover, it uses union leadership as a mechanism of control over union members, as a means of ensuring that corporatist policies are implemented. Although a corporatist approach is often associated with a wider interventionist strategy, neither can be 'read off' from a particular stage of development of capitalism; rather the key factor is the economic and political strength of labour. The greater this is, the more *market* constraints are inadequate to secure profitable accumulation. Corporatism is designed to reduce the impact of the strength of labour in periods of slow accumulation, when growth is insufficient to satisfy labour's demands, without having negative effects on accumulation.

Using a strategy of *confrontation*, the state will attempt to weaken the power of labour and so alter the balance of class forces. This may be done because of major accumulation difficulties; because corporatist policies have failed; because the state perceives union leaderships to be less malleable than union membership at large; or because the government has made a break with *compromise* policies. It can be achieved by deflationary policies which dramatically increase unemployment. This restricts union membership and funds, and leads to an increase in competition for jobs and to lower wages. Labour may be further weakened by legislation to limit trade union action, particularly on the part of shop-floor activists. This strategy is designed to increase the relative power of capital through restoring managerial authority in the workplace. The risk is that it may provoke substantial opposition from labour, even though the material basis of its strength is undermined.

4.3 The Development of Labour Policies in the UK

The policies dealt with in this section are those designed to alter the relation between capital and labour, principally legislation on industrial relations and the establishment of 'incomes' policies. Policies designed to regulate the reserve army of labour are dealt with separately in section 4.4. After dealing with the period up to 1945 (4.3.1), the post-war period is divided into several phases and each is dealt with in turn. The final part of the section (4.3.6) draws together some conclusions on the factors influencing the overall direction of policy.

4.3.1 The State and Labour up to 1945

From the sixteenth century legislation existed allowing wage levels to be fixed by local magistrates, who were also empowered under common law to prevent 'combinations' in restraint of trade. Labour was also disciplined by the operation of the Poor Law, which imposed a duty to work on the able-bodied. In the eighteenth century, workers in various trades formed unions to pursue their interests, but these were normally only based locally. In response, around forty Acts of Parliament were passed prohibiting particular trades from forming 'combinations'. With the rise of industrial capitalism came the factory, and thus the concentration of workers in the same place working for the same employer, which further stimulated workers to organise collectively and form unions. Without collective organisation by the workers, the power of capital is unassailable, given the reserve army of labour. Because of the relative weakness of the working class, the response of the state was to ban the formation of unions. This was done through the 1799 and 1800 Combination Acts, with imprisonment for those involved in combinations. This severity was related to the current economic and political crisis and the breakdown of the old system of wage regulation, which was finally abolished in 1813.

The Acts were not repealed until 1824, after nearly a quarter of a century of industrial and political struggle. Even then, although workers were to be free to organise and be members of unions for the first time without risk of criminal prosecution by the courts, their activities were almost entirely circumscribed, as they were still liable for conspiracy and subject to common law with regard to restraint of trade in their actions. In fact it was not until the Trade Union Act of 1871 that unions were granted immunity from actions for restraint of trade, and not until 1875 that they were granted immunity from conspiracy. Without these immunities, their activities in pursuing a dispute would be illegal. Union memberships doubled between 1880 and 1900, with the growth in the unionisation of unskilled workers. However, unions still only covered 12 per cent of workers. State policies to regulate and regularise their position continued, for example in the Conciliation Act 1896, which provided state assistance for the policy of 'voluntarism'. The last third of the nineteenth century saw moves by the state to form a settled relationship with labour in a period when the balance of class forces was shifting, as labour began to advance in organisation and strength.

In the mid-nineteenth century the state also introduced regulatory legislation in the form of Factory Acts, primarily with regard to hours of work, safety and the 'protection' of women and children in factories. By the Bank Holidays Act 1871 the state also provided for six days of paid holiday in a year. Legislation regulating hours and conditions of work, despite being resisted by many employers, could work in the long-term interests of capital, in so far as it ensured the reproduction of labour power and increased its long-term productivity. Although protective legislation restricted the power of individual capitalists, it also reinforced men's dominance over women in the labour market, in unions and in society at large. Skilled male workers, threatened by technical innovations in machinery, were concerned to protect their jobs from unskilled women workers. The legislation defended their jobs and their relative worth to the employer, while excluding women from them. It reinforced the tendencies towards the organisation of the labour market into men as 'breadwinners' and women as dependants and housewives, and the quest for a 'family' wage.

Trade union behaviour was still severely circumscribed by not having been granted immunity from civil liability, and judicial action could be taken against them. In the 1901 Taff Vale incident, a strike involving a railway company, which did not recognise unions, led to the use of blackleg labour and damages to the railway's property. The courts ruled against the union, and damages and costs amounted to £42,000 (at 1901 prices) by way of compensation to the employer. This event, together with the likely consequences of this kind of legal action for unions in general, was a major stimulus to the formation of a political party to represent workers' interests. The Labour Representation Committee grew rapidly between 1901 and 1906, and in 1906 the Labour Party was formed. In the same year it won 26 seats in the general election. This combination of union agitation and political success led to the Trades Disputes Act 1906, which gave total statutory immunity to unions from damages falling on companies as a result of their action. Under considerable pressure as a result of an upsurge of social conflict and the growth of union militancy, involving the unprecedented loss of 43 million person-days through strikes, the Trade Union Act 1913 was also introduced. This Act permitted union political expenditure, provided that it came from a separate political fund and that union members had the right to contract *out* of political contributions. This provided financial support for the Labour Party and financed parliamentary candidates. The combination of the legislation of 1906 and 1913, and the impact of the First World War and its aftermath led to the most rapid growth of unions in the history of the UK. By 1920, 48 per cent of all workers eligible to join unions were members (a density not to be exceeded until the early 1970s), and an increase of over 300 per cent in ten years. Membership was most numerous and dense amongst males and manual workers, with male workers dominating female by a factor of more than 5, and manual dominating white-collar by a factor of 7.

The state's response to the growing demands and strength of organised labour up to this time had been an unwilling compromise and adjustment to the underlying shift in the balance of class forces, thus further shifting it towards labour. However, despite these concessions, capital was not fundamentally threatened by the power of labour. Within the factory, the autonomy of capitalist control remained and labour-market conditions were such that competition for jobs was considerable. Furthermore, the unions themselves were limited in their capacity to use their increased power by their lack of explicit socialist consciousness, the structural limits of trade union struggle and their contradictory role as, on occasion, agencies for the *containment* of class struggle.

In the First World War, despite the growth of trade union membership, the Russian Revolution in 1917 and the labour shortages during the period, pressure was contained by the state. In the quest for national unity, strikes were banned and compulsory arbitration in disputes was introduced; trade unions co-operated in policy and the maintenance of industrial discipline. The number of days lost through strikes halved during the war. The war produced a major shift in class relations and a new turn in labour policy. Various Munitions of War Acts from 1915 led to increasing state control of the labour force in order to increase production, to free men for service in the armed forces, and to reduce the control of skilled workers and their unions over certain types of work. The state adopted a corporatist policy, inducing the TUC labour leaders to impose discipline on organised labour in return for an involvement in policy-making. This policy provided a means of challenging the growing power and militancy of shop-floor workers and the shop-steward movement, which developed out of pre-war militancy and the favourable bargaining position of labour in the manpower shortages created by the war.

In the period immediately after the First World War, however, industrial action grew as the ban of strikes was lifted. Moreover, despite the introduction of the Emergency Powers Act 1920, under which a state of emergency could be declared and action taken to ensure that 'essential' supplies were not threatened, the number of days lost through strikes reached double that of the pre-war record of 1912. However, mounting unemployment weakened the power of labour and reduced trade union membership.

The General Strike of 1926, though demonstrating the enormous potential economic and political power of the labour movement, ended in bitter and unconditional defeat for the unions. The state now confronted the unions, which were weakened by mass unemployment and demoralised by the failure of the strike. The Trade Disputes and Trade Unions Act 1927 imposed criminal sanctions on any industrial action that was not in furtherance of a trade dispute. Any action that could be considered 'political', i.e. designed to coerce or confront the government of the day, was effectively forbidden, as was any action that had the effect of 'inflicting hardship on the community'. Furthermore, members of unions were now to 'contract *in*' to unions' political funds. Membership more than halved between 1920 and 1933. With the unions weakened, the balance of power had been restored to an appropriate level for capital.

The outbreak of the Second World War saw prohibition on industrial action, compulsory arbitration and the incorporation of trade union leaders and officials onto a series of government bodies and committees. This was designed to reduce industrial and political conflict during wartime. Overall management of the labour force was undertaken by the Ministry of Labour, which was given enhanced powers under the Emergency Powers (Defence) Act 1940. A Joint Consultative Council was established, containing seven representatives each of the TUC and industry. The state employed this corporatist institution throughout the war. Free collective bargaining was retained, but disputes were to be settled by arbitration or conciliation. Strikes and lock-outs were made illegal. Strikes did occur, particularly from 1944, but in the main the policy succeeded partly because other measures to protect working-class living standards were more successful than in the First World War. Some attempts were made to improve the pay of low-paid workers, and to this end the scope of the Wage Boards was increased so that they covered 15.5 million workers by 1945. Trade union membership also increased by 25 per cent overall, although amongst women workers, whose numbers expanded substantially, the increase was 62 per cent.

4.3.2 From Legislation to Incomes Policy: 1945–68

A Labour government was elected with an overall majority for the first time in 1945. The Trades Disputes and Trade Unions Act 1927 was repealed, thus restoring unions to their legal position before the General Strike. However, economic and political circumstances were much changed. Many union leaders and officials were members of government bodies and committees as a result of the war, and this the new government wished to encourage; the government's political stance was social democratic and consensual; and most importantly, there was full employment for the first occasion ever in peacetime. Indeed by 1948 trade union membership was back to its 1920 level, from its 1933 trough. The new balance of power between capital and labour was accepted by the state, and attempts were made to further incorporate trade unions (or rather their leadership) through consultation on policy and membership of a variety of non-elected state bodies. Most union leaders shared the broad aims of the government, and taking them into state structures posed few problems. In addition, it increased the possibility that they could successfully be persuaded to co-operate in the quest for 'responsibility' in collective bargaining, particularly in response to increased government regulation of the economy as a whole.

Thus the only strategy available, given prevailing economic and political conditions, was to accept the new terms of the compromise and encourage moderation in the demands of the organised working class in return for some involvement in policy formation and in preserving a Labour government. This policy of exhortation was reasonably successful. However, the introduction of 'austerity' policies, the 1949 devaluation of the pound (by 40 per cent), and later the Korean War, resulting in inflationary pressures, caused rank-and-file agitation over moderation and wage 'restraint'. None the less, economic expansion provided the space for order in industrial relations, with relatively few strike days 'lost' and wage increases rarely out of line with inflation and productivity gains.

The first major post-war shift in policy came in 1957 with the formation of the Council on Prices, Productivity and Incomes, which announced the level of 'acceptable' pay increases. There was, however, no means of enforcing this, other than with propaganda and the management of public opinion. However, an increase in the rate of inflation, the sterling crisis of 1961, and a growing belief on the part of capital that trade unions were becoming too powerful led to the first major attempt to introduce an incomes policy. A National Incomes Commission was set up, a six-month wage freeze imposed in the public sector, and a guideline of 2.5 per cent introduced thereafter in return for the NEDC being set up. Although inflation fell, the balance of payments was still in difficulty, growth was stubbornly less than in the countries of the major competitors, and in particular productivity growth was slow. The number of days lost through strikes and disputes was slowly increasing (especially due to unofficial action), and it appeared that the terms of compromise requires a more substantial readjustment than wage guidelines and exhortation.

In 1965, the National Board for Prices and Incomes (NBPI) was set up. Its announcement of norms for pay increases was designed to achieve voluntary restraint, in conjunction with policies to control prices, extend individual rights at work (see below), introduce economic planning and other social reforms. The NBPI encouraged productivity deals in the form of changes in working practices, in return for pay increases above the norm. This was contradictory in its effects for capital. It encouraged plant-level bargaining, the longer-term consequences of which are outlined below; it got unions involved in negotiation, or at least discussion, of the organisation of work, and it led to 'comparability' problems with workers in the public sector. This was to prove particularly important, for whilst the growth of public-sector employment throughout the period in theory gave the state more direct control over the incomes of a larger proportion of workers, in practice it led to national-level centralised bargaining dominated by comparability issues, rather than by the ability to pay.

Alongside the attempt at a 'voluntary' incomes policy, two other sets of policies designed to modify the relation between capital and labour were introduced. Not only was the collective bargaining system 'failing', but other aspects of the employment relation were also creating problems. First, the training system was subject to scrutiny. Essentially, under the market, insufficient training is provided by employers, particularly in times of relatively low unemployment, as each attempts to 'free ride' on the others. This leads to shortages of labour, slow productivity growth and reduced flexibility in meeting technical change. The Industrial Training Act 1964 set up a series of Industrial Training Boards. A levy was imposed on all firms in the industries covered and grants were given to those firms reaching appropriate training standards and numbers of trainees in excess of their own individual 'needs'. Second, there was a substantial attempt by the state to extend individual rights at work, for example, with regard to periods of notice for contract termination and lump-sum payments in compensation for redundancy. These developments serve to improve workers' rights, irrespective of whether they belong to unions or not. However, redundancy legislation also assists capital by making workers more willing to adapt to changing patterns in the demand for labour power. The aim is to encourage workers to accept redundancy. Whilst redundancy payments mitigate some of the immediate financial consequences, they also significantly encourage job mobility through reducing time lost in disputes over redundancy announcements; encouraging people to move out of the labour force; reducing shop-floor resistance to job destruction; and encouraging a 'shake-out' of labour and a reduction of 'over-manning'. The legislation is based on the view not that redundancy is undesirable, but rather that it is inevitable, that employment security is secondary to profit, and that hostility to it can be and ought to be diminished in order to make dismissal easier. It thus reasserts the view of labour as a commodity, to be hired or fired at will, and diminishes resistance to it.

In the late 1960s, the continuing relative economic decline of the UK overtook *voluntary* incomes policy. The worsening balance of payments problem led to the introduction of a statutory pay freeze in 1966, followed by severe restraint as well as deflationary policies, public spending cuts and, in 1967, the devaluation of the pound by 14.3 per cent, backed by a 3.5 per cent statutory pay ceiling. The consensus with organised labour and its role as a 'partner' in policy formation was shown to be dispensable when severe economic problems had to be dealt with. The extension of a statutory policy beyond 1969 was, however, unacceptable to the unions, and indeed the number of strike days lost had increased consistently between 1967 and 1969, to the highest level since 1945. If wages cannot be limited, and rank-and-file militancy contained by the use of either a voluntary or statutory incomes policy, then the option remains for union leaderships themselves to be strengthened *vis-à-vis* their memberships and for the imposition of limitations on the right to strike. The late 1960s thus saw the beginnings of a change in state strategy from incorporation to confrontation.

The Donovan Commission, which had been set up in 1965 partly in response to employers' pressure to control unofficial strikes, reported in 1968. It recommended procedural reform to increase centralisation and bureaucratisation of collective bargaining, as a response to the growth of union power on the shop floor, which was eroding both management's power and control over the labour process, and the control of the union leadership over its rank and file, symbolised by the growth of unofficial strikes. The aim was to reform collective bargaining in order to make it more 'orderly'. Policies of this kind were proposed, along with some additional legal controls, in the attempt by the Labour government in 1969 to implement the terms of its White Paper, *In Place of Strife*. However, opposition from within the labour movement led to their abandonment.

In concluding this review of the 1945–68 period, certain strands of development can be identified. First, the processes of change within the capitalist economy exacerbated the problems of control over labour. The increasing size of plants and the increasingly multiplant nature of organisations respectively increased union strength and the power of the shop floor *vis-à-vis* management. Moreover, the growing role of the state as a direct employer of labour drew it more centrally into the conflicts between labour and capital. Second, much of the period saw a growth of 'corporatism' to deal with the changing balance of class forces. Indeed incomes policies positively require union integration and labour 'co-operation' under negotiated terms, in an attempt to paper over class divisions and put nation before class. Third, the relatively stable compromise of the period eventually began to break down, despite the Labour Party (and government's) better relations with the organised working class, and the latter's greater willingness to accept anti-working-class policy from such a government because of the organisational, financial and ideological links of the trade unions with the Labour

Party. While full employment means that the state and capital are under strong pressures to compromise with labour, voluntarism is not a viable *long-term* strategy for the state, especially if the strength of labour increases, and if *the pace of* accumulation falters. Further, given labour's strength, confrontation is not a viable alternative. The contradictions involved in corporatism for the state, labour and capital, particularly as economic decline intensifies, are considerable.

Compromise, without a major shift in the balance of class forces, is only possible if there is enough economic headroom to satisfy both capital *and* labour. State policy must otherwise create the headroom by sanctioning an increase in price inflation or by, for example, creating unemployment to *reconcile* the class interests at a different level of class forces. The post-war 'compromise', to the extent that one existed, could thus not be sustained, due to the deepening economic problems of the UK.

4.3.3 The Law Again — And Back to Incomes Policy: 1969–73

In 1969 the Labour government attempted to build on the Donovan Report of 1968 in the White Paper *In Place of Strife*. In particular, the chief concern was to reduce unofficial strikes and to increase management control at plant level. This entailed attacking shop-floor and thus shop stewards' power, and formalising collective bargaining to give increased weight to national negotiations and agreements. The proposals included the power to impose conciliation pauses on unofficial strikes and the compulsory balloting of union members prior to official strikes being called, if they were likely to 'harm the public interest'. These proposals, however, were never implemented, due to considerable union resistance, opposition from some Labour MPs, and a lack of support from capital. However, strikes had trebled between 1960 and 1970, partly due to opposition to incomes policy and the legislative proposals, and a widespread ideological offensive against 'union power' took place, which was partly responsible for Labour's electoral defeat in 1970.

The Conservative government of 1970–4 introduced the Industrial Relations Act 1971 as an alternative to what it saw as failed incomes policies. The Act attempted to confront directly union power, which was seen to emanate from the shop floor. Attempts were thus made to centralise power in unions, to enable leaders to exercise more control over their members. The Act required unions to register. Non-registered unions would lose their immunity against claims for damages, and in registering, their rules were to be vetted so that the union would now be legally responsible to the state for restraining its members from action against collective agreements. A union could be sued, if it failed to do so. These collective agreements *could* be made legally binding and a new judicial body, the National Industrial Relations Court (NIRC), would adjudicate if such agreements were broken. Emergency powers were to be available to the government to obtain a compulsory 60-day 'cooling-off' period, if a strike was thought to 'damage the economy', and to order ballots in major strikes. Furthermore, the legislation outlawed the pre-entry closed shop and effectively nullified the post-entry closed shop by giving all individual workers the right *not* to join a union.

These provisions amounted to a major legal attack on trade union action. However, these legal agreements were optional, i.e. it was up to the parties involved to decide if they were to be legally enforceable. In fact few employers insisted on legally binding contracts. Indeed the legislation failed to reduce union power and strike action. Although it had some effect in constraining union growth, the number of days lost through strikes increased by 30 per cent between 1970 and 1971 and by a further 75 per cent between 1971 and 1972, so that the number of days lost in 1971 and 1972 exceeded those lost in the whole of the 1960s. Indeed the labour movement proved too strong to be legally shackled at this time. The TUC boycotted union registration and the NIRC, thus making the Act inoperable. Moreover, the government's experience of other aspects of the Act's operation, such as cooling-off periods and ballots, was not encouraging. For example, rail workers in 1972 voted 6 to 1 in favour of industrial action, and British Rail conceded the pay claim in full. Disputes could also be escalated by action under the legislation. The docks dispute over containerisation was intensified by the NIRC jailing the so-called 'Pentonville 5' shop stewards for refusing to stop picketing a 'blacked' depot.

Consequently in 1972 a *formal* incomes policy replaced legislation as the chief means of constraining union power. This was part of a major reversal of government strategy, including tripartite discussions to reach agreement on economic policy and the operation of a voluntary incomes policy, as well as an expansionary budgetary policy. However, resistance by the union leadership was greater than with a Labour government, and hence a statutory policy was introduced in 1972. This began with a phase I wage freeze, followed by a phase II £1 plus 4 per cent and phase III (from November 1973) of

£2.25 or 7 per cent plus 'threshold' payments. Although this had some impact on moderating the rate of growth of wages and on industrial action, it failed to improve profitability, slow down inflation or reduce the power of labour. Indeed the oil-price rise of 1973, the further downward float of the pound, together with the miners' challenge to the pay policy by rejecting the maximum possible under the policy and declaring a national strike, at a time when coal stocks were low and oil prices had risen dramatically, led the Conservative government into declaring a State of Emergency, a three-day working week, and ultimately calling a general election on the theme of 'who governs?' in which it was defeated.

4.3.4 The High Tide of Corporatism: 1974–9

A Labour government was returned in 1974, after a period when incomes policies and legislative controls had failed to alter the balance of class forces in favour of capital under the preceding Conservative and Labour governments. The policy alternatives to voluntarism and consensus, which themselves had collapsed some years earlier, seemed to be closed off. Moreover, Labour was committed to repealing the existing industrial relations legislation and abolishing statutory incomes policies. Material conditions, too, gave little room for manoeuvre. Co-operation was essential and the 'social contract' was agreed upon. This involved the repeal of the 1971 Industrial Relations Act, the rejection of statutory incomes policy, and a series of 'progressive' social and labour policies, in return for voluntary pay restraint. The Trade Union and Labour Relations Act 1974 restored union immunity for inducing breaches in employment contracts, abolished the NIRC and the Commission on Industrial Relations (CIR), and established the Advisory Conciliation and Arbitration Service (ACAS). After the second general election of 1974, immunity was extended to cover commercial contracts. The Employment Protection Acts 1975 and 1978 consolidated previous legislation on individual rights with regard to unfair dismissal and redundancy pay and notification, and provided time off for union activities for shop stewards and for 'training', and introduced improved maternity provisions. Furthermore, the Sex Discrimination Act 1975 extended equal opportunities for women at the same time as the Equal Pay Act 1970 came into force (see section 4.4 below). The Health and Safety at Work Act 1974 was also part of the same package of reforming legislation associated with the social contract.

These policies further shifted the balance of power towards labour and, given both the severe economic conditions and the conventional economic polices pursued, this ensured the deepening rather than the resolution of accumulation problems. Industrial action markedly declined, and wage increases doubled from around 12 per cent in 1973 to 25 per cent in 1974. Profitability fell further, inflation increased rapidly and the pound continued to decline. In these circumstances, given the failure to develop a socialist economic strategy, the unions and the government saw the only alternative to be the negotiation of a 'voluntary' pay policy, phase I of which was introduced in 1975 as a £6 per week limit, with considerable TUC backing. Phase II (1976) was a 5 per cent norm, with a range between £2.50 and £4, whilst phase III (1977) allowed 10 per cent and phase IV (1978) a 5 per cent ceiling.

In 1976, a major shift in state policy took place. As the economic crises deepened and the pound collapsed, leading to the intervention of the International Monetary Fund (IMF), the government introduced major cuts in public spending and 'tepid' monetarism, which caused unemployment to double by 1977. Real wages also fell in 1975, 1976 and 1977. These wage cuts, along with rapidly increasing unemployment and the severity of the economic crises, weakened the unions' immediate position. However, the rate of profit by 1978 was hardly higher than in 1974, and the fourth phase of voluntary incomes policy in 1978, imposing yet another wage cut, was rejected by the TUC and Labour Party annual conferences. There followed the 'winter of discontent' with major strikes, particularly in the public services, the breaking of the pay policy, and the election of the Thatcher government in early 1979 against the backcloth of this failure of corporatism.

The period 1974–9 witnessed the strongest and most sustained period of corporatism in peacetime state-labour relations. Real wages fell, industrial militancy declined, unemployment doubled and economic policy drifted towards monetarism. Its effect therefore was to restore economic health on *capital's* terms.

4.3.5 Confronting Labour 1979 onwards

The change in government and the failures of the 1974–9 period prompted the final rejection of a corporatist approach towards labour. Unions are now effectively excluded from policy consultation, incomes policy is rejected and collective bargaining is 'freed'. The measures employed are the discipline of the market, the impos-

ition of a *de facto* public-sector pay policy through cash limits and
monetary discipline, and a legislative attack on organised labour,
backed by an ideological campaign designed to justify the strategy.
Previous policies, including legislative measures, had failed because
of the strength of organised labour. The 'crashing' of the domestic
economy, particularly of its manufacturing base, weakened the
labour movement as a prelude to legislative action. Unemployment
doubled between 1979 and 1982, and this reduced trade union
membership by over 1.3 million (or nearly 10 per cent) between 1979
and 1981. As a result, private-sector wages could be held down by the
forces of the market and industrial conflict over a formal incomes
policy avoided.

The changing balance of power within the Conservative Party, the
deepening problems of capital, and the relative weakness of the
labour movement provided a more favourable material and
ideological climate for a major legislative attack on organised
labour. The 'Prior' Employment Act 1980 restricted picketing to the
place of work where the dispute occurred. It undermined the closed
shops by providing, in effect, for the individual right to dissociate. It
also allowed employers to take legal action against individuals taking
secondary or sympathetic industrial action. The 'Tebbit'
Employment Act 1982 narrowed the legal definition of what consti-
tutes a trade dispute (in which legal immunities would apply) to those
which concern terms and conditions of employment, hence
narrowing the scope for lawful industrial action. Any action falling
outside the new narrow definition exposes unions to civil law and
action by employers, their suppliers or customers. Furthermore, it is
the *courts* which decide what falls within the new terms of a trade
dispute, and thus whether union action in any particular case is legal
or illegal. If the courts rule that a particular industrial action is
unlawful, compensation for damages may have to be paid, and if the
union has endorsed the action, then its funds are liable. If these
damages are *not* paid by the union, or if the union ignores an
injunction to refrain from action, the courts can impose unlimited
fines for contempt and seize the union's assets. It is, however, up to
the individual employer to decide whether or not to use this legislation, and many are reluctant to do so in case the effect is to increase,
rather than diminish, the conflict. The 1982 Act also restricts
sympathetic action, for example, involving action to stop the firm's
goods being supplied to another company, or involving workers
refusing to handle work diverted from a plant in the same company

overseas, where workers are having an industrial dispute. Concerning the selective dismissal of strikers, employers can now sack workers on strike whilst retaining those strikers who have returned to work. An employer can give four days' notice of sacking all workers on strike who do not return to work. This clearly weakens union solidarity and strength by encouraging the breaking of ranks, *and* discriminates against those most active and committed to the industrial action.

The 'King' Employment Act 1984 continues the legislative attack on organised labour. As well as the compulsory use of secret ballots in the election of union executives, unions will not be immune from damages unless official strikes are endorsed by a secret ballot of the union membership. The 1984 Act also attempts to weaken the ties between the Labour Party and the trade unions, as well as reducing the party's income from the unions, by requiring a ballot of union members on the political levy.

The series of Employment Acts returns to the policies pursued in the inter-war period, after the defeat of the General Strike. Should unemployment fall as accumulation conditions improve in the mid-1980s, it is this legislation rather than market conditions that will control the power of labour in the longer term.

4.3.6 Conclusions: Capitalism, Class Relations and Shifts in Labour Policy

The state has played a major role in regulating relations between capital and labour over the past 200 years. The nature of its role has varied, due to the changes in accumulation conditions, the balance of class and intra-class forces, prevailing ideologies, and relations between organised labour and the government of the day. *Non-interventionist* approaches (voluntarism) foundered in periods of weak accumulation and a relatively strong labour movement, and cannot be relied upon again without a substantial weakening of the labour movement and/or a dramatic and sustained improvement in economic conditions. The long boom provided unique accumulation conditions, allowing a stable compromise between capital and labour. However, the growth of the strength of labour during the period of non-intervention, indirectly encouraged by state policies encouraging 'professional' attitudes and formal procedures in industrial relations, threatened the terms of the compromise, whilst the end of the long boom in the world economy and the onset of absolute decline in the UK economy ensured its collapse.

An *interventionist* strategy involving either corporatism or confrontation has been pursued when accumulation conditions are threatened. *Corporatist* approaches cannot create for long the necessary consensus for their survival. Incomes policies have been unsuccessful in restraining wages growth in the longer term or in shifting the balance of class power. Corporatism requires a relatively high degree of centralisation and hierarchical power, particularly within the labour movement, so that agreements can be effectively implemented and dissident behaviour controlled or punished. However, the power of unions and employers remains too decentralised in the UK for effective control of their constituent members. Ideological conditions are also important in determining the emergence and effectiveness of corporatism. Both the state and the labour representatives require a social democratic outlook, the former to search for consensus, harmony and compromise, rather than confrontation, and the latter so that they are open to integration into policy-making. The consequences of corporatism for labour are serious. Whilst both limited gains and some purchase over policy may be achieved, these are achieved at a cost. Most notably, corporatist structures are used to legitimate and administer 'sacrifices' on behalf of the working class in the 'national interest'. Such ideological incorporation amounts to class collaboration, rather than bringing the class struggle into the state. Moreover, the divisions between union leaderships and rank-and-file members may intensify, as the former have access to decision-making structures, whereas the latter do not. Furthermore, power within the unions may become more centralised, as decisions are increasingly made by officials and national committees.

For *confrontation* to succeed, it requires, first, a high or increasing level of unemployment, in order to weaken labour's bargaining power and confidence. Second, legislation must weaken trade unions further by restricting the scope of union actions. Third, the effective organisation, militancy and solidarity of the labour movement as a whole, including its political representation, must be relatively weak. Fourth, the trade union movement, or at least a key sector of organised labour, *must* suffer a major defeat in industrial conflict. To the extent to which these factors are present, as they were in the period of the General Strike, the policy may be successfully pursued. If one or more of the factors are absent, as in the period following the Industrial Relations Act 1971, then failure and a change of policy is likely. The outcome of the period of confrontation instituted since 1979 remains to be seen.

4.4. Managing Surplus Labour: Youth, Women, Blacks and the Old

The reserve army of labour is a permanent feature of the CMP. In periods of boom, labour shortages may develop and policy is adjusted to expand the labour force to augment labour supply and contain wage increases, whereas in times of slump the labour force is contracted. These fluctuations particularly affect certain groups such as youth, women, blacks and the old, and hence policies are directed towards influencing the labour-market participation of these groups. In times of labour shortage, they have been designed to encourage their selective entry into the labour force, but in times of labour surplus, they have been designed to encourage their removal from it.

With regard to *youth*, in the long boom, the educational system and the training activities of industry were generally seen as effective means by which working-class youth could be prepared to enter the labour market. Preparation for skilled work was left to the apprenticeship system and to day-release in further education. Potential increases in youth unemployment from the mid-1960s were reduced by the growth of further and higher education, and the raising of school-leaving age in 1971. The main policy initiative came in 1974, with the establishment of the Manpower Services Commission (MSC) on corporatist lines. This was initially designed in part to provide job opportunities through the Job Creation Programme for young people experiencing unemployment as a result of what was seen as a temporary phase of slack demand for labour. As the economic crisis has intensified, the work of the MSC has been enormously expanded. At the same time, the emphasis has shifted from the provision of preparation for work, to a means of managing youth unemployment at the same time as providing cheap juvenile labour and depressing the general level of wages on entry to the labour market. The wide variety of schemes were rationalised in 1977 with the establishment of the Youth Opportunities Programme (YOP). By 1983 nearly 2 million young people had been involved in YOP. In that year, school leavers were more likely to enter a YOP scheme than full-time work.

The Conservative government elected in 1979 initially attempted to reduce state involvement directed towards youth unemployment and job-training generally. This involved the abolition of seventeen Industrial Training Boards in 1981, and the elimination of the Exchequer's subsidy to them, leaving employers free to run their own individual training programmes. However, the riots of 1981 focused attention on the threat to legitimation and security posed by the growth of youth unemployment. The MSC was given a considerable increase in funding and the Youth Training Scheme (YTS) was established. The YTS, which replaces and builds out of the YOP programme, is, at once, an attempt to reduce registered unemployment; contain young people's resentment and boredom; substitute young, poorly organised, inexperienced workers for older ones; reduce wages and worsen working conditions; provide a source of temporary, flexible workers to employers, from which to choose permanent workers; and enhance work discipline. It has little to do with training, especially in the private sector, and much to do with social control and cheap labour provision for capital. The whole scheme is funded by the state at a cost of £1,000 million per year and provides for up to 500,000 places for unemployed school-leavers. Parallel to the YTS is the Young Workers' Scheme, offering employers a subsidy of £15 per week for each one taken on, providing they are paid less than £40 per week. Not only does this weaken the Wages Councils (for many have established minima of above £40); it also reflects the view that unemployment results from wages being too high. The ideological shifts associated with the MSC schemes involve the depiction of youth unemployment as largely resulting from the inadequacies of the young people themselves. This theme was central to the 'Great Debate' on education, initiated by Labour in 1976, and has become a prominent theme of the MSC with its emphasis on the 'mismatch' of youth capacities and employers' requirements.

A number of policies have been employed to regulate the position of *women* in the labour market. Apart from the special measures employed in the Second World War, policies designed specifically to improve the position of working women were not instituted until the 1970s. These policies reflected both the growing political influence of women, as well as an attempt to improve labour productivity and a desire to reduce sex discrimination. Although the state has never pursued policies designed to allow women to participate in work on the *same* basis as men, the system of income support established by 1948, and the changing structure of employment, along with demographic changes and rising wage levels, somewhat reduced the barriers to taking paid work imposed by women's role in the family-household.

Over the post-war period, major changes have taken place in the labour-force participation of women. The proportion of women in the workforce rose until the late 1970s, with the increase in the number of working married women being particularly marked. Women now constitute 40 per cent of the labour force, and 60 per cent of married and 75 per cent of non-married women are economically active. However, they remain concentrated in a narrow range of occupations, effectively segregated into those with low pay and poor promotion opportunities; indeed there was little change in the relationship between male and female earnings between 1951 and the mid-1970s. Many women, particularly those with small children, work part-time. These workers tend to have lower pay rates, poorer promotion opportunities, and less rights in relation to holidays and sick pay. This situation reflects women's double burden of waged work, and domestic labour and child care, which in turn reflects a particular sexual division of labour at work and in the home, and the patriarchal structure of most family-households.

The Equal Pay Act 1970 did not come into force until 1975, thus allowing many employers to circumvent its provisions. It was designed to provide for equal pay for women if they did the same or like work as men, or work designated as of equivalent value under a job-evaluation scheme, in the same establishment. If a woman does not receive equal pay in such circumstances, she can take her case to an industrial tribunal. However, 'indirect' wage discrimination is not covered; the onus is on the woman to establish her case to male-dominated tribunals; the tribunal's interpretation of 'like' work is very narrow; and the major differential arising from the segregation of women workers in low-paying establishments is not tackled at all, as the woman has no one to compare herself with. Indeed the number of applications to tribunals under the act has declined from 1,742 in 1976 to only 39 in 1982. Of the 39 in 1982, only two were upheld.

The Sex Discrimination Act 1975 recognises that women's role and position are affected by factors external to the labour market, and seeks to promote equal opportunities for women through outlawing both direct discrimination, where a woman is treated less favourably than a man because of her sex or marital status, and indirect discrimination, where a condition is imposed that more men than women can comply with, for example, height or age limits. Only

150 cases were taken to tribunals in 1982, and only 24 were upheld. Indeed, despite these Acts, women's weekly earnings are still in excess of 27 per cent less than men's. Finally, maternity rights were improved by the Employment Protection Act in 1975.

The legislative pursuit of equality has proceeded without reference to the sexual division of domestic labour in particular, and the power relations between men and women in general, which structure labour-market participation. While a major challenge to the ideology of domesticity and familialism has been proposed by the women's movement, there has been little shift in the dominant ideology, which retains a contradictory stance in relation to working women. The assumption that women are responsible for child care and housework means that, when women enter the labour market, they do so on inferior terms to men. As a result, women are largely excluded from 'favoured' areas of work, and full-time employment in general. Indeed full-time employment amongst women has not increased since 1971. This benefits men by allowing them to retain their dominant position at work and at home, negotiating 'family' wages (on the assumption of a dependent wife), retaining male definitions of skill, and dominating top union positions. It is hardly surprising that the extent of sex segregation in jobs did not decline between 1973 and 1979. Public policy has not intervened to challenge the organisation of the family-household, for although reforms that allowed women's full participation would benefit capital by improving labour efficiency, a challenge to the existing family-household and to the dominant ideology would threaten legitimation, particularly in a period of high unemployment.

Policies directed towards the labour-force participation of *blacks* date from the 1950s, when large-scale Commonwealth immigration was encouraged in conditions of labour shortage. With the significant exception of a minority of professional and semi-professional employees in medicine, black immigrant workers have been concentrated in the least-sought-after, low-paid jobs, and occupationally and industrially segregated. As the labour shortage eased, policy shifted towards restrictions on immigration, starting with the Commonwealth Immigrants Act 1962. Immigration control developed in conjunction with the growth of racism, in the form of both prejudice and unequal treatment. The main policy response in the 1960s involved legislation to limit overt discrimination and some development of special educational provision. However, this approach had little impact on the racial division of labour. The Race

Relations Act 1976 covered discrimination in employment. However, the annual number of applications upheld is very small; in 1982, 19 out of 273 initial applications. The main response of the state has consisted of further controls on immigration, and the expansion of 'inner-city' policies, which were partly aimed at defusing the potential for disorder created by spatially concentrated ethnic minorities experiencing high unemployment and poor housing, who were not integrated into the existing political framework. Since the riots of 1981, the 'problem' posed by this section of the reserve army has been viewed primarily as a question of policing. Unlike some other European states that made extensive use of immigrant labour during the long boom, the UK has not employed a widespread policy of repatriation, although the restriction and harassment directed towards the ethnic minorities may have an impact on their willingness to stay in the UK.

The black population has been viewed through a complex and changing ideological lens. Initially seen as making a welcome economic contribution in a period of labour shortage, taking jobs that otherwise would not be filled, the image gradually shifted both towards 'taking our jobs' and 'scrounging', to the view of the white population being 'swamped' and suffering a major threat to physical security through the growth of 'street crime' and 'mugging'. While the race relations legislation has inhibited the public expression of overtly racist statements at least by those in positions of authority, official endorsement of racism in a 'coded' form, such as in the selective presentation of crime statistics, or in statements concerning the operation of the immigration and citizenship laws, has been widespread.

State regulation of the access of *the old* to the labour market has been mainly concerned with 'retirement', i.e. a final and permanent withdrawal from the labour force. However, retirement has only recently become the normal situation for the old. Before the Second World War the majority of men over 65 years old still worked. The Beveridge Report, and the system of retirement pensions it was used to establish, made retirement for the first time a condition for receipt of the pension. Interestingly, this provision was specifically designed to *discourage* withdrawal from work, and those who stayed on after the minimum retirement age were to be given slightly larger pensions. In 1951, the proportion of men over 65 still in work was 31 per cent. During the relative labour shortages of the 1950s no attempt was made to discourage older workers from finding employment, since they formed an important reserve of labour. However, even in this period of labour shortage, the old formed a marginal group within the workforce. Older workers often had to transfer to lower-paid jobs, as a result of a declining ability to cope with the pace or the physical demands of their normal employment. As unemployment began to increase substantially in the mid-1960s, older workers were disproportionately affected. From 1967, their rate of unemployment has been rising above the average for all workers and their prospects for part-time work have almost disappeared. State policy has accelerated this withdrawal from the labour force through the Redundancy Payments Act 1965, which increases inducements to older workers to leave their jobs; through the encouragement of additional provision of severance pay for redundant workers; through early retirement schemes, especially in the state sector; and, for those over pension age, by the maintenance of the 'earnings rule'. This rule means that pensioners returning to work have their earnings over a certain limit (at present £70 per week) deducted from their pensions.

Over the post-war period a major shift in the ideological depiction of the old has taken place. During the period of labour shortage the benefits of employing older workers in terms of their reliability, experience and 'settling influence' on the young were stressed. Retirement itself was portrayed in negative terms as a deprivation for the individual and a burden on society. Capital thus benefited from an easing of labour shortage, while trade unions would not oppose this policy so long as demand for labour was maintained. However, with rising unemployment, older workers were increasingly portrayed as unadaptable and as keeping the young out of jobs. Representatives of both capital and labour, though for different reasons, supported this ideological shift. Moving the old out of the labour force reduced registered unemployment and made it easier for firms to restructure their workforces.

The management of surplus labour, then, involves policies that are complex, due to the differing approach taken to each of the groups involved. Each of the four groups varies in terms of the extent to which its members are excluded from the labour force, the extent to which the state is actively involved in the process of exclusion, and the means used to secure exclusion. The different treatment accorded to the groups is affected by the extent and intensity with which members of the group oppose exclusion, the degree of effective organisation and solidarity possessed by the group, and the extent of public sympathy for their plight. The importance of the level of public support for the group is the reason for the substantial ideological effort put into portraying the process of exclusion as beneficial, appropriate or deserved. Unlike more favoured sectors of the labour force, many members of these groups cannot hope to secure regular and well-paid employment. The need to expand or contract the labour force imposes on them a disproportionate share of the risk of low-pay, insecure employment and joblessness, which capitalist wage labour involves.

4.5 Labour Policy and the Capitalist System

In this final section, the overall impact of labour policies on the workings of British capitalism will be briefly discussed. Despite substantial changes which have taken place in the relationship between capital and labour, the basic structure of wage labour has been maintained. Policy has succeeded generally in encouraging 'moderate' trade unionism and in containing the use of strikes for political purposes. On a number of occasions, through the use of corporatist policies, unions have been successfully brought into the process of economic planning and control. Provision to expand the labour force in times of boom has been partly successful in keeping overall labour costs down and preventing a dramatic increase in the bargaining power of labour. The main cost for capital has involved the necessity for firms to engage in active management of their workforces, although the state has assisted this through sponsoring research and education in personnel management, management science, work study, and the whole area of knowledge concerned with maintaining the power of capital in the workplace.

Labour policies have contributed to raising the level of productivity of labour, particularly by encouraging mobility, by training, by selective immigration policies designed to meet shortages of skilled or professional labour, and by policies to prevent discrimination on the basis of sex or race. Management control over the labour process has been reinforced by state encouragement of 'productivity bargaining' and in part by the specification of employee rights, which at the same time also gives legal definition to the 'prerogatives' of management.

Labour policy has contributed to both labour and generational reproduction, in so far as it has prevented wages from falling below the levels required for physical reproduction of the worker and his/her dependents. However, neither the state nor employers generally have been willing to concede the principle of a 'family wage' and wages have remained exclusively a payment for work done, rather than being adjusted by employers to the level of family needs. The main provision for financial support of generational reproduction has been outside the wages system. (See Chapter 5.)

Labour policies affect legitimation in a variety of ways. The granting of employee 'rights' is a means by which the state reinforces its claim to stand above industrial conflict, as well as reinforcing the individuation of sources of grievance. Labour policy also aids legitimation by granting legal rights and a share in political power to trade unions. More generally, the fact of wage labour itself, involving the sale of labour power to an employer as the means of obtaining a personal income, is reinforced by the way that labour policies of every kind are unquestioningly predicated on its continued existence.

Both legitimation and security are affected by policies designed to manage the size of the labour force. Particularly in periods of labour surplus, these policies play a major role in creating the ideological conditions for the acceptance of the marginal and insecure employment status of various groups. Members of these groups experience periodic shifts in the way the dominant ideology portrays their proper economic and social role, and even their personal qualities. Indeed in times of labour surplus, the responsibility for unemployment is frequently portrayed as resulting from the unsuitable qualities of the groups being excluded from work. The specific ideological constitution of these groups is also a source of major long-standing divisions within the working class, which weaken its solidarity and which can deflect discontent created by the CMP onto other members of the same class.

The characteristics of capitalist wage labour, including the direct relationship of labour and capital, the maintenance of a labour reserve, and the pattern of market-determined wage differentials, are central features of the CMP and, as such, have proved resistant to reform. Reforming governments have made little impact on wage labour beyond modifying the labour contract through the provision of employee rights. Members of the working class are still required to offer their labour power for sale at whatever wage is currently on offer, without any guarantee of obtaining employment.

Further Reading

General

Bain, G. S. (ed.) (1983) *Industrial Relations in Britain*, Blackwell
Palmer, G. (1983) *British Industrial Relations*, George Allen and Unwin

4.1

Hyman, R. (1975) *Industrial Relations: A Marxist Introduction*, Macmillan
Strinati, D. (1982) *Capitalism, the State and Industrial Relations*, Croom Helm
Thompson, P. (1983) *The Nature of Work*, Macmillan

4.2

Crouch, C. (1979) *The Politics of Industrial Relations*, Fontana
Panitch, L. (1981) 'Trade Unions and the State', *New Left Review*, no. 125.

4.3

Burgess, K. (1980) *The Challenge of Labour*, Croom Helm
Coates, D. (1980) *Labour in Power?*, Longman, ch. 2

4.4

Beechey, V. (1984) *The Changing Experience of Women*, U221, Units 10–11, Open University Press
Braham, P. (1980) *Class, Race and Immigration*, D207, Unit 14, Open University Press
Evans, M. (ed.) (1982) *The Woman Question*, Fontana
Phillipson, C. (1982) *Capitalism and the Construction of Old Age*, Macmillan
Schofield, P., Preston, E. and Jacques, E. (1983) *Youth Training: The Tories Poisoned Apple*, ILP

5 INCOME SUPPORT POLICY

5.1 Income Support and the Capitalist Mode of Production

This chapter will examine the role played by the state in the modification of living standards through measures to increase or decrease the disposable money income of individuals and families. The major reason for these policies lies in the nature of wage labour. In the basic model of the CMP, the sale of labour power for a wage is the sole means by which the labourer obtains an income sufficient to reproduce the ability to labour, and to finance the upbringing of the future generations of labourers. However, in the CMP those forced to rely for subsistence on wage labour are not guaranteed to obtain an adequate wage, or even employment at all, hence threatening legitimacy and security and the reproduction of capitalist relations of production. The existence of a possible favourable impact on accumulation, legitimation and security provides a general framework for understanding the development of state policies designed to support incomes. However, the pattern of policy which develops in any particular capitalist society will depend on the form and the extent of the threats to accumulation, legitimation and security resulting from the distribution of personal incomes, as well as the level of development of productive forces, which affects the available surplus, the capacity of the state to organise a system of income support, the balance of class forces, and the nature of the dominant ideology.

The remainder of the chapter will be organised as follows: the development of policy up to the present will be dealt with in section 5.2. In section 5.3, the general features of the development of policy in relation to the growth of capitalism will be examined. In section 5.4, the effect of income support on income distribution and on sexual inequality will be discussed, and finally, in section 5.5, the overall impact of the system on the operation of capitalism in the UK will be evaluated.

5.2 The Development of Income Support Policies

5.2.1 The Poor Laws and the Development of Capitalism up to 1900

Many features of the present system of state income support can be traced back to the Poor Law Act 1601, which was a response to the periodic disorders resulting from the existence of a substantial mobile destitute population. This was due to agricultural enclosures, the threat of starvation arising from food shortages caused by bad harvests, population growth and inflation. Poor relief was to be the responsibility of individual parishes, controlled by the local JP and financed by the poor rate. The legislation provided for separate treatment for each of three categories. The able-bodied were to be set to work with materials provided by the parish, possibly in a workhouse. Those who had proved unwilling to support themselves would be subject to a disciplinary regime in a 'house of correction', the 'impotent' poor, unable to maintain themselves, would be maintained by income supports and/or the provision of almshouses. The fundamental principles of the scheme thus rested on a system of administration controlled by local representatives of the dominant class, the classification of the poor according to their adjudged ability to perform wage labour, a combination of income support and institutional provision, and the denial of any relief to the working poor.

The Poor Law was established in a period in which the transition to capitalist relations of production was taking place. While wage labour was becoming a major source of subsistence, substantial barriers existed to the organisation of production solely for profit and to the use of state power to support the process of capital accumulation. Since control of poor relief was highly localised, enormous variations existed in the levels and forms of relief provided, and the provision of separate poorhouses, workhouses and houses of correction was not widespread. However, the framework provided by the 1601 legislation continued to govern the administration of poor relief at least until the end of the eighteenth century.

After 1795, a shift in the administration of poor relief took place involving the adoption by many parishes of the so-called 'Speenhamland' system. This involved the extension of the use of supplements to income in cash and kind, both to the poor and to those in work, linked to the price of bread. This system was established at a time when wages in many areas were falling below subsistence level, due to the inflation caused by the Napoleonic war and to a series of bad harvests. In addition, the authorities were concerned to minimise the growth of radicalism in the aftermath of the French Revolution. The adoption of the allowance system was an attempt to re-establish a degree of economic security for the rural working class, based on a gentry paternalism which still showed some resistance to purely capitalist values.

The allowance system led to increases in expenditure on poor relief, and thus to higher rates, which provoked the opposition of the ratepayers. The allowance system also led to low wages, since employers could pay them in the knowledge that they would be supplemented by the parish. The resistance of rural ratepayers led to increasing pressure to reform, or even abolish, the Poor Law. The allowance system also offended the tenets of classical political economy by interfering with the free determination of wages and by failing to impose the sole responsibility for financing generational reproduction on parents. The outbreak of widespread rural violence in 1830, precisely in those areas where the allowance system was most used, further increased the demand for reform.

The principles of classical political economy, along with those of Benthamism, formed the basis for the Poor Law (Amendment) Act 1834. The Act was designed to reduce expenditure on poor relief by preventing cash payments, known as 'outdoor relief', to the able-bodied poor. In future such persons would either have to find some means of supporting themselves or enter a workhouse, in which conditions were designed to be so unpleasant that almost any alternative would be preferable. As a result, it was believed that the incentive to work would be reinforced. The Act also transferred the responsibility for the poor to some 600 Poor Law Unions, run by Guardians elected by the ratepayers, from whom the necessary rates were collected. Central control was undertaken by a Poor Law Commission using circulars and instructions to local Guardians, and through an Inspectorate.

The Act had a substantial impact on the nature of poor relief. The initial aim of reducing expenditure was achieved. However, out-relief to the able-bodied continued to be given in many unions, sometimes because ratepayers and Guardians resisted imposing the increased rates required to finance workhouse construction. There was also popular resistance to attempts to abolish out-relief which came to a head during the trade depression of 1837 in the industrial cities of the north of England. In some areas, neither out-relief nor the allowance system was ever abolished. In the industrial towns and cities, the instability of employment led to massive fluctuations in the numbers claiming relief and the workhouses could not cater for the numbers involved. The recommended solution was to impose a 'labour test', involving a spell of menial labour such as stone-breaking, as a condition of relief to the able-bodied.

Following the 1834 Act, the proportion of paupers resident in workhouses grew throughout the century. At the same time, the population in receipt of poor relief showed a downward trend, due to the growth of working-class institutions of self-help, and the increase in real wages which took place, as well as the deterrent effect of the workhouse. A high proportion of workhouse inmates were not able-bodied, but consisted of the sick, the handicapped and the old. In 1871, the central administration of the Poor Law was transferred to a newly created Local Government Board. A renewed drive to reduce out-relief was undertaken. More 'Relieving Officers' were appointed to investigate the claims of those seeking relief, in particular women, who made up the great majority of those receiving outdoor relief in the form of cash benefits.

Reliance on the Poor Law as the sole means used by the state to deal with the unemployed came under challenge in the 1880s. In February 1886, major rioting broke out as a result of the severe unemployment in London, and the Lord Mayor organised a programme of fund raising. In March of the same year, the President of the Local Government Board allowed local authorities to provide relief work for the 'exceptional' unemployed outside of the Poor Law administration. This policy was later formalised in the Unemployed Workman's Act 1905, which allowed local authorities to set up 'Distress Committees' to provide relief work, but not financial assistance alone.

By the end of the century, the operation of the Poor Law was still uneven. Out-relief remained, and resistance to the deterrent approach was growing, as a result of the removal of the property qualification for participation in the election of Boards of Guardians. This led, in some working-class areas, to the election of Guardians sympathetic to the poor. However, overall expenditure on poor relief remained relatively low, at £8.6 million in 1906. The workhouse remained as a potent symbol of class dominance. It was viewed as a warning of the consequences of the inability to secure subsistence independently. Claimants were deterred by the fact that the receipt of any form of relief from the Poor Law authorities normally involved subjection to humiliating investigatory procedures as well as disenfranchisement, for that small minority of applicants to relief who were entitled to vote.

5.2.2 The Transition from the Poor Law: 1900–40

By the first decade of the twentieth century, considerable political opposition to the existing Poor Law was developing as part of the general ideological shift related, to the growing external political, military and economic threat from the newer industrial capitalist states, to the growing scale and technological advance of British industry, and to the expanding influence of labour. The Liberal government of 1906–14 incorporated many of the contradictory currents arising from this ideological turbulence, which was intensified by the growing socio-political crisis that developed in the decade preceding the outbreak of war in 1914. During this period the Poor Laws themselves were investigated by a Royal Commission which, in 1909, published a Majority and a Minority Report. The different proposals of the two reports reflected the deeply opposed viewpoints within ruling-class opinion. In consequence, the Poor Law was retained, but state policy on income support was expanded to include limited schemes for old age pensions and insurance for health and unemployment.

The Old Age Pensions Act 1908 provided a means-tested pension of 5 shillings per week at the age of 70. The high qualifying age and the low level of benefit were designed to minimise expenditure. In the event, 490,000 pensioners — mainly women — qualified, constituting about *half* of the over-70 age-group. The National Insurance Act 1911 provided for compulsory health insurance for those earning below £160 per annum. The Act also provided compulsory insurance against unemployment for some 2.5 million workers in seven occupations, most importantly, building, mechanical engineering and shipbuilding.

Although the pensions and insurance schemes represented a move away from the deterrent approach of the Poor Law, considerable elements of continuity were maintained. All three schemes were designed to restrict benefits to a category of deserving individuals. Pensions could be refused to those who could not show that they had not habitually failed to work. The insurance schemes used the alternative approach of restricting the duration of benefit so as to exclude 'malingerers'. The low level of benefits was designed to provide a continuing market for private insurance schemes. The insurance scheme involved the encouragement of thrift through placing it on a compulsory state-organised basis. Health insurance was widely supported for the favourable effects it was hoped it would have on labour efficiency. The restriction of the scheme to workers, with their families excluded, particularly emphasised this. The long-term chronic sick were also excluded. Unemployment insurance excluded the lowest paid, the unorganised and the casually employed.

Several features of the schemes have retained a place in subsequent income support policy. First, the division between recipients of insurance benefits and those only given assistance subject to means tests or other conditions has continued. Second, the funding principle used in the 1911 Act, where contributions from employed workers were supplemented by a contribution from their employers and the state, has remained the basis of later insurance schemes. Finally, the principle that benefits were limited in duration and only earned by a certain level of contribution has been retained.

While the Poor Law continued to be financed from the rates and thus involved some redistribution from better-off ratepayers to those in receipt of relief, the system of finance used in the insurance schemes mainly involved a redistribution within the wage-earning population (from those in regular work to those who were not) with a small Exchequer contribution. In the 1911 budget, income taxes were made more progressive and since death duties were only levied on large estates, some redistribution took place. However, the poor still paid indirect taxes such as excise duties, and these, with flat-rate insurance contributions, tended to be regressive. During the First World War the income tax system was made more progressive, but since most war-spending was financed by borrowing, the main beneficiaries were the owners of loanable funds.

Throughout the inter-war period, income support policies were primarily concerned with the unemployed. The rapidly changing economic and political situation led to a complex series of shifts of policy. At the end of the First World War, the government introduced a temporary benefit for the unemployed known as the Out-of-Work Donation. The relative generosity of this benefit, set at a level sufficient for subsistence, was due to fears of the consequences of forcing large numbers of demobilised troops and unemployed munitions workers to apply for relief from the Poor Law Guardians. For the longer term, the governing Liberal-Conservative coalition introduced the National Insurance Act 1920. This provided for the compulsory insurance of all workers earning below £250 p.a. except for teachers, civil servants, agricultural labourers and domestic servants. However, by 1921 the scheme was unable to function, because of a considerable rise in unemployment. Large numbers of unemployed workers were disqualified from receipt of benefit by the contribution rules. Rather than force them to apply for poor relief, 'uncovenanted' benefits were, from 1921, allowed to insured workers. These benefits however, could be refused by the Local Employment Committee if the applicant was found to be Not Genuinely Seeking Work (NGSW). From 1922, uncovenanted benefit could be refused if the aggregate income of all the members of the household exceeded a limit set by the Local Insurance Committee. In 1923, the minority Labour government abolished this extremely unpopular household means-test, but retained the NGSW regulations.

In 1925, national insurance underwent substantial expansion as a result of the Widow's Orphan's and Old Age Contributory Pensions Act of that year. This provided for contributory non-means-tested pensions for those already covered by the health insurance scheme. The means-test for unemployment benefit was reimposed from 1925 to 1927. From 1927, in addition to the retention of the NGSW rules, benefit could also be refused for those adjudged to have an unsatisfactory employment record in the previous two years. The NGSW provision remained a focus of criticism and a source of a large number of appeals. Those of the unemployed who did not qualify for benefits could apply for poor relief, which remained under local control and hence varied greatly. In addition, the operation of the national insurance scheme was causing an increase in the numbers applying for poor relief. The NGSW rules were being applied with increasing severity in the wake of the defeat of the General Strike. In some areas, as many as 40 per cent of claims were refused. Those refused often applied in desperation to the Poor Law Relieving Officer and in many areas, especially where there was a substantial Labour presence on the Board of Guardians, they were given relief, normally in some combination of cash and kind. The government gave itself powers to penalise over-generous boards under the terms of the Board of Guardians Default Act 1926, which was used against a number of boards after the General Strike. In 1929, the Conservative government abolished the Boards of Guardians altogether and transferred the function of administering the Poor Law to 146 newly created Public Assistance Committees to be established by local authorities.

The new Labour government elected in 1929 relaxed the administration of insurance benefits by the abolition in 1930 of the NGSW rules, which were the main target of the hunger marches of that and the previous year. This led to some increase in the number of people receiving benefit, particularly amongst women. This once again created concern about national insurance funding. A press campaign against abuse of benefit led the Labour government to appoint a Royal Commission in late 1930. In June 1931, the commission published a recommendation for benefit cuts and other changes. The Anomalies Act 1931 was passed in July. Within 18 months 300,000 people, 83.7 per cent of them married women, were refused benefit as a result. In August, a major financial crisis occurred in which the Labour Cabinet split over the required measures, including a proposed cut in benefits, and the National government was formed.

Unemployment climbed to 22.4 per cent in September 1931. In the same month, the total deficit of the Insurance fund reached £114 million. The National government immediately moved to reduce expenditure on income support. Under the National Economy Act 1931 the contribution rules were tightened, the duration of benefit was cut, and its value was reduced by 10 per cent. After 26 weeks, claimants had to apply for 'transitional payment' to the Public Assistance Committee (PAC), which employed a household means test. In the first seven weeks after the scheme came into operation, 440,000 out of 800,000 people who had previously received benefit had their benefit refused or reduced on application to the PAC. As a result, increasing numbers applied for relief under the Poor Law. The changes introduced by the National government led to substantial opposition from the unemployed. The membership of the National Unemployed Workers Movement reached its peak in 1932, and riots took place in Liverpool and London. A few PACs refused to implement the new policies and were replaced by commissioners. Substantial local variations continued to exist, and in 1934 legislation was introduced to impose a uniform national system.

The Unemployment Act 1934 transferred responsibility for *all* those registered as unemployed to the Ministry of Labour. The 10 per cent cut in insurance benefit levels made in 1931 was restored and an Unemployment Insurance Statutory Committee with Beveridge as its chairman (see the following subsection) was set up to oversee the scheme. Insured workers were given an entitlement to benefit strictly limited to 26 weeks. Others had to apply to a newly created Unemployment Assistance Board (UAB). This was intended to apply a single national means test, distributing benefits on a uniform scale. The local authority PACs, however, were retained to provide relief under the Poor Law to the non-able-bodied. The low benefit level initially chosen by the UAB led to major public disorders. As a result, the new scheme was phased in over three years. In 1937, the insurance scheme was expanded to include all non-manual workers earning less than £250 per annum. No further major changes in income support policies were made before 1940.

5.2.3 *War and Social Security: 1940–8*

During the Second World War unemployment almost completely disappeared, and this issue, which was at the centre of the numerous policy changes of the inter-war period, was no longer a major concern. The war also brought about a substantial shift in the balance of class forces. In particular, the participation of the Labour Party in the coalition government from 1940, the growth in the membership and political influence of the trade unions, and the upsurge of popular radicalism which took place, all increased the forces in favour of reform.

The Old Age and Widow's Pensions Act 1940 reduced reliance on the Poor Law by providing supplementary pensions in cases of need. The Act established the pensionable age at 60 for women and 65 for men. The UAB was renamed the Assistance Board and administered the scheme on uniform lines. The war transformed the work of the Assistance Board, due both to the virtual disappearance of the unemployed and to its new role with the old. It also took on responsibility for blitz victims, evacuees and others with special wartime needs under the Prevention and Relief of Distress scheme. The household means test was replaced with a test of individual incomes by the Determination of Needs Act 1941 as part of the price exacted by the Labour Party for entering the coalition government. The numbers on outdoor relief under the Poor Law declined, due both to supplementary pensions and to the absence of mass unemployment. Wartime tax changes were also used to support family incomes. The budget of 1941 reduced tax allowances and increased tax rates. Inflation led to increasing numbers of working-class taxpayers and child tax allowances thus came to benefit many better-paid workers.

The reforming currents which developed during the Second World War were given direction by the Beveridge Report of 1942. Beveridge proposed a scheme based on social insurance in which a single weekly contribution would provide a right to receive a comprehensive range of benefits set at subsistence level, covering all interruptions of income and exceptional expenses. Everyone was to be covered by the scheme and both the benefits and contributions were to be set at a single rate applying to all, although some differences in entitlement were to exist between the different classes of contributions. A single department was to administer all the benefits available in a uniform fashion. Beveridge also maintained that a national health service, a system of family allowances and the pursuit of full-employment policies were essential preconditions for his scheme.

Prior to, and on its publication, the report received considerable publicity and attracted widespread popular support. The attraction of the report lay chiefly in the proposal for benefits at a level adequate for subsistence, and in the promise of the eventual abolition of the means test. The proposals for a national health service, full employment and family allowances were viewed by the public as integral parts of the plan. The insurance scheme did represent an important advance over existing provision, which was uneven in coverage, in the value of benefits provided, and in the extent to which means-testing was used. It involved the completion of a pattern of provision that had largely crystallised by 1940, with the imposition of dual national schemes for unemployment insurance benefit, and for the means-tested relief of the uninsured unemployed in the UAB.

Beveridge himself saw his plan as a means by which the state could abolish 'want' at the same time as increasing the efficiency of the CMP, without undermining the central features of private ownership and individual responsibility. Accordingly, key features of the scheme were portrayed by Beveridge as consistent with the values necessary for the continuation of capitalism in the UK. The insurance principle would reinforce self-help. Contribution rules would prevent 'abuse' by malingerers. The funding system, involving contributions from the employer and the state, would symbolise the acceptance by capital and the state of a concern for employee welfare. The existence of a 'national minimum' would give concrete expression to the obligation of the state to maintain for everyone an acceptable national standard of life. The 'universal' nature of the scheme, that is its inclusion of everyone, would symbolise its centrality as part of the rights of citizenship. Setting benefits at subsistence level would maintain work incentives and encourage the development of private provision of income support and thrift to pay for it. In addition, it would keep the cost low. Finally, the overall disturbance to the existing pattern of income inequality would be minimised.

The Beveridge proposals were not fully endorsed on publication, despite considerable popular support for them. However, in 1944, a White Paper on social insurance was produced which accepted many of the details of the Beveridge scheme, although it rejected the central provision that benefits should be set at subsistence level. The 1944 White Paper also accepted the proposal for family allowances, and the coalition government legislated for them in the Family Allowances Act 1945. Under this Act, an allowance of 5 shillings per week was paid to the mother for each child after the first. Family allowances were to be paid to all families on a non-contributory and non-means-tested basis. Beveridge supported family allowances for a number of reasons. Insurance benefits could be kept down, since larger families with greater needs would have them met by family allowances. Incentives to obtain work would be increased for those larger families who had previously received unemployment insurance benefits with allowances for dependants. The Treasury and many employers supported family allowances, because they hoped they would reduce the pressure for higher wages by improving the living standards of families with children who were living on low earnings. They were also viewed as a means of neutralising demands for a minimum wage. Finally, family allowances were supported by imperialists, worried about the continuation of the 'British race' and the evidence in the 1930s of a declining birth rate. By the end of 1946 allowances were being paid for some 4 million children at an annual cost of about £50 million. In the same year, pensions for all were introduced in advance of the implementation of the main national insurance legislation.

The National Insurance Act 1946 enacted a scheme based largely on the details of the Beveridge plan. However, the failure to set insurance benefits at subsistence level negated the key objective of reducing reliance on means tests. The proposed benefits for marriage and for desertion were not included, and Beveridge's proposal that unemployment benefits should be of unlimited duration was not followed. Although insured workers in relatively regular work were adequately covered by the scheme, many other people were not. The self-employed were excluded from unemployment benefit, the non-employed were excluded from both unemployment and sickness benefit. Married women were not treated on the same basis as men (see subsection 5.4.2). Those unable to enter the labour force, such as the handicapped, were not able to obtain any insurance benefits. These, along with those whose benefit had run out, had to undergo a means test to obtain additional funds. Means-tested benefits were made available under the National Assistance Act 1948. This abolished the Poor Law and transferred its institutional functions to the NHS and the local authorities. The Act established a National Assistance Board (NAB), which replaced the existing Assistance Board and took on its work along with the functions previously performed by the PACs. The national insurance (NI) and national assurance (NA) schemes came into effect in July 1948. In 1948, the NAB paid benefits to just over 1 million clients (see Table 5.1). Of this total, two-thirds were also receiving insurance benefits and 63 per cent were pensioners. The day on which the income support schemes came into operation was also the 'appointed day' for the start of the NHS. Thus, on the same day began a programme of reforms that sought to incorporate the working class as full citizens of a democratic welfare capitalist state.

5.2.4 Income Support from 1948

The social security system established in 1948 provided a degree of economic security for male workers and their dependants in a period of relatively low unemployment. The subsequent development of state policy, however, proceeded in the opposite direction to that anticipated by Beveridge. The long boom and low levels of unemployment came to an end and the means-tested assistance scheme, far from disappearing, grew substantially. Other economic and demographic changes led to rises in expenditure on income support. Increased taxation, partly to finance this expenditure, also had an adverse impact on working-class living standards.

During the 1950s the numbers receiving national assistance increased (see Table 5.1). By the late 1950s, the Conservatives were becoming concerned at the rising level of NI expenditure on the old. The first major modification to the 1948 scheme was undertaken by the Graduated Pensions Act 1959. In return for a contribution graduated according to income level, a supplement to the ordinary NI pension would be given. However, the Act also encouraged the growing private insurance sector by allowing employees to contract out of the state scheme if they belonged to an approved private superannuation scheme. This Act also represented a move away from the principles of flat-rate benefits and contributions and of universal provision.

The Labour government in 1966 introduced an earning-related supplement (ERS) payable to those on NI sickness or unemployment benefit under the Social Security Act 1966. This also renamed NAB the Supplementary Benefits Commission (SBC). The introduction of ERS was part of an attempt to use cash benefits to contribute to the 'modernisation' strategy by increasing 'flexibility' in the utilisation of labour. As unemployment rose from July 1966, when deflationary measures were introduced, the rhetoric of 'shake-out' and 'redeployment' began to be widely used. Rising unemployment also led to an ideological offensive against 'shirkers' and 'scroungers' in 1968. Partly in response, the government introduced the 'four-week rule', under which unemployed single unskilled workers under 45 years of age could be deprived of benefit after four weeks, if jobs were deemed to be available in the locality. The procedure represented the return of the not genuinely seeking work rule.

The composition of the clientele of the SBC was changing rapidly in the 1960s (see Table 5.1). The proportion of pensioners was

Table 5.1: Persons Receiving Supplementary Benefit in the UK, 1948–82

	National Assistance (thousands)			Supplementary Benefits (thousands)		
	1948	1951	1961	1971	1981	1982
Retirement pensioners and						
NI widows 60 years and over	495	767	1,089	1,820	1,640	1,700
Others over pension age	143	202	234	103	95	82
Unemployed with NI benefit	19	33	48	129	234	285
Unemployed without NI benefit	34	33	94	258	1,084	1,437
Sick and disabled with NI						
benefit	80	121	138	146	66	83
Sick and disabled without NI						
benefit	64	98	142	159	155	157
One-parent families not in						
other groups	32	41	78	213	369	415
National insurance widows						
under 60	81	86	60	65	16	20
Others	63	81	18	20	61	90
Total persons receiving						
supplementary benefit	1,011	1,462	1,902	2,910	3,720	4,270

Note: Figures for 1948 and 1951 are for Great Britain only.

falling, partly due to the wider availability of occupational pensions, whereas the number of unemployed and of single-parent families was increasing. The unemployed, unlike the sick, were excluded from the entitlement to a 'long-term' addition after two years on benefit, which the 1966 Act had introduced.

In 1971, the Conservative government introduced a Family Income Supplement (FIS), which provided a supplement to low wage-earners. This was the first direct subsidy to low wages since the allowance system which operated before 1834. The number of recipients has remained low, and many of those eligible fail to claim the benefit. A number of other new means-tested schemes were also being introduced at about this time, most notably rate rebates from 1966, and rent rebates from 1972. Free prescriptions and school meals were also available on a means-tested basis.

The major reforms carried out by the 1974–9 Labour governments involved the finance of the NI fund, pensions and family allowances. In 1975, the flat-rate NI contribution was replaced by a weekly contribution of 5.5 per cent of weekly income, falling within a band from £11 to £69 per week. The Pensions Act 1975 established a scheme, to be phased in over twenty years, to provide a basic flat-rate pension with an earnings-related supplement. This supplement can be provided by an approved private-sector scheme. The Child Benefit Act 1977 brought in a weekly benefit for every child at the same time as child tax allowances were being withdrawn. The main feature of income support in this period of Labour government involved the expansion of the clientele of the SBC (see Table 5.1). This resulted mainly from the growth in unemployment. The rise in fuel costs in this period also led to an increased use of 'exceptional needs payments' and was also partly responsible for a large increase in appeals. In order to cope with an increased workload, the staff of the SBC more than doubled in the decade after 1966. The SBC was also put under some pressure by the activities of claimants' unions and by criticism of secrecy in the administration of the rules governing benefit entitlement. In 1976, an ideological campaign against 'scroungers' led to an increase in the number of fraud investigators.

The wide-ranging expenditure cuts introduced by the Labour government in 1976 did not have a major immediate effect on income support schemes. However, a review of the SBC was undertaken, which reported in 1978. The proposals made in this review formed the basis for the Social Security Act 1980, introduced by the new Conservative government. This Act abolished the SBC and brought supplementary benefit under the direct control of the DHSS. It substantially reduced the scope for discretionary payments, leaving many claimants worse off. While it reduced the qualifying period for the long-term addition (worth £10.60 to a couple in 1983) to one year, the unemployed were still excluded from this payment. Cuts were also instituted in November 1980, and sickness, unemployment, maternity, and industrial injury benefits were increased by 5 per cent less than the current rate of inflation. Further cuts were achieved by the abolition of the ERS from the end of 1981. The benefit system was also modified to penalise those involved in strikes. The supplementary benefit payable to the families of strikers was reduced by £12 (now £16), which was deemed to allow for strike pay from a trade union, whether or not this was actually received. In addition, from 1982 tax rebates due to striking workers have been withheld until the end of the dispute. Payments to the unemployed were also made subject to tax in 1982.

Two major changes were introduced in the Social Security and Housing Benefits Act 1982. This Act abolished short-term NI Sickness Benefit and gave employers the responsibility for paying Employers' Statutory Sick Pay for the first eight weeks of benefit. The Act also established a Housing Benefit (HB) to combine the previous rent rebates, rent allowances and rate rebates. Over 6 million households, a *third* of the total, receive HB. Those who are council tenants will now have their rent and rates paid direct to their council's housing department by the DHSS.

The changes introduced since 1979 had, by 1982–3, reduced expenditure by about £2,000 million from what it would otherwise have been. The overall pattern of expenditure on benefits is shown in Table 5.2. Despite the cuts, real expenditure on social security has risen by 25 per cent in the period 1979–83. The main reason has been the increase in unemployment, which accounted for 17 per cent of the social security budget by 1983 as compared with 8 per cent in 1979. This increase has taken place despite substantial cuts in the value of benefits to the unemployed. In 1979, an unemployed male worker, previously receiving average earnings, would receive NI benefits, including ERS, worth 34.6 per cent of his normal pay. By 1983, with the cuts and the abolition of ERS, the value of benefit would be only 18.2 per cent of his normal pay. However, a decreasing proportion are maintained by insurance benefits. The rest are forced to rely on supplementary benefit (SB) or do not obtain any benefit at all (see Table 5.3).

Table 5.2: Major Benefits — Expenditure (percentage) and Numbers of Recipients in Great Britain 1982–3

	Expenditure (£ million)	Percentage of total expenditure	Number of recipients per week (millions)
National Insurance benefits (60.8% of total expenditure)			
Pensions	13,688	44.0	9.075
Invalidity and Industrial Disablement Benefit	1,951	6.3	0.89
Unemployment Benefits	1,650	5.3	1.2
Other: maternity, sickness, injury, widows and death	1,617	5.2	—
Means-tested benefits (22.8% of total expenditure)			
Supplementary Benefits — pensions	1,408	4.5	1.73
Supplementary Benefits — other (unemployed, sick, etc.)	4,609	14.8	2.325
Family Income Supplement (FIS)	92	0.3	0.160
Housing Benefit/Rent Rebates and Allowances	995	3.2	3.315
Non-contributory benefits (16.4% of total expenditure)			
Child benefits	3,704	11.9	12.935
War and other pensions	508	1.6	0.330
Invalid pensions and care allowances, attendance and mobility allowances	792	2.6	—
One-parent benefit	90	0.3	0.505
Total	31,104	100	—

Notes: These figures are indicative rather than definitive, since they are calculated from estimates.
Administrative costs are not included.
The number maintained wholly or partly by these benefits is larger than the number of recipients, since in many cases these have dependants.
Source: Adapted from CSO *Social Trends* (HMSO, 1983) Table 5.6 and DHSS, *Social Security Statistics* (HMSO 1983), Table 34.31.

Income Support Policy

Table 5.3: Benefits for the Unemployed in Great Britain, 1961–82: numbers and percentages in each category

	1961 thousand%	1971 thousand%	1982 thousand%
Unemployment benefit only	133 (47.0)	295 (40.9)	448 (21.3)
Unemployment benefit & SB	27 (9.5)	98 (13.6)	231 (11.0)
SB only	62 (21.9)	195 (27.0)	1100 (52.4)
No benefit	61 (21.6)	133 (18.5)	321 (15.3)
Total	283 (100)	721 (100)	2100 (100)

Source: Adapted from CSO, *Social Trends* (HMSO, 1983), Table 5.7.

Throughout much of the post-war period the dominant ideological representation of the unacceptable aspect of income inequality has rested on the notion of 'poverty'. This was based on an income standard (poverty line) designed to be just adequate to maintain the capacity to perform productive or reproductive labour, or, in the case of children, to continue normal physical development. Within this framework it was possible for the inadequate provision made for particular groups, such as the old and the disabled, to be made the subject of campaigns for reform without the overall extent and nature of inequality becoming a major issue. Up until the mid-1960s this conception of poverty dominated both political debate and academic research on the subject. As the post-war consensus began to break up in the late 1960s, this dominant conception of poverty was called into question. The Labour government of 1964–70 began to adopt the notion of multi-deprivation as a basis for its experimental area-based Urban Programme and Educational Priority Area policies. A wider range of measurable inequalities, involving such factors as health, housing and education, were to be tackled by a range of 'urban' policies. These apparently more radical approaches were paralleled on the right by a revival of the notion of poverty as being caused by the failings of those who experienced it. In the form of the 'cycle of deprivation' theory, this approach to poverty could be combined with the elements of the multi-deprivation approach to portray the urban poor as trapped by their own inadequacies in a style of life which perpetuated itself from one generation to another. Such approaches tend to be given increased prominence in periods of economic crisis, since they help to shift the responsibility for failure to secure an adequate income onto those involved, and to reduce opposition to cuts in benefits.

While the social security system has remained the major means by which the state has supported incomes, a growing role has been played by the tax system. Contrary to popular belief, direct personal taxation is not the main source of tax revenue. The proportion of total tax revenue from income tax peaked at 37.3 per cent in 1976. Income tax has, however, had a major effect on working-class incomes. The level at which households start to pay income tax (the tax threshold) has tended to fall throughout the post-war period. Income taxation has continued to be operated on an allowance system, under which income recipients are entitled to a certain income free of tax. The most valuable allowances are the 'personal' allowance, and that given for mortgage interest relief. Tax rates have been set in bands, with an increasing proportion of additional income being paid in tax the higher the taxpayer's total income. The precise details have been frequently changed, although Labour governments have generally been more willing to increase the tax on high incomes. Unlike income, wealth has not been taxed, except by estate duty and by capital transfer tax, which was established in 1975 to replace estate duty. The yield of these taxes has continually fallen as a proportion of total tax revenue. A capital gains tax was established in 1965, but in 1980 it yielded only £410 million of revenue. The period since 1979 has seen substantial cuts in personal direct taxation, due to increases in personal allowances and in the higher-rate tax threshold, and reductions in the higher rates. There have also been reductions in the investment-income surcharge and in capital transfer tax and capital gains tax. In 1982–3, the value of these tax cuts was £2,400 million, most of which went to those in receipt of high incomes.

Indirect taxation, i.e. taxation on expenditure, has been an important source of revenue in the post-war period. The major expenditure taxes are excise duties on drink and tobacco, fuel tax, and until 1973 purchase tax, which was then replaced by VAT. Conservative governments have been particularly prone to raise revenue in this way and, especially since 1979, there has been a major shift from direct to indirect taxation. Labour governments have tried to use expenditure taxes to increase the real incomes of low-income recipients. When VAT replaced purchase tax, it was not levied on food, fuel or public transport.

A major change in taxation in the post-war period has been the increase in the sums raised by NI contributions. These made up to 4.7 per cent of central government tax revenues in 1946 and 17.1 per cent in 1979. The introduction of a percentage payment from 1975 means that the yield of these taxes now automatically increases if incomes rise.

Over the post-war period the contribution of company taxation to total tax revenue has fallen substantially, due both to falling profitability and to a series of changes in the taxation system. During this period, companies have expanded their own involvement in state-subsidised systems of income support. Many employers have had sick-pay schemes, and all are now involved since the introduction of Employers Statutory Sick Pay in 1982. In the private sector, top employees may also receive subsidies for travel, health and life insurance, loans, share purchases, and meals. A wider range of employees receive company cars, which have been subject to taxation since 1977, but at a rate that underestimates their real value. The most significant area of company-organised income support has been pensions. About 12 million employees are covered by company pensions. They are more common in the public sector than the private sector. Better-paid employees, men and white-collar workers are those most likely to receive them. The pensions are normally earnings-related. Company pensions, along with all forms of company-financed income support, are subsidised in that the sums contributed by employers are not subject to tax. In addition, considerable sums of money capital are channelled into the financial system through the pension funds, which have now become major holders of financial assets. Policy has encouraged the growth of private pension provision through setting state pensions below subsistence, through tax reliefs, and by allowing contracting out of state earnings-related schemes (since 1959) in favour of approved private schemes. The massive growth of tax-subsidised and earnings-related private provision has been a key feature of income support in the post-war period. As a result, the relative importance of direct state provision based on a uniform scale of payments for all recipients has declined, having been partly replaced by a company-run, tax-subsidised system of income support which closely reflects and reinforces the pattern of income inequalities resulting from the existence of wage labour.

5.3 Capitalism, Class Relations and Income Support

This section of the chapter will outline the way in which various aspects of the growth of capitalism in the UK have acted together to produce the complex pattern of development of income support policy described in the previous section. The direct influence of the CMP is particularly evident in the case of income support due to the central role played in capitalism by the system of wage labour. Income support policies have normally reinforced the incentive to work, with benefits kept well below wage levels. Only exceptionally have substantial benefits been made available to those in paid employment. Policies have normally been designed to hold expenditure to the minimum consistent with the maintenance of the degree of legitimation and security necessary for the continuation of capitalist accumulation. In consequence, the extent of redistribution of real income from the rich to the poor has also been limited. Policies have also consistently been employed to reduce the necessity for state assistance by imposing the obligation to maintain those without resources on 'liable relatives'. Policies that support the family-household system also maintain existing sexual divisions, in particular by reinforcing the role of women in labour and generational reproduction, and in caring for the old and the handicapped.

Although income support policies have normally operated to reinforce the CMP, the extent to which policy has conformed exclusively to this pattern has varied. The balance of class forces affects the degree to which income support is governed by the material needs of the recipients, rather than the requirements of the capitalist labour market. Popular protest and social disorder may lead to concessions, unless the subordinate classes are not politically organised, when they are more likely to be met by repression. The relative weight of purely bourgeois interests within the ruling bloc will affect the kinds of concessions that are made and the extent to which these are withdrawn in periods of class dominance. In the UK, aristocratic and professional influences within the ruling bloc have often prevented the rigorous imposition of capitalist values. Where social democratic values are also incorporated into the dominant ideology in the form of an emphasis on 'citizenship', then further concessions will be likely.

The influence of the form and extent of existing barriers to accumulation on income support is complex, although of central importance is the stage of development of the CMP. In Britain, in the transitional phase in which capitalist relations of production were being established, the Poor Law was intended to prevent the development of a level of disorder which might threaten the security of property, and to reinforce a form of labour discipline based on regulated wages and stable employment in small-scale craft and agricultural production. The beginnings of competitive industrial capitalism created new problems of labour control, associated with the subjection of the labour force to factory discipline. However, the growth of the allowance system at the end of the eighteenth century reflected a concern with the potential for disorder arising from the growth of popular radicalism. In these emergency conditions, a substantial relaxation temporarily took place in the administration of poor relief. The attempt in 1834 to establish a national deterrent workhouse system was a return to the pattern developing before the establishment of the allowance system. Its adoption reflected the growing influence of capitalist values, although working-class resistance prevented the full imposition of the workhouse system. In the second half of the nineteenth century, the problems associated with the initial establishment of factory labour receded and it was becoming evident that wage labour could operate without the deterrent workhouse. In the twentieth century, the development of a wide-ranging system of income support based on a combination of means-tested and insurance benefits has been associated with the existence of a strong labour movement. In the early years of the century, when some of the enduring features of the present system of income support were established, the transition from competitive to monopoly capitalism was in process. This weakened the resistance of capital in general to state expenditure on labour reproduction.

Throughout the twentieth century, the system of income support has been periodically adjusted. Periods of popular radicalism, such as the Second World War and its aftermath, have led to increases in the level of benefits, their coverage and to a relaxation of the rules governing their distribution. Widespread protests and disorders have also led to limited concessions on occasion. Periods of economic crisis have led to reductions in benefits, to increases in the stringency of rules governing their distribution, and often to ideological offensives against claimants and the benefit system. The effect of the political party in power has been to modify the influence of the balance of class forces and the conditions for accumulation, in the case of the Conservative Party by increasing the application of capitalist values, and in the case of the Labour and Liberal Parties by reducing this tendency.

5.4 Income Support and Inequality

5.4.1 Income Support and the Distribution of Personal Incomes

The effects of income support policies on personal incomes are not governed by the application of any single unambiguous policy objective. Instead, policies are directed towards a variety of conflicting and partially realised aims such as setting an income floor below which no household should fall, maintaining work incentives and labour discipline, and reinforcing the pattern of income distribution produced by the labour market.

The redistributive effects of the benefit system are a complex amalgam of *vertical* (between-income groups) and *horizontal* (within-income groups) effects. Vertical redistribution may be *progressive* (from rich to poor) or *regressive* (from poor to rich). All flat-rate NI and non-contributory benefits involve a progressive vertical redistribution in that they represent a higher proportion of the income of poorer recipients. However, vertical redistribution can also be viewed as requiring a disproportionate chance of receiving a given benefit. Unemployment benefit, for example, is progressively redistributive, since low-paid workers, who have a higher chance of unemployment, are thus more likely to receive it. However, most of the expenditure on NI benefits goes on pensions (see Table 5.2). These have a regressive redistributive effect because they involve a disproportionate payment to the better-off, since this group lives longer. Other benefits, such as that paid for sickness, redistribute income horizontally, i.e. from the healthy to the sick, within each income group. Means-tested benefits such as SB involve progressive redistribution, since they are only paid to those who can demonstrate a low or non-existent income level. However, the very low level of payments should be noted. Those dependent on SB (see Table 5.4) are maintained at a minimal standard. About 54 per cent are pensioners or children; these are required to exist at this level in order to preserve 'work incentives' and hold down public expenditure.

Although means-tested benefits involve progressive redistribution, a quarter or more of those eligible for supplementary benefits and/or housing benefit, FIS, and free school meals do not claim

Table 5.4: Supplementary Benefits — Numbers of Recipients and Dependants, December 1982 (Thousands)

Numbers maintained by supplementary benefits	All pensioners	Unemployed		Sick and Disabled		NI widows under 60 years	Single parents not in other groups	Others	Totals
		With NI	Without NI	With NI	Without NI				
Persons receiving benefit (i.e. number of payments made per week) (thousand)	1781	285	1437	83	157	20	415	90	4267
Numbers of dependent wives maintained (thousand)	308	178	435	42	11	—	—	36	1010
Numbers of dependent children under 16 maintained (thousand)	8	283	665	36	11	5	700	14	1721
Number of other dependants 16+ maintained (thousand)	2	10	29	2	2	1	19	5	70
Total provided for (thousand)	2099	756	2566	163	181	26	1134	145	7068
Average value of each weekly payment made (£)	£10.75	19.19	34.82	14.45	26.74	14.59	39.86	41.48	

Source: DHSS, *Social Security Statistics* (HMSO, 1983), adapted from Tables 34.31 and 34.38.

them. This is due to the complexity of the procedures involved in claiming, ignorance of the benefits available, the humiliation and invasion of privacy involved in means-testing, the stigma associated with the status of claimant and the low level of many of the benefits. The effect of non-receipt of these benefits reduces substantially the extent of progressive vertical redistribution.

The redistributive impact of direct personal taxation is complex. The system of income tax allowances is regressive, since these are most valuable to those with taxable incomes high enough to attract the higher marginal tax rates. The 'personal' tax allowances have a partly progressive effect, since they reduce the average rate of tax per unit of income for lower-income recipients. Higher rates of tax levied on high incomes are progressive, but less than 2 per cent of all income recipients pay these, and since 1979 the top rate has been reduced to 60 per cent. As a result of the small number of higher-rate taxpayers, the percentage of income paid in tax is very similar for most of those subject to it. The level of earned income is now also the basis for the payment of NI contributions. These are progressive up to the upper-income limit, where the maximum weekly payment is made, but regressive thereafter, since their value as a percentage of earned income falls. Domestic rates are a highly regressive tax. Expenditure taxes vary in their redistributive effects according to the pattern of consumption. Thus excise duties on tobacco and on most alcoholic drinks are regressive, since working-class consumers spend a higher proportion of their incomes on these products. In contrast, VAT, for which food, fuel and public transport are zero-rated, has a mildly progressive effect, since working-class households spend a higher proportion of their incomes on these products.

Official figures for the redistributive impact of direct and indirect personal taxation are based on statistics from the tax authorities. Particularly in the case of direct taxation, an element of progressive vertical redistribution is evident, although this is slight except for those on the very lowest incomes. The extent to which the tax statistics underestimate incomes is unknown, since the self-employed and small businesses have ample opportunity to defraud the tax authorities. Effective tax rates levied on those in receipt of large incomes from business, employment or property also tend to be reduced by the numerous opportunities for legal evasion which exist.

The overall redistributive pattern produced by state policy results from the joint effect of the benefit and personal tax systems. Vertical redistribution mainly helps those with little or no independent income, who receive benefits substantially greater than their tax payments. Overall, the system does not involve substantial progressive redistribution. For example, Table 5.5 shows that the effect of the tax system is to leave the distribution of income between income groups more or less unchanged. The major effects are horizontal. Funds are transferred from the healthy to the sick, and from the employed to the unemployed. However, the main element of transfer is to the old through retirement pensions. In addition, substantial sums are directed to children through the child allowance and because NI and SB payments are adjusted for household size. From the standpoint of the individual worker, the effect is to redistribute lifetime income so that funds are available for childhood and retirement.

The redistributive effects of income support policies have changed in recent years, due to the increased availability of means-tested benefits to those in work. The existence of these benefits has created a 'poverty trap'. Benefits such as FIS, rent allowances and rent and rate rebates (now housing benefit), and free school meals are available to households dependent on a low-paid worker. To the extent that a worker receives these benefits, he or she will be unable to gain much extra income from a pay increase, since this will lead to loss of benefits. Because of the low-income tax threshold, extra income is also likely to attract tax as well as an increased NI contribution. As a result, additional wage income can be reduced by up to 100 per cent. In consequence, many lower-paid workers are trapped at a disposable income level at, or only marginally above, that of those

Table 5.5: Distribution of Income Before and After Tax in the UK, 1974

Income group	Percentage of gross income, including state income support	Percentage of income remaining after tax	Percentage of income paid in tax
Top 10%	20.8	21.0	32.7
11–20%	13.6	13.6	33.4
81–90%	6.1	6.2	32.0
Bottom 10%	4.5	4.6	33.1

Source: M. Campbell, *Capitalism in the UK* (Croom Helm, 1981), Table 4.5, p. 99.

whose main or sole source of income is state benefits. The addition of those subject to the poverty trap to the large number dependent on state benefits, which has itself increased substantially due to the current high levels of unemployment, means that a major section of the working class is forced to live at a minimal material level with little immediate prospect of any improvement.

5.4.2 Income Support and Sexual Inequality

State income support policies provide differential treatment for men and women in a variety of ways through both the benefit and the tax systems. The post-war treatment of women by the benefit system was undertaken largely in accordance with the recommendations made in the Beveridge Report. Beveridge assumed that women's main role should involve domestic reproductive labour in the family-household. He recommended that, in cases where they worked, they could choose to pay a lower contribution and become ineligible for certain benefits. Even where they paid a full contribution, their benefit levels for sickness and unemployment would be below those for men. Thus the proposals maintained the economic dependence of married women on their husbands. The report also recommended inferior provision for cohabitees, separated women and unsupported mothers. This rested on orthodox assumptions about domesticity, motherhood and the importance of the family, and linked these to a desire to maintain capitalist relations of production and Britain's imperial role.

The scheme established by 1948 allowed women workers to contract out and pay a reduced insurance contribution, and 75 per cent did so. The minority of women eligible for unemployment or sickness benefit not only received a lower rate of payment, but could not claim the allowances for a dependent spouse or dependent children that were available to men. Married women who had children were discouraged from staying in work by the provision that they could only have a right to retain their existing job if they returned to it seven weeks after the birth of a child. The system of basing rights to benefit on the continuity of insurance contributions also worked to the disadvantage of women who experienced absence from work due to childbirth. The only insurance benefit available to a family unsupported by a man was the widow's benefit. Unmarried, deserted and separated mothers were required to apply for national assistance. Women have been harassed over the operation of the 'cohabitation rule' under which benefit can be denied to them if they have a continuing sexual relationship with a particular man. However, women did benefit relative to men with respect to retirement pensions, which they could draw at the age of 60. In addition, women benefited from a restriction in the definition of 'liable relatives' such that, after 1948, families were no longer obliged by law to maintain elderly or incapacitated relatives.

The dependence of women on men is also built into the tax system. Until recently, a women's income was presumed to belong to her husband. Married men pay less tax on a given income than either married women or single people of either sex, due to the 'married man's allowance'. Marriage itself is rewarded (for men) by the denial of this allowance to male cohabitees. Tax returns have to be filled in by husbands, and wives are required to reveal their incomes to their spouse, but not vice versa.

In the post-war period, the assumptions made in the Beveridge Report about women's economic participation and about the nature of the typical family-household have proved incorrect. The proportion of economically active married women has continued to increase, from 10 per cent in 1931 to 62 per cent in 1980. The full-time housewife has become a rarity. In about one-sixth of all households, the earnings of a working woman are the main source of family income. The growing participation of women was assisted by a reduction in family size, and by the availability of commodities that could reduce the socially necessary labour time required for the performance of reproductive tasks. Moves have taken place to reduce some of the more obvious discriminations against women in income support. The Employment Protection Act 1975 increased to 29 weeks the maximum time a woman could stay off work after the birth of a child and still have a right to return to her job. From 1977, women were no longer given the option of contracting out of the insurance scheme, although those already doing so were allowed to continue. In 1978, an EEC directive required the abolition of some forms of discrimination against women. As a result, married women on insurance benefit can obtain an allowance for a dependent husband (from November 1983) and dependent children (from November 1984). The introduction of child benefit in 1978 and the additional payment for single-parent families have increased the revenues independently available to women. Since 1971, it has been possible for a married couple to be treated for tax purposes as if each were single. Since 1978, tax rebates may be paid to wives. However, the married man's allowance is still retained. Recently, conditions for women have worsened, due to restrictions on the right to maternity leave for women working in small firms that are contained in the Employment Act 1980. In addition, from 1981 women claiming unemployment benefit must give proof of 'availability for work' by demonstrating the existence of adequate child-care arrangements.

Overall, the post-war period has seen some decrease in the extent to which income support policies assume and reinforce the dependence of women on men, in the extent of discrimination against women, and in the extent of discrimination against households not conforming to the orthodox nuclear-family pattern. Policy towards women is contradictory, since it reflects attempts made at various times both to reinforce women's domestic reproductive role and to reduce barriers to their labour-market participation. The extent to which one or the other of these elements influences policy-making at any given time depends on the overall level of demand for female labour, the strength of the labour movement, and the strength and form of the demands pursued by and on behalf of women. In the present period of economic crisis, the long-standing tendency of the state to respond with policies designed to shift women into the reserve army of labour and to emphasise domestic reproductive roles is operating. At the same time, however, the current relative strength of the women's movement inhibits attempts to increase direct discrimination against women in the benefit system.

5.5 Income Support and the Capitalist System

The impact of income support policies on accumulation, legitimation and security in the context of British capitalism will be discussed in this final section of the chapter. The impact of policy on capital in general has been subject to considerable controversy. Undoubtedly the cost of social security payments and in particular their tendency to rise in periods of economic crisis, may create public expenditure problems. At the same time, this is partly counteracted by the increased prospects for realisation resulting from the maintenance of purchasing power. Income support does not involve widespread direct competition with the private sector for resources, apart from those required for the administration of the scheme. The main impact on particular capitals is to redistribute demand. Opportunities for private profit in the provision of private insurance and other savings-based benefits are restricted, while capitals involved in the markets for commodities purchased by those whose incomes are supplemented will gain.

Income support policies have important implications for the efficient utilisation of labour. The linking of benefits to regular and continuous employment rewards compliant workers. The existence of benefits for dependants may reduce pressure for increased wages. Offsetting this, incentives to work may be reduced. The ease with which firms can expand or contract their labour forces is increased by the existence of provision for the unemployed, since this reduces resistance to job loss and maintains an industrial reserve army in a physical condition for work (see section 4.4). The reproduction of labour is aided by provision for periods of sickness or unemployment, while the general costs of labour reproduction are reduced in so far as policy increases the pressure on women to perform domestic reproductive tasks at low cost. Income support for dependants aids both labour and generational reproduction, since it increases the resources available to the family-household.

The impact on legitimation is complex. Expenditure on the maintenance of those who can play little part in productive or reproductive activities, such as the old and the handicapped, tends to aid legitimation. Income supports for those with low incomes, and the definition of the unacceptable aspect of inequality as poverty, tend to reduce the salience of the overall distribution of income and wealth as a political issue. The classification of benefit recipients, and their unequal treatment, tends to reinforce social divisions and encourages the identification of negative stereotypes, such as 'scroungers', which form the basis for recurrent ideological campaigns. Finally, the way that income support is adjusted to precisely defined individual 'needs' tends to individualise inadequacy of income as a particular problem facing particular individuals, rather than as a general feature of the operation of the CMP. Income support policies tend to increase internal security, since they reduce the likelihood of widespread hunger and physical distress.

In the post-war period, there has been little attempt to challenge the dominant role of wage labour, and of a benefit and tax system largely designed to accommodate to it, as the means of distributing personal incomes. The only significant departure from this principle has involved family or child benefits, which do distribute income according to need. The influence of the need to maintain and reinforce wage labour, intensified in periods of economic crisis by demands for reductions in expenditure, has left income support as the area of social policy least penetrated by non-capitalist values.

Further Reading

General

George, V. (1973) *Social Security and Society*, Routledge and Kegan Paul

5.1

Ginsburg, N. (1979) *Class, Capital and Social Policy*, Macmillan
Gough, I. (1979) *The Political Economy of the Welfare State*, Macmillan

5.2.1–5.2.2

Deacon, A. (1976) *In Search of the Scrounger*, G. Bell
Fraser, D. (1973) *The Evolution of the British Welfare State*, Macmillan
Golding, P. and Middleton, S. (1982) *Images of Welfare*, Martin Robertson, ch. 2
Hay, J. R. (1975) *The Origins of the Liberal Welfare Reforms, 1906–1914*, Macmillan
Marshall, J. D. (1968) *The Old Poor Law, 1795–1834*, Macmillan
Rose, M. E. (1972) *The Relief of Poverty 1834–1914*, Macmillan

5.2.3–5.2.4

Deacon, A. and Bradshaw, J. (1983) *Reserved for the Poor*, Basil Blackwell
Kincaid, J. (1973) *Poverty and Equality in Britain*, Penguin
Showler, B. and Sinfield, A. (eds.) (1981) *The Workless State*, Martin Robertson

5.4

Barrett, M. (1980) *Women's Oppression Today*, Verso, ch. 5
Field, F. (1981) *Inequality in Britain*, Fontana
Field, F., Meacher, M. and Pond, C. (1977) *To Him Who Hath*, Penguin

5.5

George, V. and Wilding, P. (1984) *The Impact of Social Policy*, Routledge and Kegan Paul

6 HOUSING POLICY

6.1 The Marxist Approach to Housing

In this chapter, the role played by the state in the provision of housing in the UK is discussed. This section introduces the distinctive contribution of Marxism to the study of housing.

For the working class, the 'housing question' has normally focused on the quality and cost of housing. This concern arises from the inability of the CMP to provide good-quality housing at a price affordable by all members of the working class. Throughout the nineteenth century, the standard of housing that could be profitably provided for working-class tenants was extremely poor, because low wages and irregular employment kept rents to a minimum. Housing conditions were also lowered by the uneven development of capitalist industry, which led to extremely rapid phases of urban growth in those towns and cities where particular industries were concentrated. Housing conditions were particularly bad where industrial growth and a population increase took place in established towns such as London or Liverpool, where the opportunities for new building were limited. Housing affects the capitalist class and the CMP by providing opportunities for production and for redistributing the existing pool of surplus value through loan finance. It is also a major element in reproduction, in that it provides the shelter within which the family-household functions. The reproductive role of housing depends on its quality and its location. Adequate housing is also central to the maintenance of legitimation.

An important part in housing and housing policy is played by the legal forms through which the occupancy of a dwelling is secured, which is known as tenure. The three main forms of tenure in the UK are based on the ownership of the dwelling by the occupier, the ownership of the dwelling by a landlord who lets it to a tenant, and the ownership by a local authority which lets it to a tenant. Tenure is important for several reasons. First, the property rights of the occupiers are defined by tenure, in particular their freedom to use and dispose of the property. Second, housing policy is normally directed towards a particular tenure, rather than to housing as a whole. Third, tenure plays a part in structuring interests and consciousness, and is a major factor in conflict generated around the question of housing. Fourth, tenure influences the ways in which surplus value is realised or acquired through the production or finance of housing. Finally, the actual legal provisions defining the rights of the parties involved in the different tenures reflect the impact of class relations on housing provision.

Housing policies cannot be viewed simply as a response to working-class demands for improved living conditions. Housing policy is to be seen in terms of its relation to the processes of accumulation, legitimation and security. Complexity arises from the range of policies that are pursued. Housing policies typically involve some combination of the following: temporary accommodation for the homeless; the improvement of housing quality; increases in the size of the housing stock; and reductions in the price of housing. The particular form, phasing and combination of these elements obviously varies according to historical circumstances in any given capitalist society.

The discussion of housing policy in this chapter is organised as follows. Section 6.2 describes the development of housing policy since the mid-nineteenth century. This is followed in section 6.3 by a brief analysis of the impact of the development of capitalism on housing policies. Existing patterns of inequality in housing are then examined in section 6.4. Finally, the effects of housing policies on the workings of the capitalist system are discussed in section 6.5.

6.2 The Development of Housing Policies

Any attempt to give an account of the overall development of housing policy is faced by three major difficulties. First, housing policy does not exhibit a clear directional character. Second, housing policies have been subject to a high degree of local authority control, which has led to considerable variations in the policies pursued in different areas. Third, although all housing policies can be seen as being involved with either the homeless, the quality of housing, the quantity of housing, or the price of housing, a number of different forms of intervention have been developed relating to each of these areas. In order to overcome these difficulties, the two subsections below (6.2.1 and 6.2.2) give particular attention to the establishment of the major features of contemporary housing policies. Analytical issues concerning the impact of the CMP on housing policies is then discussed in section 6.3.

6.2.1 State Housing Policies: 1840–1940

Throughout the nineteenth century almost all working-class housing was rented from private landlords and built speculatively by small-scale enterprises, although some large employers financed the building of houses for their workers. At best, housing standards were low. The worst conditions were encountered during periods of very rapid urban growth, when extreme overcrowding, the occupation of cellars polluted by human and animal waste, damp, disrepair, and lack of sanitation were common. Rural housing conditions also deteriorated in the first half of the century, due to the abandonment of the practice of farm servants boarding-in with their employers, and the destruction of homes due to enclosures and to prevent their possible occupation by new residents who might have to be supported by poor relief.

The earliest forms of national housing policy were directed towards those unable to obtain any shelter at all. The homeless could obtain workhouse accommodation. Commercial provision for them existed in 'common lodging houses', and the Common Lodging Houses Act and the Labouring Classes Lodging Houses Act, both of 1851, provided a system of regulation of private lodging houses. Policies affecting the housing of a wider range of working-class people were also beginning at this time. In the 1840s, a number of local improvement Acts allowed by-laws stipulating standards of house construction, street layout and sanitation. A whole series of Acts in the 1850s and 1860s extended the powers of local authorities to inspect, improve, purchase or demolish unfit houses. The Artisans' and Labourers' Dwellings Act 1868 allowed local authorities in towns with a population in excess of 10,000 to force property owners to repair insanitary dwellings and to undertake compulsory purchase if this was not done. Much of the existing housing legislation concerning insanitary and overcrowded accommodation and the establishment of building regulations through local by-laws was codified by the Public Health Act 1875. The Artisans' and Labourers' Dwellings Improvement Act 1875 further extended the scope of policy by permitting local authorities themselves to build new houses, but only in districts where slums had been cleared. These Acts, together with the Building Societies Act 1874, which gave 'permanent' building societies a legal basis, constituted the framework within which future housing policies were to develop.

Indeed in the second half of the century, housing conditions, especially overcrowding, were worsening in many cities. This was due to the destruction of working-class housing in order to allow extensive commercial development of central sites and to clearance undertaken by local authorities. By-laws governing house building certainly improved the quality of houses built after 1875, but at the cost of increasing rents so that better-quality housing remained beyond the reach of much of the working class.

Although the state was becoming more involved in housing, the general assumption was that housing should be left to the market, self-help and private philanthropy. The building of 'model dwellings' designed to provide working-class accommodation of an adequate standard was encouraged by the Labouring Classes Dwelling Houses Act 1866. This Act enabled companies to construct working-class dwellings. The flat accommodation they set up exercised some influence over the forms taken later by local authority housing. Another influential innovation was the development of a new form of landlord-tenant relationship, particularly by Octavia Hill and her followers. This approach was closely linked to the casework methods pioneered by the Charity Organisation Society. It required the careful selection and grading of tenants, and their supervision in the matter of regular rent payment and domestic skills by the worker responsible for rent collection.

The findings of the Royal Commission on the Housing of the Working Classes, published in 1885, demonstrated the marginal impact of existing policies and of philanthropic initiatives. Under the Housing of the Working Classes Act 1890, local authorities could borrow to undertake house building that was not done as part of a clearance scheme. However, few local authority houses were built before 1914. The major exception involved the London County Council which was established in 1888 and which, by 1914, possessed about half of the national total of around 20,000 local authority-built houses. Apart from the reliance on permissive rather than mandatory powers, the main reason for the lack of impact of housing policies on working-class housing standards was the refusal to allow any form of subsidy that would lower the cost of housing. As a result, local authority housing could only benefit better-off members of the working class.

The Housing Act 1914 allowed subsidies to be given for rural housing, and there is evidence that wider schemes for subsidised housing were being planned, although the war delayed their intro- duction. During and immediately after the First World War, attempts were made for the first time to reduce the housing costs of the working class. Rents were frozen at pre-war levels, partly in response to rent strikes in Glasgow, by the Increase of Rent and Mortgage Interest (War Restriction) Act 1915. Subsidised local authority housing was established by the Housing and Town Planning Act 1919. The housing built was generally of a high standard, and with the rent controls introduced in 1915, it estab- lished a continuing, if fluctuating, state policy of reducing the costs of working-class housing. About 214,000 houses were built before the economic crisis of 1921 brought a reduction in further building. The Housing Act 1923 represented a move back towards financial stringency. Financial aid was made available both to private builders and to local authorities, but the subsidy and the required standards were lowered. The Housing Act 1924, passed by the first minority Labour government, increased the subsidies for local authority housing, but maintained the building standards employed in the administration of the 1923 Act. By the end of the 1920s, local authority house building began to decrease both as a result of the general economic crisis and because subsidies were reduced. This shift away from the provision of subsidised local authority housing for 'general needs' continued. The National government's Housing (Financial Provisions) Act 1933 abolished remaining subsidies, reduced standards further, and allowed building solely when slum clearance took place. The issue of overcrowding was pursued by the Housing Act 1935, which defined overcrowding, made it an offence, and provided subsidies for house building to abate it. The financial administration of local authority housing was rationalised by the Housing Act 1936, which abolished the existing practice by which the rents for individual dwellings depended on the provisions of the Act under which they were built. All rents and subsidies were pooled in a 'Housing Revenue Account' and rents were set irrespective of the original cost of building.

In the period 1919–39, the distinctive organisation of council housing was established. The use of long-term loans to finance housing, which originated with the Victorian 'model dwellings' movement, was universally adopted. A system of housing management based on that developed by Octavia Hill was crystal- lised in the practice of local authorities and the new profession of housing management that began to emerge. The practice of building local authority homes in massive estates was established. The extensive use of flats became popular in cities, and council housing was used to build 'model' communities. In the early 1920s, this was reflected in an emphasis on cottage homes based on the garden-city concept. In the 1930s, the notion of a 'model estate' became influenced by the 'modern movement' in architecture and the large-scale development of workers' flats in Vienna, outstandingly in the case of Quarry Hill flats in Leeds. In the inter-war period, 28 per cent of all building was of local authority dwellings. Private renting, although it remained the most common tenure for members of the working class, underwent a relative decline. Owner-occupation, particularly in the 1930s, when interest rates and building costs were low, expanded substantially.

Overall housing standards improved in this period. However, the effect of state intervention on working-class housing was variable and complex. Rent restrictions simultaneously reduced the cost, quality and level of investment in private rented housing. The extent, form and standard of local authority housing policies in terms of slum clearance, rehousing and rents varied considerably. Generally, the level of subsidy was such that only better-off members of the working class could afford council rents. The attempt in the 1930s to concentrate policy on slum clearance and overcrowding failed to allow for the effects of high unemployment and low wages, which were creating new slums as fast as the old disappeared. The outbreak of war in 1939 brought to an end the period in which slum clearance formed the major focus of policy, and at the same time it led to a massive deterioration in the quality and quantity of the housing stock, which contributed to a new housing crisis at the end of the war.

6.2.2 Housing Policy in the Welfare State: 1940–83

During the Second World War, extensive controls were placed over the building industry and house building was considerably reduced. Special wartime provision included rent controls, compulsory billeting, and a system of makeshift repairs for damaged buildings. During the war over 3.5 million dwellings were damaged and 475,000 destroyed or made uninhabitable. At the end of the war housing was a major issue and, following the 1945 election at which Labour, for the first time, won an overall majority, an extensive housing programme was undertaken.

The major housing legislation was the Housing (Financial and

Miscellaneous Provisions) Act 1946, which provided for large subsidies for council building. As a result, over 800,000 local authority houses were completed by 1951. Although this Act was a return to policies employed in the early phase of rapid local authority building, the New Towns Act 1946, which started the new towns programme, and the Town and Country Planning Act 1947, which established a mandatory basis for local authority land-use planning, were new departures.

The Housing Repairs and Rents Act 1954 returned to the policy of restricting council housing to the replacement of cleared slums. This Act was part of a general attempt to encourage private housing. Controls on building for owner-occupation were reduced and, in 1963, the Schedule A tax on the imputed rental income of owner-occupiers was abolished. The Rent Act 1957 reduced the number of controlled tenancies to stimulate the private rented sector by allowing rents to rise.

The Labour government of 1964–70 began by reversing these policies. The Rent Act 1965 reintroduced controlled or 'fair' rents, housing costs for low-income buyers were reduced by the option mortgage scheme established in 1966, and those with low incomes could also benefit from a scheme of means-tested rate rebates introduced that year. The Housing Subsidies Act 1967 attempted to control expenditure by a system of 'cost-yardsticks' for council houses. The Act also reduced the extra subsidy that had been available for high-rise flats. Partly in response to opposition to some features of urban housing and planning policies, the planning system was modified and opportunities within it for 'public participation' were increased by the Town and Country Planning Act 1968. The Housing Act 1969 involved a shift away from both slum clearance and council building, and instead introduced grants for the rehabilitation of existing dwellings, and a scheme for 'General Improvement Areas'.

The Conservative government of 1970–4 substantially increased the value of these grants. It also encouraged council-house sales. The Housing Finance Act 1972 was a major attempt to restrict subsidies to council housing to those with low incomes and to areas of housing need. A new system of 'fair' rents, based on market rent, was introduced, along with means-tested rent allowances for private tenants.

The Labour government of 1974–9 repealed this Act and replaced it with the Housing Rents and Subsidies Act 1975, which allowed rents to be set below the level sufficient to cover the cost of newly built houses. The Rent Act 1974, passed by the same government, restored security of tenure to furnished tenants. Tax relief for mortgage interest payments on second homes and on that part of any mortgage over £25,000 was abolished. The government also encouraged local authorities to grant mortgages. These totalled 100,000 in 1974, but declined to 28,000 by 1976. Improvement policies also continued with the provision for the designation of Housing Action Areas from 1974.

The Housing Act 1980, which was passed by the Conservative government elected in 1979, introduced a number of changes. Financial incentives for council-house sales were increased. Local authority rents were increased and tenants were given increased statutory rights. Council-house building itself has been severely cut, with only 21,000 starts in 1981. Private rents were allowed to be increased, and provision was made for a new 'shorthold' tenancy for temporary lettings. In 1983, the upper house-value limit for tax relief on mortgage interest payments was raised to £30,000.

Although a number of new departures in housing policy in the period since 1940 have taken place, considerable continuity with the earlier period remains. This is most evident in the continued use of loan finance for council housing, and the maintenance of existing practices of administration and control in housing management. The overall structure of state control, based on centralised loan sanction, national building standards and cost controls, but with considerable local influence over rents and levels of house building, was also retained except for the period 1970–2.

However, some changes took place in the kinds of housing that were provided. Whereas in the 1950s and 1960s very large estates were being built, the cutback in new building and the move away from wholesale clearance has resulted in more emphasis on smaller housing developments and 'infilling' in vacant central city sites. The building of high-rise flats was another significant feature of post-war policy. It seemed to offer a solution to rehousing after slum clearance that reduced urban sprawl and cut land costs by permitting high densities. High-rise building peaked in 1966, when it accounted for 25.7 per cent of all new council dwellings. However, high-rise buildings remained unpopular and expensive. During the period 1940–83, the balance between the three tenures changed substantially and the total stock of dwellings almost doubled (see Table 6.1).

The figures in Table 6.1 conceal substantial regional and national variations within the UK; in particular, both Scotland and Northern

Table 6.1: Housing Tenure in the UK, 1938–80

	1938	1950	1960	1970	1980
Owner-occupied (%)	33	29	42	50	55
Council rented (%)	10	18	27	30	32
Private rented and					
miscellaneous (%)	58	53	31	20	13
Total stock (millions)	11.4	13.9	16.2	18.7	21.0

Ireland have a higher proportion of local authority housing. After 1953, owner-occupation was strongly encouraged by both major political parties through tax reliefs, option mortgages and, later, local authority mortgages. Council-house building, while it continued throughout the period, was subject to rather greater fluctuations. The drastic decline of private renting mainly involved small working-class houses. Since many of these were demolished or transferred to owner-occupation, the remaining dwellings were mainly furnished and unfurnished flats of greatly varying quality. In recent years the activities of housing associations have added to the private rented stock. The Housing Act 1974 provided for a huge increase in the funds available for the Housing Corporation to dispense to housing associations. Housing associations in essence provide for the private building and management of publicly-financed rented housing. With the rundown of council housing in the late 1970s, they constitute about a quarter of all publicly-financed housing starts. Another major change in policy has involved the sale of council houses. Although sales occurred in the 1960s, the numbers sold in any one year never exceeded 8,500. In the years 1970–3, however, a total of nearly 96,000 were sold and, more recently, sales have continued at an even higher rate, reaching 214,000 in 1982. As a result, the size of the total stock of state-owned housing has, for the first time, begun to decline.

6.3 Capitalism, Class Relations and Housing Policy

This section discusses in turn the part played by the overall development of the CMP, particularly the changing pattern of investment in housing, the role played by associated shifts in ideology, and the effects of changes in the balance of class forces. The pattern of investment in housing has had a major impact on housing policy by determining the quality and quantity of housing made available in pursuit of profit. In the nineteenth century, house building for private renting was a major outlet for small-scale local investment, but by the early twentieth century investment in housing was slowing down. Rent controls served to accelerate further the relative decline of private renting. However, during the inter-war period other investment opportunities in housing finance expanded appreciably. Loans to local authorities formed a major outlet for investable funds. The house-building boom of the 1930s involved a massive growth of mortgage finance for house-buying and bank-lending for construction.

The supply of adequate housing has been further restricted by the small scale of the industry, and by the existence of archaic working methods and employment practices. The structure of the industry itself has reflected the peculiarly volatile demand for house-building, which has resulted in large numbers of small under-capitalised firms. Although the practice of erecting council housing in massive estates stimulated the formation of larger companies, improvements in technology have been slow, except in the case of high-rise buildings, where costs have nevertheless remained high. Direct state involvement in building has been minimal. There is no centralised house-construction agency, and the 'direct labour' departments of local authorities have been used mainly for repairs and rehabilitation, rather than building.

A further element in housing costs, particularly in central city areas, is land. High land values and the prospect of substantial capital gains in the land market have resulted in considerable speculative activity. In the post-war period, Labour governments on three occasions have attempted to restrict speculative gains from land, particularly where these result from changes in designated land-use. However, these attempts have each been repealed by succeeding Conservative governments. Speculation in property has sometimes led to extremely rapid price rises as in the boom of 1972–4. Some planning policies, such as 'green belts', have further restricted the availability of land for housing. The implications for housing are generally to encourage high-density developments. Even so, in the period 1963–75 the proportion of the cost of new council housing accounted for by land rose from 7.1 per cent to 19 per cent. In large cities, and particularly in London, the figures are far higher. The joint impact of changes in patterns of investment in housing, in the house-building industry and in the land market has been to maintain or increase the cost of housing relative to wages.

Within the framework provided by these long-term changes, other patterns may be observed in housing policy which relate to changes in class relations and shifts in the dominant ideology. A recurrent theme in housing policy has been a 'sanitary' approach, where policy concentrates on slum clearance. This policy has also often been associated with attempts to reduce public expenditure on housing by cutting house building, by reducing housing standards, and stimulating private provision. Another major phase in housing policy has involved construction drives to meet housing shortages. This has normally required a combination of popular radicalism and a widespread acceptance of the need for state intervention. Apart from the period immediately following the Second World War, each of the phases of expansion has ended as a result of public expenditure cuts resulting from economic and financial crises.

In the post-war period, the ideological framework within which housing policy has developed has become more complex. There has been a noticeable shift in emphasis away from a quantitative, 'engineering' and sanitary approach towards a concern for 'community' and 'neighbourhood units'. The failure to achieve 'social' objectives and the considerable criticism levelled at many commonly pursued policies such as massive clearance schemes, peripheral estates, high-rise and deck-access were accompanied by a further shift, which became apparent in the late 1960s. This involved the attempt to develop a more effective version of 'social planning', to encourage 'participation', to preserve existing 'communities', along with a move back to building houses rather than flats, and an increased emphasis in public housing on meeting 'needs'.

Shifts in housing policy are partly explicable in terms of the alternation between Labour and Conservative governments. Labour has generally been more in favour of expansive policies, and the Conservatives have tended to support a 'sanitary' policy. Labour, however, has abandoned its expansive approach during periods of crisis. Overall, policy has been dominated by the 'sanitary' approach, and periods of substantial additions to the public housing stock have been exceptional.

The exceptional nature of policies designed to expand the public housing stock is reflected in the arrangements through which they are administered. Both local authority housing and the regulation of private renting are not subject to detailed or uniform central control. As a result, major variations in rent levels for similar-quality housing have remained and no attempt has been made to enforce a uniform national system of provision. Private-sector provision remains dominant, although it has shifted from renting to ownership. The establishment of a substantial stock of publicly owned housing has itself relied heavily on private capital so that, in effect, local authorities undertake public management of housing built and financed by the private sector. Finally, local authority housing management has involved the retention of the traditional powers of property owners and landlords over tenants.

6.4 State Policy and the Distribution of Housing Inequalities

In this section, the impact of state policies on the allocation, rights of occupancy, the standard and cost of housing is examined. This is then followed by a brief account of existing inequalities in housing between various social groups.

There is no uniform national system of council housing allocation, although most councils use a 'points' system of some kind, based on existing housing conditions, family size, etc., while others employ a waiting list. The chances of obtaining a council house depend on the local level of building, of moves out, of slum clearance, and of homelessness. Given that the last two categories enjoy statutory preference, the number of other new tenancies may be quite low. The allocation process also extends to the quality of housing that is offered. Prospective tenants are likely to be graded formally or informally and the quality of accommodation offered adjusted accordingly. As a result, the 'undeserving' are offered 'hard-to-let' accommodation in 'sink estates'.

In both private renting and owner-occupation, allocation and occupancy are closely related to ability to maintain the necessary financial outlay. Tenants who fail to pay rent may be evicted and those who do not keep up mortgage repayments may have their mortgages foreclosed. Little state regulation of private-sector allocation exists, except for the laws on race and sex discrimination and for tied housing, where agricultural labourers since 1976 have security of tenure. Tenants of private rented accommodation have some security of tenure. However, many landlords, in order to avoid being subject to these and other provisions, require those occupying their property to sign 'licence' agreements, under which the occupants do not count legally as tenants under the Rent Acts. The most secure occupants are those owner-occupiers who are outright owners (about 45 per cent), who can only be removed if their houses are compulsorily purchased or condemned as unfit.

Building societies and banks generally prefer to lend funds to those in professional rather than manual occupations on the grounds of greater job security, and also fail to give equal weight to women's earnings in assessing ability to pay. Building societies use a system of 'red-lining' to prevent loans in some areas, usually in the inner city, where they think house values may fall. As a result, houses deteriorate because some existing owners have to remain in housing they cannot afford to maintain, while those who wish to buy are forced to rely on alternative (and more expensive) sources of finance with a resulting greater risk of foreclosure.

Housing standards have been an object of policy for over a century. Conventionally, housing standards have been measured with reference both to the physical qualities of dwellings and to the number of occupants. There is no doubt that standards have improved substantially, especially in the post-war period. Between 1951 and 1976, the percentage of households living in unfit or substandard houses, suffering overcrowding (i.e. densities above 1.5 persons per room), sharing accommodation, or living as 'concealed households', decreased from 69 per cent to 15 per cent. The major inequalities in housing today concern the kind of accommodation that is occupied. The poor occupy the smallest houses and are particularly likely to live in flats (see Table 6.2 below). In terms of the traditional measures of amenity (sole use of bath, toilet and kitchen), inequalities have been reduced substantially, though not eliminated. Differences in housing standards are closely related to tenure. In general, the worst conditions are found in the private rented sector, where the housing stock is older and where many houses have been converted into flats, often with shared kitchens and bathrooms.

The long-term reduction in overcrowding has been due both to a decrease in household size and to an increase in the number of dwellings available, relative to the number of households. While overall there has been a long-term improvement in measured housing standards, the pattern of change has not been unilinear. The space standards for new council housing, for example, have varied from 860 sq. ft in 1920 to 720 sq. ft in 1932, up again to 1,050 sq. ft in

Table 6.2: House-type by Socio-economic Group (percentage) in Great Britain, 1982

Socio-economic group of economically active heads heads of household	Detached	Semi-detached	Terrace	Flat
Professional	51	26	13	10
Employers and managers	38	32	19	9
Intermediate non-manual	25	34	24	17
Junior non-manual	15	34	28	23
Skilled manual	12	35	38	16
Semi-skilled manual	7	30	40	23
Unskilled manual	2	26	43	29

Source: OPCS, *General Household Survey* (HMSO, 1984), Table 5.17.

1948, and down to 900 sq. ft in 1960, since when they have risen again. Although in terms of conventional measures of amenity council accommodation is of a high standard, much of the high-rise flatted accommodation and some other council housing, especially in 'sink' estates, is little sought after. Finally, there is evidence of a recent acceleration of the deterioration of the housing stock, due to the effects of unemployment, high interest rates, and stagnating incomes from unemployment.

The impact of state policy on the cost of housing is also complex. Direct funding by the state in the form of a large Exchequer payment and a smaller rate-fund contribution to the costs of council housing would appear to be a direct subsidy to local authority tenants. Indeed, in 1975/6 these payments were almost equal to the value of rents paid per dwelling. However, it must be remembered that a very high proportion of all local authority housing expenditure goes on debt charges (70 per cent in 1975/6), through which council building is financed. It is thus the system of financing council-house building through loans rather than from current income that necessitates the subsidies that therefore benefit the lenders rather than the tenants. In the case of private tenants, there is no direct general subsidy, although rent controls in effect require landlords to let property at below market rents. Landlords are also disadvantaged by the tax system relative to other small businesses and to owner-occupiers, since they cannot claim tax relief on repairs to houses they let, or on mortgages taken out to buy property to let. Since 1972 both local authority and private tenants have been entitled to a means-tested benefit towards their rent, and recipients of supplementary benefit normally have their rent paid in full. These separate schemes have now been replaced by a single housing benefit (see section 5.2.4). Owner-occupiers with a mortgage receive tax relief on that part of their repayments which consists of interest on the loan. Thus those with high incomes buying expensive houses gain most. Inflation also enables them to repay capital with money of a lower value than that which they initially borrowed. All house-owners benefit from the opportunity to realise untaxable capital gains when the price of their house increases, particularly when the increase is greater than that of the general price level.

The overall impact of state policies on housing costs thus differs considerably between income groups and between tenures. High-income buyers benefit substantially from tax relief, while low-income renters may receive some reduction in the rent they have to pay. Those who rent privately may benefit from past and present rent restrictions. Council tenants in new property benefit from the system of rent pooling, while those who occupy older accommodation pay more than the cost of production of their accommodation. Council housing costs in total involve a substantial transfer of existing surplus value to those who lend to local authorities. Overall patterns of inequality in housing are reflected in the relationships of socio-economic group to tenure as Table 6.3 shows.

Higher-income groups tend to be found overwhelmingly in the owner-occupied sector. The decline of private renting and the expansion of council housing means that, in contrast to the inter-war period, those with the lowest incomes are now mainly accommodated in the local authority sector. The social composition of the private rented sector is the most varied. Some groups, such as students and young middle-class couples, may use it temporarily, before entering owner-occupation. Others, such as ethnic minorities, immigrant workers and their families, low-paid single workers and poor families unable to obtain council accommodation due to local shortages, constitute a longer-term population.

Although housing patterns reflect the nature of capitalist relations of production and their impact on inequalities in the labour market and in the distribution of wealth, they are also influenced by race and sex. Ethnic minorities occupy a distinctive place in the housing system and have experienced barriers to entry into owner-occupation and council housing. Women are subject to

Table 6.3: Tenure by Socio-economic Group (percentage), Great Britain, 1982

Socio-economic groups with economically active head of household	Owner- occupier	Local authority renting	Private renting
Professional, employers and managers	87	5	8
Intermediate non-manual	77	10	12
Junior non-manual	63	21	15
Skilled manual	56	35	9
Semi-skilled manual	35	48	17
Unskilled	27	60	13
All	56	32	11

Source: CSO, *Social Trends* No. 15 (HMSO, 1985), Table 8.7.

unfavourable treatment in the granting of loans for house purchase and through the unwillingness of many councils to provide good-quality accommodation for one-parent families, most of which are headed by women.

The most extreme manifestation of inequality in housing involves those who are unable to find permanent individual accommodation within the normal tenure system, including squatters, those who live in mobile homes, the homeless and institutional residents. Although squatting takes place on a relatively small scale, recent policy has involved attempts to reassert the right of property owners to repossess premises subject to squatting, and the invention of the new offence of criminal trespass in 1977 has simplified the process. Occupants of mobile homes historically have been subject to considerable harassment by local authorities, and although the Caravan Sites Act 1968 established a framework for the provision of permanent sites, the standard of facilities provided has generally been low. The treatment of the homeless has often followed the traditions of workhouse 'casual wards'. Temporary emergency accommodation has been provided under part III of the National Assistance Act 1948, and in addition there are reception centres for the single homeless. However, during the post-war period a significant cause of homelessness has been eviction from local authority dwellings, following which the welfare department of the same council became responsible for those evicted. In 1977 the law was changed, and now local authority housing departments are responsible for the homeless in their areas. Homelessness is very unevenly distributed, being concentrated in large cities, particularly London. The standard of accommodation provided for the homeless varies substantially: at worst, punitive workhouse traditions of 'less eligibility' and segregation remain. Institutional residents experience the worst housing conditions of all, and though the vogue for community care could provide the opportunity for greater privacy, independence, and personal control over space for those previously held in institutions, the lack of resources available makes this unlikely.

The account of inequalities in housing given in this section illustrates the ways in which housing provision reflects the nature of capitalism. In terms of allocation and occupancy, ownership confers a degree of security not available to those who rent. Although housing standards have improved considerably, those with the lowest incomes are likely to occupy housing of a lower quality. Though there exists a massive stock of state-owned housing, housing construction and housing finance is almost wholly undertaken by, and to the benefit of, private capital. The impact of policy on housing costs varies considerably between tenures and income groups, and there is no consistent pattern of vertical redistribution towards recipients of low incomes. As a result of all this, massive inequalities in housing continue to exist, which closely reflect the general distribution of income and wealth that results from the operation of the CMP.

6.5 Housing Policies and the Capitalist System

The effect of housing policies on accumulation, legitimation and security in the context of British capitalism is discussed below. There is also a brief examination of the extent to which some recent issues involving housing offer a radical challenge to the existing framework of policy.

State housing policies clearly have some unfavourable effects on accumulation by capital in general, in so far as they are financed out of taxation. In addition, where policies lead to increased expenditure on house construction, they involve a transfer of surplus to a relatively inefficient section of capital. Policies also work in favour of those in possession of loanable funds, and in effect operate as a means whereby surplus is transferred to this sector of capital. Other sectors, such as land ownership and firms that provide services for housing developments, also gain. In contrast, the private rented sector has generally seen returns on its capital diminish and substantial aggregate de-investment has taken place. Housing policies also affect labour productivity by influencing the mobility of labour. While private renting and owner-occupation do not form major barriers to labour mobility, local authority housing does. Although transfers within a local authority are normally possible, transfers between authorities are not and most local authority allocation schemes treat new in-migrants unfavourably. Housing policies, especially in their favourable overall effect on housing quality, contribute to the process of labour and generational reproduction. The threat to health posed by poor housing has been considerably reduced. However, it remains the case that many of those on the margins of the labour market, and their families, live in conditions which are below those officially defined as acceptable. These conditions affect both the learning ability of children in the household and the health of all members of the the family. Health can also be affected when housing costs are high, since expenditure on other essentials, such as food, will be reduced.

The impact of housing policies on legitimation is highly complex and involves a number of unresolved issues. It has often been suggested that home ownership reinforces commitment to the capitalist mode of production. Home ownership has been seen as buttressing individualism, tying the buyer to a large debt, which he must work hard to service, and turning him/her into a property owner. Undoubtedly in the UK, ownership has received political encouragement from the right, because it is believed that it will have these effects. Cross-national comparisons, however, suggest that the supposed ideological effects of ownership may not be universal. In addition, the extent to which house buying is seen as involving the ownership of a wealth-producing asset seems to vary. In the US, for example, decisions on house purchase tend to be based on a form of investment appraisal, and buyers, in effect, become part of the residential real-estate industry. In the UK, house buying tends to be treated more as a form of consumption expenditure. The link between ownership and support for the existing order would seem to be dependent upon distinctive ideological factors, in particular the role played in the UK by state housing.

To a large extent, working-class pressures for municipal housing arose in the context of the decline of private renting, to which it was seen as an alternative. In some periods council housing has been seen as a radical alternative to other forms of housing provision and has appeared to offer considerable advantages in terms of high standards and low costs. However, the prevailing mode of housing management, the replacement of private renting by owner-occupation, with all its advantages, as the main alternative tenure, the emphasis on unpopular forms of development such as high-rise and deck-access, and periodic attempts to raise council rents to 'economic' levels have all contributed to the unpopularity of council housing. Although council housing involves a partial supersession of provision by private capital, along with some degree of collective democratic control through local councils, it does not seem to form the basis for any widespread preference for public provision.

The impact of housing policies on divisions in the working class is an important aspect of their ideological effects. If the stock of public housing shrinks further, it is likely to be generally seen as a 'residual' form of accommodation. The ideological portrayal of public housing would shift from a focus on affluent tenants who should not be in 'subsidised' housing, to the degraded nature of the inhabitants of the tenure as a whole.

The impact of housing policies on internal security is nowadays relatively small, although concern about security has historically been an important element in clearance policies. There have been some attempts to modify the design of housing schemes in order to reduce the likelihood of crime directed against residents or their property. More broadly, housing schemes have been designed with the aim of encouraging 'community' and discouraging 'anti-social' behaviour, but this form of 'architectural determinism' has been rather unsuccessful.

The substantial improvement in housing amenities and the massive post-war growth of owner-occupation have completely transformed the nature of political controversy over housing. The near-extinction of private landlordism, the growth of working-class owner-occupation, and the unpopularity of much council housing, have reduced the appeal of the traditional Labour policy, based primarily on the expansion of council housing and the control of private renting. The left remains reluctant to give wholehearted support to owner-occupation, because of its presumed ideological effects. At the same time, no solution has been offered to forestall the residualisation of local authority housing. The commodity status of housing remains strong and is little challenged by any notion of a 'right' to housing. Challenges to prevailing patterns of management and control of public-sector housing provision are fragmented and localised. To a far greater extent than in other areas of social policy, such as education and health, housing remains dominated by private capital.

Further Reading

General

Dear, M. and Scott, A. J. (eds.) (1981) *Urbanisation and Urban Planning in Capitalist Society*, Methuen
Merrett, S. (1979) *State Housing in Britain*, Routledge and Kegan Paul

6.1

Ball, M. (1983) *Housing Policy and Economic Power*, Methuen

6.2.1

Bowley, M. (1945) *Housing and the State 1919–1944*, Allen and Unwin
Gauldie, E. (1974) *Cruel Habitations*, Allen and Unwin

6.2.2

Ball, M. (1982) 'Housing Provision and the Economic Crisis', *Capital and Class*, no. 17
Darke, J. and Darke, R. (1979) *Who Needs Housing?*, Macmillan
Donnison, D. and Ungerson, C. (1982) *Housing Policy*, Penguin

6.4

Lansley, S. (1979) *Housing and Public Policy*, Croom Helm

6.5

Ginsburg, N. (1979) *Class, Capital and Social Policy*, Macmillan, chs. 5 and 6

7 HEALTH AND WELFARE POLICIES

7.1 The Marxist Approach to Health and Welfare

This chapter examines the role played by the state in the provision of health and welfare services within the UK. The Marxist approach focuses on the relationship between capitalism and the nature of health and welfare provision, including the conception of health and welfare, the organisation, control and scientific basis of provision, the processes by which ill health and diswelfare are generated, and their distribution.

Acceptable levels of health and welfare are defined by the ability to undertake normal social functions. In capitalist societies this involves, for adults, the capacity to undertake wage labour or the tasks of domestic reproduction. For those without the capacity for wage labour or domestic reproductive labour, it involves being in a position to live independently. The distinction between health and welfare is socially determined. Physical ill health normally involves identifiable pathologies, although this is not generally true of mental illness. Welfare conditions generally involve the absence or breakdown of the family-household, leading to an inability to reproduce wage labour, to maintain dependants or to live independently. Whether and in what form the impairment of productive and reproductive capacity comes to merit health or welfare intervention depends substantially on the degree to which this is viewed by the state as a threat to accumulation, legitimation and security.

The account in this chapter is organised as follows. The development of the health and welfare services is examined in section 7.2. The economic and social factors determining inequalities in the distribution of ill health and 'diswelfare' are then examined in section 7.3. The impact of health and welfare policies on women, the old and the mentally handicapped is explained in section 7.4. Finally, the overall impact of health and welfare provision on the workings of the capitalist system is discussed in section 7.5.

7.2 The Development of Health and Welfare Services

Throughout the following account, emphasis has been put on the impact of the development of the CMP, the response to the appearance of various barriers to further accumulation, the role played by class conflict, the role of private capital in shaping patterns of provision, and the impact of the various occupational groups that emerged in the process of development of health and welfare services.

7.2.1 Early Patterns of State Intervention

While a degree of state intervention in the fields of health and welfare was in existence prior to the appearance of industrial capitalism, it was not until the nineteenth century that these services took on a recognisably modern form involving institutional provision for the sick and helpless, the development and utilisation of scientific knowledge for health and welfare problems, and the monopolisation of the delivery of services by professional groups regulated by the power of the state. State involvement in medicine goes back at least as far as an Act of 1518, which established the Royal College of Physicians. By 1800 its fellows and licentiates represented the most influential medical practitioners, serving an upper-class clientele and living on private practice. In 1800 the College of Surgeons was founded. Catering for a less exclusive clientele, surgeons, along with apothecaries, constituted the lower ranks of the medical profession. For most working-class people, medical services were also provided by local helpers.

Medical knowledge was relatively primitive with little attempt to treat particular diseases. Few effective medicines existed, and even by the late nineteenth century extensive use was still made of such treatments as purging and bleeding. Medical education was not particularly rigorous, except in Scotland, and membership of the Royal College of Physicians was regulated mainly by ability to pay and 'connections'. The Medical Registration Act 1858 was the first comprehensive attempt by the state to regulate medical standards.

Until the nineteenth century, there was little provision for institutional care for either the physically or mentally ill. Only about 3,000 beds were available in England and Wales, in the mainly charitable 'voluntary' hospitals. These catered almost exclusively for the poor and doctors gave their services free, using the prestige of their position as honorary hospital physicians as a means of enhancing their reputation for the purposes of pursuing private practice. Some state provision existed in workhouses, where the chronic sick, particularly those who were old, were likely to be found. Little provision existed for the insane before the mid-eighteenth century, apart from a small number of asylums. The first major state intervention in this area came in an Act of 1808, which permitted magistrates to establish asylums for the insane in their areas. This Act was an early consequence of a sustained campaign to reform private madhouses, which were later subject to regulation under the Madhouse Act 1828. The major impetus towards the state provision of institutional medical care came from the Poor Law (Amendment) Act 1834 (see subsection 5.2.1). As a result of the attempt to abolish cash payments, many old, sick, disabled and insane people found their way into the workhouses, and these formed the core of the long-term workhouse population, augmented by labourers and their families during periods of economic dislocation. This Act helped establish the central role of institutionalism.

There was a relationship between the development of capitalism and the growth of widespread support amongst the ruling class for institutional solutions to social problems such as crime, illness and pauperism. Traditional community patterns and family-based systems of care and control began to be severely disrupted by urbanisation and increased economic fluctuations. Health and welfare institutions were designed to cater exclusively for working-class inmates. Indeed, until the late nineteenth century physically sick members of the middle and upper classes would receive medical treatment at home, although private madhouses, some extremely luxurious, existed for moneyed 'lunatics'.

Policies directed towards the health of all members of society did develop in the nineteenth century, but they involved public health rather than individual health care. Knowledge of the relationship between environmental conditions such as water, sewage disposal and the incidence of disease developed towards the mid-century. The development of a system of local government, following the Municipal Corporations Act 1835, and the advance of techniques in water provision and the water-borne disposal of sewage provided the basis of a public health system. The danger posed to the health of members of other classes by epidemics originating in working-class areas and a belief that the prevention of ill health would reduce the numbers on poor relief and improve the efficiency of the workforce allowed sufficient support to be obtained for the passing of the Public

Health Act 1848. This Act allowed any local authority to set up a Public Health Committee and appoint a Medical Officer of Health. A General Board of Health was set up which could require this to be done where the annual death rate exceeded 23 per 1,000. Similar provisions to these were made compulsory by the Public Health Act 1875.

7.2.2 The Growth of the State Hospital System

The development of the hospital system was very rapid in the second half of the nineteenth century. The total number of hospital beds in England and Wales increased from under 8,000 in 1851 to 113,000 in 1891, and 197,000 in 1911, of which over 78 per cent were provided by the state. Most beds for the physically sick were provided under the Poor Law. Although the sick wards in the workhouses generally provided a low level of care, towards the end of the century some areas built separate Poor Law infirmaries and were able to attract paying patients. The state was also involved in the provision of hospitals for the insane, particularly following the Lunatics Act 1845, which required those counties that had not already done so to erect asylums for pauper lunatics. The Act represented the view that lunacy was amenable to medical intervention rather than 'moral treatment', which involved placing lunatics in carefully regulated small-scale, humane and comfortable institutions under lay control. A massive programme of asylum building ensued and the numbers certified as insane increased substantially, especially in industrial regions.

From the mid-nineteenth century substantial changes also took place in the voluntary hospitals. These were charitable foundations, not capitalist enterprises, generally providing free out-patient services for the poor who could not afford to pay a GP. In-patient care was also made available for the poor if they had a letter of recommendation from someone connected with the raising of charitable funds for the hospital. Since the senior hospital doctors received no salary, they were not easily subjected to the authority of the boards that governed the hospitals. They used their position to limit the number of senior hospital medical posts, to control the disposition of medical resources, and to control admissions to the 'beds' they had assigned to them.

Much of the present-day organisation of medicine was established at this time, including the existence of a range of medical specialisms, the subordination of junior hospital doctors to seniors in their specialism, the exclusion of GPs from hospitals and their inferior status within the profession, and the practice by which patients could only obtain consultation with a hospital doctor by referral by a GP. The establishment of nursing in its modern form also developed within the voluntary hospital system. The system of nurse training was largely modelled on the school started by Nightingale at St Thomas's Hospital in 1860. The role of nurses in relation to doctors reflected the relationship between husband and wife in the patriarchal Victorian family. Partly due to the substantial involvement of upper-class women in the movement for nursing reform, however, nurses were able to establish a separate hierarchy of control within the voluntary hospitals so that nursing services were not under the direct management of doctors. The function of the boards of the voluntary hospitals was mainly limited to the raising of funds and the control of everyday administrative and domestic matters. This system of management was eventually that chosen for hospitals in the NHS.

An important feature of the organisation of medical care in the second half of the last century was the role played by paying patients. Doctors outside the salaried public sector of hospital provision lived mainly on the fees from paying patients. The practice of charging patients was a minor source of income for most hospitals, largely due to the opposition of doctors, who objected to hospitals receiving payment that patients might otherwise have made to them if a hospital place had not been made available. The income of most voluntary hospitals came overwhelmingly from donations, bequests, and fund raising.

Many of the main features of the modern system of medical care were established at this time. Institutional provision was overwhelmingly provided by the state. The view that the provision of personal health care, preferably in a hospital, was the most effective means of dealing with ill health had begun to gain acceptance. The dominant position of the medical profession in general, and of hospital doctors in particular, was established. Medical effort became concentrated on acute conditions and a low priority was accorded to the care of the chronically sick, who were channelled to the workhouse sick wards, which became little more than custodial institutions for hopeless cases. In the field of mental health, the county lunatic asylums became large-scale custodial establishments, providing little hope of cure and a minimal standard of care. Finally, the existing geographical pattern of economic inequality was reflected in the uneven distribution of voluntary hospital provision.

This major growth of institutional provision brought few benefits to patients. The effectiveness of the best available in-patient treatment in the voluntary hospitals was low, although advances in scientific knowledge improved conditions towards the end of the century. However, the decrease in mortality rates which occurred in the late nineteenth century was due more to public health improvements and higher disposable incomes than to the growth of institutional medical provision.

7.2.3 Twentieth-Century Health and Welfare before the Welfare State

In the first half of the twentieth century, state involvement in non-institutional forms of provision developed. The Liberal Governments of 1906–14 played an important role in initiating this process, and introduced a wide range of reforms which reflected the willingness of the ruling bloc at this time to undertake an extension of state activity in order to reduce the developing threat of socialism and to increase industrial and military efficiency.

The major innovation of the Liberal government was to make provision for health and welfare that was not administered through the Poor Law. From 1906, local authorities were enabled to provide school meals, and in 1907 medical inspection of schoolchildren was instituted. The major reform in the area of health was the provision of compulsory health insurance under the National Insurance Act 1911. This provided free family doctor care and a weekly sickness benefit for workers (but not their families) who earned less than £160 p.a. The scheme was administered by appointed Insurance Committees, but private Friendly Societies still dispensed the benefits. GPs were paid a capitation fee, and thus acquired an assured income and remained self-employed, rather than becoming state employees. The 1911 Act also encouraged expenditure on isolation hospitals for tuberculosis victims, resulting in nearly 28,000 new beds in the period 1911–34.

Another major change in institutional provision occurred as a result of the Mental Deficiency Act 1913. Until this time, most mentally handicapped people were confined in workhouses or lunatic asylums. This Act established compulsory certification for the 'mentally defective' and set up a system of subnormality hospitals. The Act was strongly influenced by eugenicist beliefs in the dangers of biological deterioration and also by the new 'science' of intelligence testing, which provided the basis for a complex classification of degrees of 'mental deficiency'. By 1939 some 32,000 patients were held under this Act, including some women who were certified as a result of giving birth to an illegitimate child.

It was also in this period that important features of the organisation and practice of social work were established. The origins of social work lie in the activities of the Charity Organisation Society (COS), founded in 1869 as a means of regulating the disposition of charitable funds to the poor. Applicants for funds who applied to the COS were interviewed in order to establish their status as 'deserving' or 'undeserving'. The undeserving were recommended for the workhouse, while the deserving were assisted through casework and occasional dispensations of cash. The COS attempted to ensure that charitable funds were only dispensed through its workers. The COS was also instrumental from 1895 in securing the appointment of almoners in the voluntary hospitals. Their role was to establish the 'deserving' status of those offered free treatment. The development of social work was also influenced by the 'settlement' movement. The first settlement, Toynbee Hall, was established in East London in 1884. This movement was an attempt to remoralise the working class by exposing them to the example and influence of their social betters, in the form of volunteers from the universities. The settlements co-operated with the COS in the provision of social-work training. In 1903 the COS founded a School of Sociology to train its workers. The syllabus reflected a strong attachment to a *laissez-faire* ideology. Emphasis was placed on the role played by personality as a determinant of poverty, the importance of early socialisation in the family, and the desirability of casework rather than material aid. These patterns were continued when the state eventually became heavily involved in this area.

The general pattern of state health and welfare provision in existence by 1914 did not change fundamentally in the period up to 1939, although the First World War produced substantial, but temporary modification of services. No centralised system of hospital planning was established, and after the war little control was exercised. In the reorganisation of the state apparatus that took place at the end of the war, a Ministry of Health was set up (in 1919) and a report on health care was commissioned. The Dawson Report of 1920 made some relatively radical proposals, but by the time of its publication the brief radical upsurge that took place at the end of the war was over and orthodox policies were being reasserted.

In the inter-war period, the cost of the most advanced forms of hospital care increased substantially as new techniques and equipment were developed, and by 1938 about a third of voluntary hospitals were running at a deficit. With the partial exception of the Poor Law infirmaries, the public sector of hospital provision continued to cater almost wholly for chronic or fever cases, and provided a low level of care. Some changes took place in mental health. The Mental Treatment Act 1930 put more emphasis on treatment and required local authorities to make provision for out-patients and after-care. State provision of social work also began in the area of mental welfare. The Child Guidance Council was established in 1927, and by 1939 over 40 clinics had been established, some funded by local authorities. The movement was associated with the employment of 'scientific' therapeutic knowledge in the form of Freudian theory. The training of psychiatric social workers was undertaken and an effective governing body for this new profession was set up in 1930. This created a model of professionalism that was to strongly influence other social workers.

Medical services outside the hospital system underwent little development in this period. Although the numbers insured rose from 13 million in 1914 to 20 million in 1939, this was achieved mainly by raising the income threshold below which workers were compulsorily insured. The uninsured members of working-class families, however, were often deterred from obtaining care by the charges made by GPs. Some improvements had occurred in maternity services, where the Midwives Act 1936 had required local authorities to provide midwifery services. However, in the early 1930s, infant mortality amongst working-class babies remained at similar levels to those recorded in 1911. More generally, class differences in mortality and morbidity were maintained or intensified in this period.

The Second World War played a major role in the creation of the conditions that led to the NHS and the establishment of a wide-ranging welfare system based on social work. Prior to the outbreak of the war, the Ministry of Health undertook a survey of the hospital system and began planning for the expansion of the number of hospital beds in an Emergency Hospital Service. This also involved attempts to equalise the distribution of medical staff and equipment. Considerable changes were also made in policies affecting nutrition as a means of improving health. Rationing, vitamin supplements, milk for schoolchildren, the expansion of school meals, factory canteen and local authority-run restaurants ('British Restaurants') were all part of a comprehensive nutrition and food policy that had a major impact on diet-related diseases. The war also created an increase in welfare work organised or regulated by the state. The supervision of evacuated children, work with the bereaved and those made homeless, and rehabilitative work with those injured in the war all developed. Popular radicalism grew during the war and a major shift in ruling-class opinion took place, including support for a National Health Service from the wartime coalition government (see subsection 5.2.3).

7.2.4 Health and Welfare and the Foundation of the Welfare State

The National Health Service was established by the National Health Service Acts of 1946 and 1947 (for Scotland). It provided a universal and free system of health care covering hospital medicine and general practice. The NHS was the first major reform of the Labour government elected in 1945 on a tide of radicalism largely generated by the war. The abolition of charges for medical consultations and treatment was the major change from the standpoint of patients, and it created a substantial improvement in the access of working-class people, especially women and children, to medical care. Another major change was that health provision was now to be financed almost wholly by taxation. Given the absence of any threat to powerful capitalist interests, there was little outright opposition to the scheme. The organisational and administrative arrangements were strongly influenced by the top ranks of the medical profession, whose dominance within medicine had originally been established in the nineteenth century. Moreover, of the hospital beds that were brought under control of the NHS over 80 per cent were already within the public sector; the rest came from the take-over of the voluntary hospitals.

The organisational framework which had developed in the voluntary hospitals was established in the state sector except in mental hospitals, where the local authority system based on a Medical Superintendent was retained. Consultants kept control over 'their' beds, were given the right to practise privately and to use NHS facilities for this purpose, and received salaries for previously unpaid hospital work as well as the chance of substantial 'merit awards' dispensed by their representatives. The system was run centrally from the ministry through a system of appointed boards at regional and hospital level. These boards had a substantial upper and middle-class representation, and anyway wielded little control over the provision of hospital care. Teaching hospitals were not even subject to this degree of control.

General practice, along with dentistry and ophthalmic services, was provided through local Executive Committees, which replaced the existing local Insurance Committees. Practitioners remained self-employed and contracted their services. Apart from controls over the distribution of GPs, few changes were made in the form of service provided. The third branch of the NHS was assigned to local authorities, whose health committees became responsible for a number of services that did not involve the extensive use of doctors, such as home nursing, health visiting, ambulances, health centres, midwifery, and the mentally and physically disabled.

Welfare services also came under the control of local authorities at this time. While the NHS took medical services provided under the Poor Law, workhouse provision for children, the old and the homeless was assigned to the welfare departments of local authorities. The Children Act 1948 required local authorities to establish a children's department to provide residential accommo-dation and to regulate adoption and fostering. Considerable inequality in the range and quality of local authority provision existed. No overall attempt was made to reduce this, and in many cases the change in the system of control had little effect on the treatment of clients.

With the major exceptions of the new form of hospital management for the former local authority hospitals and, outstand-ingly, the provision of free treatment, few changes had been made in the health and welfare system. Hospital medicine and its senior practitioners retained their dominant status and influence. No effective system of health service planning was established. The existing pattern of priorities, which emphasised acute medicine at the expense of preventive provision and care for the chronically sick, was maintained. Welfare provision, in practice, made no radical break with custodialism and 'less eligibility'.

The formation of state health and welfare services up to the estab-lishment of the welfare state demonstrates the importance of the factors outlined at the beginning of section 7.2. While the overall development of the CMP was associated with the increasing availa-bility of resources and the growth of scientific knowledge, the key role was played by changes that occurred in the major barriers to accumulation and the ideological shifts to which these led. The growth of institutionalism to deal with those who failed to maintain themselves through the market was part of an attempt to maintain the subordination of the emerging working class in the period of the early growth of industrial capitalism. The reforms of the 1906–14 Liberal governments reflected a heightened concern with industrial efficiency and military security, as well as a continuation of the preoccupation with the maintenance of working-class subordination. The reforms of the Second World War and its aftermath reflected a concern to further incorporate the working class as well as to maintain legitimacy and industrial/military efficiency in a period of working-class strength. Private economic interests have also played a part by providing senior hospital doctors with a basis for a high degree of control in voluntary hospitals, and later by obtaining state sanction for their dominance over medical organisation and practice.

7.2.5 Post-War Capitalism and the Changing Pattern of Health and Welfare Provision

Considerable changes have taken place in health and welfare provision since 1948. For the first twenty years of the NHS, the main thrust of policy remained committed to public-sector provision and to expansion. It was widely expected at its inception that the operation of the NHS would lead to a healthier population and an eventual reduction in expenditure. However, medical intervention was often able to preserve the life of patients who then required further regular and more expensive treatment. Expenditure was also increased by the rising numbers of old people. Another factor has been the advance of medical science and technology. The research which forms the basis for this is mainly financed by private companies, charitable organisations and the Medical Research Council. There is no overall co-ordination of research effort, and the organisation and control of research generally follows the pattern typical of large-scale scientific projects (see subsection 8.3.2). The work is overwhelmingly concentrated on physical medicine, and priorities are determined jointly by the commercial interests of private capital and the attachment of influential doctors to high technology medicine.

The increased capital-intensiveness of hospital medical procedures has also been associated with the growth in the para-medical professions such as radiography, physiotherapy, occupational therapy, dietetics and orthoptics. Professionalisation has also occurred in social work, where it has rested on the claim to possess a 'generic' or core set of skills applicable to a wide range of problems. Social workers, however, have failed to gain a sufficient measure of professional status to exclude untrained workers or to gain acceptance of the view that their goals are desirable and their methods effective. The tension between 'care' and 'control' in their work, in particular the existence of a range of coercive powers over parents and children, means that clients frequently resist social work intervention.

The proportion of expenditure on institutional provision in health and welfare has increased during the post-war period, and substantial changes in the pattern of care have taken place. In physical medicine, the trend towards hospital treatment has continued. In the fields of mental illness and handicap, and social welfare generally, however, a significant move from institutionalism has taken place. The Mental Health Act 1959 encouraged an 'open-door' policy and a voluntary admissions policy. The Act also promoted the idea of 'community care' and allowed local authorities to make day and hostel provision for mental patients, though few did. New drugs increased the capacity of patients to live relatively independent lives. The medical profession offered little resistance to the proposed reduction in mental hospital provision, since mental hospital medicine was a very low status specialism, largely staffed by foreign doctors. Community care also provided an answer to the critique of institutionalism in mental health that developed in the 1960s. Finally, it appeared to offer an opportunity to cut costs by transferring patients from the state to the 'community', that is, where available, the family-household of the patient. In line with this policy, the number of mental hospital residents declined from a peak of 140,000 in 1954 to 96,000 by 1974. Although many handicapped patients are still kept in old, low-standard institutions, new psychiatric units are being established in some general hospitals and new forms of treatment regime such as the therapeutic community are being employed. This represents a partial return to the approach of 'moral treatment', though the 'medical' model involving reliance on chemotherapy and other physical treatments such as ECT remains influential. In the welfare services, the reaction against institutionalism was not so strong, though by the 1960s more emphasis on forms of domiciliary provision such as home helps and meals on wheels occurred. Some experimentation in new forms of residential accommodation, such as smaller 'homes' for the old and the handicapped, the establishment of forms of sheltered accommodation with separate flats and a resident warden, and the greater use of fostering for children in care also took place.

7.2.6 Health and Welfare and the End of the Long Boom

The first form taken by the changes resulting from the developing crisis in British capitalism was the reorganisation of the NHS and the local authority welfare services, initiated by the Labour government of 1964–70. These reorganisations were part of a wider restructuring of the state apparatus, which formed part of an overall strategy aimed at modernising British capitalism. The reorganisation of both the NHS and the local authority welfare services was strongly influenced by concurrent processes of restructuring in the private sector. Reformists saw reorganisation as a means of securing social betterment without increased expenditure, while capital approved of the application of private-sector management techniques to the public sector. The reorganisation proposals generally reflected the view that the existing forms of provision were satisfactory, but that problems of co-ordination, duplication, unevenness of provision, and inadequate planning constituted barriers to effective services.

The reorganisation of the local authority welfare services was examined by the Seebohm Committee, which reported in 1968. Its membership and its recommendations were strongly influenced by the desire to establish a firm basis for social work professionalism. The NHS reorganisation was not preceded by a formal inquiry. Instead, a series of proposals were published by the DHSS in the late 1960s and early 1970s, under both Labour and Conservative governments. While the NHS plans were more strongly influenced by explicitly managerialist ideas, the major role of medical professionalism was not questioned. In neither case was research undertaken to evaluate the existing pattern of provision, or to seek the views of clients.

The reorganisation of the local authority welfare services was undertaken by the Local Authority Social Services Act 1970. The main aim was to unify the control of provision. The Act required local authorities to establish a social services committee, to undertake the welfare functions previously carried out by the children's, welfare, and public health departments. The existing system of specialisation in social work was to be replaced by the 'generic' approach. More stress was to be put on 'community development' and the provision of a 'community-based and family-oriented' service.

The NHS (Reorganisation) Act 1973 established a new structure for health provision which was implemented in 1974. The three arms of the existing service were brought under a single organisational framework. In effect, the reorganisation amounted to adding the local authority health functions to the Regional Hospital Boards, and adding two additional tiers of control at area and district level. The local Executive Committees were now to be called Family Practitioner Committees. A system of extensive professional consultation, amounting to a medical veto, was established throughout the various levels of control. The 'participation' of the public was to be secured by appointed Community Health Councils with limited powers of review and investigation.

For a variety of reasons, neither of these reorganisations achieved their ostensible objectives of improving services and increasing efficiency. The process of reorganisation itself was in each case severely disruptive, and the new administrative arrangements proved more bureaucratic, while the system of generic social work involved the deskilling of many specialised workers. In the NHS, the new administration involved considerable duplication and, since 1982, 200 new District Health Authorities have replaced the Area Health Authorities.

The failure of the reorganisations coincided with a major ideological shift away from the largely bipartisan centrist policies of the post-war boom and the expansive period of welfare statism. Only two substantive changes in the nature of health and welfare provision resulted from the reorganisations: the attempt to create a more even pattern of health provision by the work of the Resources Allocation Working Party (RAWP), and the increased focus on community work and community care for the local authority welfare services. Both these changes were to play a significant part in the policy of cutting spending plans that developed in the mid to late 1970s.

The initial impetus for the cuts in expenditure plans came from the Labour government in the aftermath of the crisis of 1976. Spending on welfare was cut substantially and health spending was budgeted to rise at its slowest rate since the inception of the NHS. These cuts, particularly in capital spending, were in addition to severe pressure on budgets due to the RAWP exercise. The cuts have taken place at the same time as an increase in the size of the private health sector. This remained small throughout the post-war period of expansion, although private medicine continued in the hospital sector, helped by the availability of part-time contracts for consultants, and NHS pay-beds. In 1974, the Labour government attempted to alter these arrangements. After considerable conflict, a Health Services Board was established to phase out pay-beds. In the meantime, partly as a consequence, a considerable growth in the number of private hospital beds took place.

The attempt by Labour to separate NHS and private medicine has been reversed by the Conservative government's National Health Service Act 1980. This Act ended the phasing out of pay-beds, reduced restrictions on the development of private hospitals, and required health authorities to seek co-operation with the private sector. It allowed health authorities to undertake fund-raising activities and ended the commitment of the 1946 Act to fund *all* essential expenditure. This government has also encouraged the privatisation of domestic services such as catering and laundry. Private hospital medicine is increasing, due to dissatisfaction with NHS provision, the popularity of private medical insurance as a form of employee remuneration, the support of top doctors and substantial international demand. Public provision of health and welfare is also threatened by the continued promotion of 'community care', since the effect is almost invariably to shift the cost from the state on to the families of patients, that is, normally, on to women.

7.3 The CMP and Threats to Health and Welfare

Patterns of mortality, morbidity and usage of NHS facilities closely follow the overall pattern of class inequality (see Table 7.1). Working-class people live shorter lives and suffer more from both chronic and acute diseases. For the vast majority of recorded causes of death in old age and earlier, the highest rates are found amongst the working class (see Table 7.2). These differences have been a feature of the capitalist mode of production at least since the early decades of the last century. However, life expectancy has increased and major changes have occurred in the pattern of morbidity and in the major causes of death. In the nineteenth century, the major immediate causes of death were TB and the infective fevers. Insanitary conditions, poverty and poor housing were major reasons for the prevalence of infections. These diseases are no longer a major threat due to improved housing, diet and, to a lesser extent, vaccination and inoculation and effective forms of treatment. The major

Table 7.1: Standardised Mortality Ratios (SMRs) for Children, Women and Men by Occupational Class in England and Wales

	Professional	Intermediate	Skilled non-manual	Skilled manual	Semi-skilled manual	Unskilled manual
	I	II	IIIn	IIIm	IV	V
Children aged 1–14						
Male	74	79	95	98	112	162
Female	89	84	93	93	120	156
Single women aged 15–64	110	79	92	108	114	138
Married women aged 15–64 (by husband's occupation)	82	87	92	115	119	135
Men aged 15–64	77	81	99	106	114	137

Note: Standard mortality ratios indicate the divergence of the death rate for a given category from the average of all groups, which is set at 100 (i.e. they show a percentage of the average).

Source: OPCS, *Occupational Mortality. 1970–72* (HMSO, 1978), App. 2, Table A.

Table 7.2: Selected Major Causes of Death (SMRs) for Men Aged 15–64 and 65–74 and Survival Rates, by Occupational Class in England and Wales

Cause of Death	Percentage of total deaths from this cause in the age-group	Standard mortality ratios for Classes I–V					
		Professional I	Intermediate II	Skilled non-manual IIIn	Skilled manual IIIm	Semi-skilled manual IV	Unskilled manual V
Cancers							
Men aged 15–64	26.9	75	80	91	113	116	131
Men aged 65–74	25.1	96	98	99	102	100	101
Cardio-vascular diseases							
Men aged 15–64	46.6	86	89	110	106	110	118
Men aged 65–74	51.0	114	109	106	98	98	91
Respiratory diseases							
Men aged 15–64	9.9	37	53	80	106	123	187
Men aged 65–74	16.1	60	74	82	105	108	123
Accidents, etc.							
Men aged 15–64	8.7	78	78	83	94	122	197
Men aged 65–74	1.6	94	95	91	87	102	125
Percentage of those alive at 15 who die by age 64		22.5	23.4	27.3	29.3	30.7	35.7

Source: OPCS, *Occupational Mortality, 1970–72,* (HMSO, 1978), Tables 4A and 8A.

causes of death today are cancers, heart disease and cerebro-vascular conditions such as strokes. These are diseases in which severe and often irreversibly damaging conditions develop in major organs.

The modern pattern of mortality and morbidity is shaped by various features of the capitalist system. A number of threats to health and welfare arise within the labour process. The most important of these involves occupational disease. Dangerous substances encountered at work are also known to damage members of the families of workers. Numerous accidents also occur at work. These cause up to 2,000 deaths per annum and numerous injuries. Many jobs, particularly those involving extreme physical or climatic conditions, also exhaust workers and affect their general health. Stress caused by pace, tedium, noise and oppressive supervision also represents a threat to health. The statutory control of hazards at work by the Health and Safety Executive, however, is based on the principle of attempting to protect workers from dangerous processes, rather than seeking safe methods of production. The Executive has also continued the practice of viewing violations of the regulations as a matter for negotiation rather than prosecution, and the courts generally impose light sentences on employers who break the regulations.

Other features of the CMP also damage health and welfare. Fluctuations in the level of economic activity, and hence in employment levels and living standards, are associated with fluctuations in a variety of causes of death. Some, such as suicide, increase when unemployment rises. High mortality rates are found in industries subject to substantial cyclical fluctuations or to rapid structural change. The CMP also causes a number of environmental threats to health. The health hazards that result from the growth of cities, caused by the centralisation and growth of production, are well known. Housing standards have an effect on health; damp, cold, overcrowding, sharing kitchen and bathroom facilities, lack of gardens and secure play space, and isolation all increase the risk of accidents, mental illness and physical disease. Industrial processes create localised contamination. Road traffic also creates major threats to health. The lead in petrol engine exhausts can cause brain damage, especially in children, while diesel exhausts are a likely cause of various respiratory diseases. In addition, traffic accidents kill up to 7,000 people and seriously injure many more every year. Due to the proximity of industry, high-density housing, lack of open space and high traffic levels, urban working-class areas are particularly subject to environmental dangers involving risk of disease and injury.

Major avoidable threats to health arise from personal consumption. For capital, consumption is a major means of realisation of surplus value and hence profit. In addition, food forms a major part of expenditure for reproductive purposes. Modern dietary patterns fail to maximise the possible favourable effects of diet on health and welfare. Consumption of sugar and fat is extremely high, especially amongst those with low incomes. This, together with lack of knowledge of appropriate dietary patterns and stress, combines to produce high levels of obesity, which itself threatens health. Levels of consumption of vegetable fibre are low, and the use of chemicals to flavour, colour, preserve and texturise food is widespread. In the production of food for profit, the promotion of health through diet is often neglected. Overconsumption of alcoholic drinks and tobacco products also damages health. Overconsumption of alcohol is responsible for numerous admissions to mental hospitals and is associated with obesity, heart disease and other conditions; very strong drinks are also likely to cause liver and kidney damage. Tobacco products cause substantial damage to users and to those in their vicinity, especially in the form of lung cancer, bronchitis and heart disease. Close links between exercise and health are known to exist, but no concerted attempt is made to encourage improved levels of adult personal fitness, although physical education is included in the school curriculum.

It is clear that major threats to health and welfare arise from the way that the labour process, the environment and consumption are organised under capitalism. The effort accorded to the discovery and control of threats to health and welfare, where this would interfere with profitable production or raise the costs of reproduction, is relatively low.

7.4 Health and Welfare Provision: Women, Old Age and Mental Handicap

Health and welfare provision accords priority to those with present or future productive and reproductive capacities. Those who do not fall into these categories receive a lower priority. In order to illustrate this, the health and welfare provision made for women, the old and the mentally handicapped will be examined.

The health and welfare services have played a major role in the reinforcement of the family-household system through the maintenance of the capacity of women to provide domestic care for men, children and elderly dependants. In the post-war period, the domestic child-rearing role of mothers has been reinforced by the notion of maternal deprivation as a source of developmental problems in children. The welfare services have been strongly attached to the maintenance of the nuclear family unit. The tensions created by the nuclear family, however, have been evidenced by child abuse and wife-battering, while links between mental illness and working-class motherhood, resulting from social isolation and lack of child-care facilities, have recently been established.

Health and welfare interventions in the areas of female sexuality, gynaecology and obstetrics have been used to reinforce women's domestic role and to enforce the general subordination of women. Victorian denials of female sexual pleasure and contemporary notions of the normality of heterosexual monogamy have each served to tie women to the home and to reinforce their domestic subordination. Gynaecology has been the source of interpretations of complaints such as pre-menstrual tension and menstrual pain and symptoms of neurosis. The provision of contraceptive advice has only been freely available through the NHS since 1973. The contraceptive pill and other hormone-based techniques have caused considerable health risks. Abortions under the Abortion Act 1967 are controlled by medical decisions and, largely due to lack of NHS facilities and the unwillingness of many doctors to undertake them, about half are carried out in the private sector of medicine. The process of birth itself has been thoroughly medicalised. Almost all births now take place in hospitals, and in many of these a system of 'active management of labour' is employed. This involves the frequent use of induction, anaesthesia, and control of the birth posture by the doctor, which many women experience as an attempt to reinforce their subordination under the guise of meeting their needs.

The old are another group who are accorded distinctive treatment (see section 4.4). The experience of old age under capitalism involves an intensification of the patterns of inequality that exist amongst the working population. Many working-class old people suffer extreme deprivation, often involving inadequate heating, social isolation and a sense of uselessness resulting from exclusion from the labour market. These factors contribute to a general deterioration of their health and welfare. In addition, many forms of physical degeneration commonly affect the old, including defects of sight, hearing and mobility. Some 35 per cent of all expenditure on health and welfare goes on the old, and members of this group occupy 57 per cent of all non-maternity hospital beds. Many old people benefit from the high standard of medical care available for accident cases and acute episodes or conditions. However, those suffering from conditions unamenable to effective medical intervention receive less favourable treatment. Geriatric medicine is a low-status specialism with few merit awards and little opportunity for private practice. Medical research into the problems of the old is also relatively underdeveloped.

Extensive welfare provision is made for the old. About 20 per cent of all referrals to area offices of local authority social services departments involve people over 75 years of age. The techniques of social work, however, are primarily designed to deal with the problems of children and families. The provision of domiciliary services is low and charges are sometimes made for home helps, even when the old person is a recipient of supplementary benefit. The frequent absence of suitable sheltered housing means that many more old people than necessary live in institutions in which standards are low. The shift from institutions to community care can involve considerable hardship when domiciliary services are not improved at the same time. The low standard of many of the services provided for the old reflects their exclusion from the key process of production and reproduction in a capitalist society.

The mentally handicapped constitute a group who are permanently excluded from productive and reproductive roles. This exclusion has been imposed upon this group by the institutional and custodial policies that have been pursued towards them. Medical and legislative depictions of them as 'defective' or 'subnormal' reflect a view that mental handicap creates an insurmountable barrier to the development of ordinary human cognitive and emotional capacities. Conventional forms of medical treatment have had little positive impact on mental handicap, and medical control over provision has brought few benefits. Medication is frequently used mainly to control behaviour that itself often results from the tensions and frustration of institutional life. Conditions in long-stay hospitals for the mentally ill and handicapped are very poor. A large number of patients live in dormitories, have few personal possessions, wear institutional clothing, and have few opportunities for creative mental or physical activity. Segregation of men and women, strict discipline, understaffing, poor food, few visits and few opportunities to leave the hospital are common as well as, in some cases, the abuse and exploitation of patients.

Since the mid-1960s, an attempt has been made to improve conditions in hospitals and to make more use of non-hospital forms of provision. However, the existing forms of local authority provision such as day centres have often failed to provide stimulating activities for the handicapped and, in common with other slow learners, although they may receive special educational assistance, their education is insufficiently prolonged to develop fully their cognitive potential. The handicapped suffer from the cultural legacy of over a century of exclusion, institutionalism and negative evaluation, based on their inability to survive without assistance in the social environment of the capitalist economic system. The lack of provision of opportunities for employment, family life and political participation, along with social rejection, which these reinforce, maintains the position of this group at the extreme margin of society.

The examples given in this section of the treatment of women, the old and the mentally handicapped illustrate a number of general features of the health and welfare system. First, the quality of the care and treatment made available to different groups varies considerably. Second, the beneficial effects of provision often fall short of what might have been achieved, due to the form taken by health and welfare professionalism. Finally, the implicit priorities governing provision reinforce the capacity of the capitalist system for production and reproduction. Those who do not contribute to these processes receive the poorest services.

7.5 Health and Welfare Services and the Capitalist System

This final section of the chapter outlines the overall impact of the health and welfare services on accumulation, legitimation and security in the capitalist system. The economic impact on capital accumulation in general is unfavourable, since a considerable proportion of expenditure, which is financed out of taxation, is directed towards groups such as the old and the severely handicapped, who do not play any part in production or reproduction. However, particular industries that provide medical equipment and supplies, such as pharmaceutics, as well as the building industry, benefit. Commercially-provided health and welfare facilities benefit from a largely parasitic relationship with the NHS, which provides trained staff, services such as blood, and the use of facilities in emergencies. The services have a positive effect on labour efficiency through their impact on the general level of health and the recuperative capacity of workers. They contribute to reproduction both by helping to maintain women's health and by reinforcing the family-household. The changes being pursued by the 1979–83 and post-1983 Conservative governments involve an attempt to reduce the negative effect on accumulation by encouraging private-sector provision, cutting public-sector services, and by increasing the productivity of the health labour force by wage cuts and the intensification of work.

Modern health and welfare services play a major role in legitimation. The emphasis on provision of health and welfare services to individuals and the rhetoric of distribution according to need draw attention to apparently benevolent features of the existing order. The emphasis on personal health care and the stress on the modification of life-style as the key to the prevention of ill health individualise health and welfare problems by blaming them on personal choices in consumption. Health and welfare services further contribute to legitimation by reinforcing the class structure. Many senior doctors come from upper-class families and their social proximity to this class helps to distance it from a purely entrepreneurial ethos. The implicit priorities of the health and welfare services both reflect and reinforce the scale of values that legitimates the present structure of income distribution.

Health and welfare services have a significant impact on security, most importantly in so far as they are able to overcome threats to health and life from disease and accident. In addition, commonly used therapies in health and welfare can be adapted for control purposes. The most obvious cases are the use of drugs, psychosurgery, and a variety of psychologically-based techniques for interrogation or behaviour modification in the 'treatment' of offenders.

Health and welfare provision is not organised on a capitalist basis, although the pattern of provision has been strongly influenced by the capitalist system and continues to embody many principles which operate to support it. The present forms of provision rest on particular and limited notions of the nature of health and welfare, and of the services which should serve to promote them. Although the system has many positive features, further advance awaits a broader conception of health and welfare services as a collectively controlled attempt to provide conditions that will ensure a minimisation of threats to health and welfare, and a system of care and treatment in the control of which the recipients share.

Further Reading

General

Doyal, L. (1979) *The Political Economy of Health*, Pluto
Parry, N., Rustin, M. and Satyamurti, C. (1979) *Social Work, Welfare and the State*, Edward Arnold
Thunhurst, C. (1982) *It Makes You Sick: The Politics of the NHS*, Pluto
Tuckett, D. (ed.) (1976) *An Introduction to Medical Sociology*, Tavistock

7.1

Navarro, V. (1976) *Medicine Under Capitalism*, Prodist

7.2.1–7.2.3

Abel-Smith, B. (1964) *The Hospitals 1800–1948*, Heinemann Educational Books
Parry, N. C. A. and Parry, J. (1976) *The Rise of the Medical Profession*, Croom Helm
Scull, A. (1982) *Museums of Madness*, Penguin

7.2.5–7.2.6

Allsop, J. (1984) *Health Policy and the National Health Service*, Longman
Jones, C. (1983) *State Social Work and the Working Class*, Macmillan

7.3–7.4

Leeson, J. and Gray, J. (1978) *Women and Medicine*, Tavistock
OPCS (1978) *Occupational Mortality 1970–72*, HMSO
Phillipson, C. (1982) *Capitalism and the Construction of Old Age*, Macmillan
Ryan, J. and Thomas, F. (1980) *The Politics of Mental Handicap*, Penguin
Townsend, P. and Davidson, N. (1982) *Inequalities in Health: The Black Report*, Penguin

7.5

Fightback and the Politics of Health Group (n.d.), *Going Private: The Case Against Private Medicine*, Fightback and Politics of Health Group

8 CULTURAL POLICY — EDUCATION, SCIENCE AND THE MEDIA

8.1 Capitalism, Culture and Consciousness

This chapter examines the role played by the state in the production and reproduction of culture. In the simple model of the CMP, it is assumed that all areas of culture, including social and natural science, the visual arts, literature and common-sense understanding of economic, political and social affairs, serve the interests of capital through the contribution they make to accumulation, legitimation and security. However, the overall nature of culture, the institutions involved in its production and the form and extent of state involvement are subject to considerable historical variation and to change as the CMP develops.

A number of approaches to the question of knowledge, belief and values have developed within Marxism. The first is most pithily expressed in the phrase 'the ideas of the ruling class are in every epoch the ruling ideas'. This approach focuses on the means by which cultural dominance is exercised in the interests of capital in general. A second approach is summarised by the phrase 'social being . . . determines . . . consciousness'. This viewpoint seeks to understand culture as a response to the direct material conditions of life and thus points to sources outside the control of the capital. A third approach starts from the development of the forces of production and examines how the process of capital accumulation influences the development of natural and social science. The cultural dominance of the capitalist class, the response of the classes to everyday living conditions and the cultural changes associated with the development of the forces of production are the major elements in the overall production of bourgeois or capitalist culture.

In this culture, the depiction of economic, political and social organisation stresses competitive individualism and rationalism. Capitalist rationalism in economic life involves the systematic pursuit of personal advantage. In the sphere of cultural production, it involves the elaboration of knowledge into coherent and internally consistent forms. This process is seen at its most intense in the development of the positivist methodology of the natural sciences, involving the development of clear-cut differentiation between separate areas of enquiry, the use of methods of classification and experimentation, and the pursuit of 'scientific' laws. This methodology also penetrates other areas of thought and those cultural products which approximate most closely to it are accorded far greater significance than those, like various forms of art or crafts, which do not.

In any particular capitalist society, the nature of individualism and rationalism is modified by specific historical circumstances. Analysis of a particular culture involves a simplified account of its general features. However, in order to understand consciousness, that is, the ideas which lie in people's minds, it is necessary to outline the variety of levels on which the ideas may be presented and communicated. The level of cultural production most accessible to analysis is the systematic treatise, in which knowledge is presented in a coherent and organised form by members of a stratum of intellectuals. Simplified versions of knowledge, though still in relatively systematic form, form a second level of analysis. These may involve schooling or some form of publication or mass communication in which a process of popularisation takes place. The third level of presentation involves verbal and non-verbal imagery operating at a largely unconscious level. Language itself is a code which structures what may be expressed and which frequently builds concealed evaluations into apparently neutral descriptions. Non-verbal symbolism, such as that used in religious or civic rituals, is also important. Any area of culture may be presented and communicated at varying levels.

Access to culture in its elaborated and explicit form is distributed very unequally, usually in close correspondence to the overall economic distribution of resources in society. A high degree of cultural diversity results from the division of intellectual labour that exists both within the institutions of cultural production and in those groups, such as the professions, through which this knowledge receives its material application. Within the limits of an overall cultural consensus, variants of the dominant culture may develop that are related to the structural divisions within the dominant classes and to variations in patterns of socialisation.

In the basic Marxist approach, analyses of the transmission of the dominant culture to the working class employ the concept of *false consciousness* to explain the misperception of the real nature of classes, class conflict, inequality and political power. A more satisfactory approach focuses on the production of *hegemony*, which involves the generation of a consciousness that prevents radical challenge to the existing order. This is a continuous and arduous process. A hegemonic culture must not only unite the various segments of the dominant class and its immediate allies into a *ruling bloc*, it must attach the working class to the existing order by integrating those elements of culture derived from its traditions and direct experience with a commitment to the social order as a whole. The concept of false consciousness does not give sufficient weight to the role of ambiguity and instability in working-class culture. Gramsci's notion of *'contradictory consciousness'* is a more adequate term.

Working-class consciousness can be seen as contradictory since everyday experience as well as working-class organisations frequently emphasise aspirations which challenge parts of the existing order. Conflicts exist between these elements of working-class culture and those transmitted through the cultural domination of the capitalist class. In periods of crisis, rapid changes can occur as 'residual' or 'emergent' elements in consciousness are evoked. These new elements may be reactionary or progressive. Various forms of authoritarianism or populism may activate subterranean cultural traditions that are normally not given public expression. On the other hand, elements of a socialist culture may also be embedded in the subterranean traditions of a working class apparently thoroughly enveloped in the hegemonic culture. Elements of this socialist culture may be found in the traditions of major working-class parties and trade unions, in the radical culture of some working-class communities and occupations, as well as in the ideas developed in a variety of groups formed around particular issues, such as racism, sexism, and militarism.

The nature of bourgeois culture, its relation to the capitalist class and the CMP, the forms of cultural presentation, and the complexity of the determination of working-class consciousness are underlying themes in the examination of the cultural role of the state that is undertaken in the remainder of this chapter. Section 8.2 examines the education system, and is followed (in section 8.3) by an analysis of science and science policy. In section 8.4, the state information system is analysed. The concluding section, 8.5, gives an assessment of the relationships between capitalism and the cultural policies of the state.

8.2 Capitalism and Formal Education

8.2.1 The Development of State Education until 1944

The history of state intervention in education is usually dated from 1833, when grants of public money were first given to finance schooling, although it should be remembered that some state-provided education in workhouses, prisons and the armed forces existed before this. The development of industrial capitalism led to the growth of Sunday School education, organised by religious societies from the 1780s. The development of the 'monitorial' system of education in the first two decades of the nineteenth century was an attempt to expose working-class children in the industrial towns to middle-class influence. A single teacher would teach an enormous class using 'monitors' (older children), whom he/she had trained, to teach the other children. In some workplaces employers provided factory schools. The formation of Mechanics Institutes from the 1820s was again a middle-class attempt to exert some cultural influence over the artisan stratum of the working class. At the same time, working-class cultural institutions, including schools, corresponding societies and a variety of reading and discussion groups, were becoming established so that by the 1830s something of a dual system of education, divided by class lines, existed.

The period from the first educational grants in 1833 to the legislation of 1870 involved the intervention of the state to encourage the adoption of a system of 'rational' schooling, designed largely to adapt working-class children to the requirements of capitalist wage labour by habituating them to obedience and providing them with the rudiments of literacy and numeracy. The establishment of an inspectorate, the regulation of teacher training, and the distribution of grants were used to promote this version of education. Most importantly, the 'Revised Code' issued in 1862 established a system of external state control of subsidised private-sector schooling through 'payment by results', based on tests of levels of pupil attainment, and figures for school attendance.

The Education Act 1870 and a similar Act of 1872 for Scotland were designed to ensure that all working-class children had access to this kind of education. The Department of Education was to provide for elected School Boards to run schools in areas where the provision of voluntary schools was inadequate. In 1880, school attendance was made compulsory from the ages of 5 to 10. In 1891, all charges for schooling up to the age of 11 were abolished, and in 1893 attendance until 11 became compulsory. Most working-class children continued to receive a minimal education, although in the 1890s some 'higher-grade' elementary schools were established which were, in effect, a form of secondary education.

Some middle-class children attended independent day 'grammar' schools, while upper-class children were educated in the 'public schools' which were private fee-charging boarding schools. Both grammar and public schools were regulated by the state on the basis respectively of the proposals of the Clarendon Commission (1864) and the Taunton Commission (1867). The universities of Oxford and Cambridge were also reformed on the basis of inquiries published in 1852. Clerical influence was reduced and admissions were made more meritocratic. Several new universities and university colleges were established alongside the ancient English and Scottish universities, particularly in the expanding industrial cities.

In the remainder of the last century, many features of the present system were formed. These included the local administration of schooling within a framework laid down by central government, a system of schooling for the middle and upper classes outside the state system, the emergence of the teaching labour force as an influence on policy, the form of school organisation, the curriculum, and the role of examinations (see subsection 8.2.4).

The Education Act 1902 brought all elementary schools under the control of local education authorities, although 'voluntary' schools were not fully financed by the state and retained the right to give denominational instruction. The Act also, for the first time, made provision for some working-class access to secondary education, while amendments to the regulations in 1907 provided for 25 per cent of the places in secondary schools to be free. Education was to last until 13 years of age, although exemptions to the rule were made. The welfare of schoolchildren was advanced by the Education (Provision of Meals) Act 1906, which allowed local education authorities (LEAs) to provide meals. By 1912 about 30 per cent were doing so. Medical inspection in schools was introduced in 1907.

These reforms made up part of the attempt to use state action to improve economic efficiency during this period. The Education Act 1918 formed part of the same process, although it also owed something to the mood of radicalism created by the First World War. It made attendance from the age of 5 to 14 compulsory and abolished exemptions from education. It provided for part-time 'continuation class' from 14 to 16, and for nursery education. It also increased the central government contribution to the financing of education, which rose from £19 million in 1918 to £32 million in 1919, although cuts were introduced in 1920 and intensified in 1922 as part of the Geddes package. In 1924, Labour introduced an increase in the proportion of free secondary places from 25 per cent to 40 per cent and a few areas abolished fees for secondary education, but by 1926 there were no LEA nursery schools, and only one LEA provided compulsory continuing education for 14 to 16-year-olds.

In the inter-war period, many LEAs reorganised their schools on the basis of the proposals of the Hadow Report of 1926, which provided for new secondary schools to be set up alongside the existing grammar schools. However, the 1931 cuts reduced the education budget, cut teachers' pay by 10 per cent, and put the free-places scheme on a means-tested basis. In the 1930s, class sizes fell, although by 1938 there were still over 2,000 classes containing more than 50 children. Streaming in elementary schools was encouraged by the Board of Education, and some LEAs began to use intelligence tests for selection at 11 years of age.

The Second World War led to major changes in education. The evacuation of children from threatened areas led to considerable disruption of schooling, and by 1940 about 0.5 million children were receiving no education at all. The war led to more support for the view of education as a right that should be available to all, rather than a privilege obtained by wealth or ability. The impact of change was felt particularly in the armed forces. The Army Education Corps was expanded and the Army Bureau of Current Affairs was established in 1941. Up to three hours per week of time previously assigned to military training was now used for educational purposes. Plans for the reform of the school system were also put forward. These finally resulted in the 1943 White Paper, *Educational Reconstruction*, which sought to retain different kinds of secondary school, but to give them 'equal esteem'. In effect it recognised the strength of the forces making for reform, but sought to channel these into an extension of the form of schooling that had developed in the 1930s. Resistance to any more radical change was strong, particularly from the churches who sought, and obtained, an increased degree of state subsidy for denominational schooling.

8.2.2 *Education and the Long Boom: 1944–76*

The Education Act 1944 abolished the category of 'elementary' education, and provided for all children to receive compulsory 'secondary' education from the age of 11 until 15 (from 1947). The Act divided education into three stages: primary, secondary and further. Education was to be 'child-centred' and to be adjusted to the 'ages, abilities, and aptitudes' of the children; it was also to include the provision of 'special schools' for those who needed them. The existing administrative framework was retained. The Ministry of Education had no direct control of the curriculum or examinations, but it was able to regulate teacher training, capital expenditure and standards (through the Inspectorate). Considerable emphasis was put on the physical welfare of children. LEAs were required to provide dental and medical inspection and treatment, school meals, and free transport for those travelling over a certain distance. Independent schools could seek 'recognition' and 'registration', although this provision was not activated until 1957. Those independent day schools that provided 25 per cent of their places free for children who had attended LEA primary schools were given a 'direct grant'. 'Voluntary' schools were given the opportunity to obtain state funds by adopting 'controlled' or 'aided' status. For the first time, religious education and daily worship was made compulsory in all LEA schools. The Act did not specify how education was to be organised, but the Ministry of Education promoted a system of modern, technical and grammar schools. In most areas, however, secondary education was divided between modern and grammar schools.

The period from 1944 to the mid-1970s was a time of expansion in education. The percentage of GDP spent on education rose from 3.3 per cent in 1950 to reach a peak of 7.0 per cent in 1975. However, the nature of schooling continued largely unchanged. A distinctive feature of the post-war period was the dominance exercised by the progressive reformist, social democratic view stressing equality of opportunity combined with a concern to aid accumulation by associating educational expenditure and economic growth. This consensus on education was indicated by the support for increases in provision in a succession of reports dealing with almost every area of education. The Robbins Report (1963) recommended an expansion of the universities to increase the percentage of the age-group receiving higher education from 8 per cent to 17 per cent. New universities were established and some existing colleges of advanced technology were given university status. From 1968, polytechnics were also set up. Part-time further education has developed very unevenly, subject largely to local initiative. Partly as a result, a high percentage of working-class children leave school at the earliest opportunity and receive no further formal education.

During the long boom, the relatively low educational achievement of working-class children was the subject of a number of major reports. These addressed the problems of the working-class child in terms of the 'need' for an educated population to meet the challenge of advanced technology, and the 'wastage' caused by lack of opportunity. Under-achievement was seen as related to living conditions and family life. The reports also evinced a strong concern to increase attachment to conventional morality as a means of dealing with the problems of 'youth'. The solution was to be more and better education. The comprehensive school also appeared to many to offer a solution to the failure to achieve the egalitarian aspirations of 1944, which was ascribed to the operation of selection at the age of 11.

The attempt to establish a system of comprehensive schools in the state sector was begun by the Labour government with the issue of Circular 10/65 to LEAs, asking them to submit plans. Since then the process has been long and uneven. In 1970 the Conservative government withdrew the circular, and it was not until 1976 that legislative compulsion was established. The impact of comprehensive reorganisation on education is hard to assess. Many schools have continued to classify and stream pupils, and in many areas selection is retained. Large numbers of middle-class pupils are educated outside the state sector. In recent years many colleges of further education have taken larger numbers of A-level students, while some areas have established 'sixth-form colleges'. Certainly the overall pattern of educational inequality does not seem to have changed dramatically (see subsection 8.2.5 below). Apart from these structural changes, there have been changes in the organisation of schooling with some increase in parent and pupil participation in the running of schools, a broadening of the curriculum, and some changes in the examination system, in particular the introduction of the Certificate of Secondary Education (CSE), which has increased the percentage of school-leavers obtaining a qualification. In primary education there has been a move away from formal teaching methods and some experimentation with new forms of school design, such as open plan. Following the Plowden Report of 1967, there were experimental projects in 'positive discrimination', designed to improve the primary schooling of working-class children in inner-city areas, although these projects had little general impact on schooling.

At the end of the 1960s signs of the disintegration of the post-war education consensus began to appear. In 1969, the first of the 'Black Papers' provided a coherent right-wing alternative to the prevailing viewpoint. The Conservative government elected in 1970 made a number of cuts, including the abolition of free milk to those over 7 years old, and major cuts in teacher training that were initiated in 1973. These cuts led to college closures and mergers, and to reduced opportunities for women in higher education. The Labour government elected in 1974 at first pursued the traditional policy of improving working-class access to education. The direct grant to independent day schools was abolished in 1974. This led to an expansion of private schooling, since few of the affected schools chose to be incorporated into LEA-provided education. The Education Act 1976 gave powers to compel comprehensive re-organisation. However, in 1976 a major change in educational policy took place, which was related to the economic crisis of that year.

8.2.3 Education and the Crisis from 1976

In 1976, cuts in the education budget were undertaken after the financial crisis and the intervention of the International Monetary Fund (IMF). Over the period 1975–9 the proportion of GDP spent on education fell from 7.0 per cent to 5.8 per cent. The Labour government also initiated a 'Great Debate' on education. This moved away from the traditional social democratic concern with access to education, and brought to the fore issues raised in the various 'Black Papers', in particular, the curriculum, 'standards', teacher competence, and vocational preparation. It was also accompanied by a broader ideological campaign against 'progressive' teaching methods and left-wing teachers. At a time when unemployment was rapidly increasing, the Great Debate served to blame it on those who experienced it and to reduce resistance to further education cuts. Cuts in university education were made from 1981. The polytechnics' budgets were also cut and a process of restructuring has been initiated by the National Advisory Board. The government has also undertaken a campaign against social science education in general, and sociology in particular.

Courses in further education have been reorganised through the establishment of the Business and Technical Education Council (BTEC). The Manpower Services Commission (MSC) has also become heavily involved, and by 1986 it will finance about 25 per cent of all courses in colleges of further education. The MSC's 'New

Training Initiative' (1981) includes proposals for an 'Open Tech', using 'distance-learning' techniques and the provision of 'Pickup' courses (Professional, Industrial and Community Updating). A feature of all MSC courses is the exclusion of any critical social, economic or political analysis and the removal of control of the curriculum from those who teach.

Since 1976 considerable changes have taken place in schooling. The Conservative government in 1979 repealed the 1976 legislation requiring comprehensive secondary schooling. In the period 1979–83, the number of teachers fell by 38,000 and 800 schools were closed. Expenditure on adult education, libraries and nursery schooling was cut. The Education Act 1980 required LEAs to allow parents to state a preference for the school their child would attend. An 'assisted-places' scheme was established to finance attendance at independent day schools, and provision was made for parents and teachers to be represented on school governing bodies. Finally, the schools meals service was put back to the pre-1944 basis: LEAs were no longer required to provide meals, except for those receiving them free, nutritional standards were no longer specified, and LEAs could levy whatever charge they wished. There have also been moves to make changes in the school curriculum. In 1981 the School's Council was abolished, and the government has also expressed support for a 'core curriculum' and 'curriculum development', using the language and approach of the MSC. This has involved an emphasis on 'transferable skills', 'life skills', etc. The MSC has also become directly involved in secondary schools through the Technical and Vocational Training Initiative, which involves a pilot four-year technical curriculum involving 14,000 children in 147 schools.

Since the mid-1970s, the extent of central control has been increased, and this has been used both to institute cuts and to shift provision in the direction of vocationalism. The attempt to narrow the curriculum has also involved a move to establish a higher degree of consonance with the dominant ideology in the broad area of social and historical studies.

8.2.4 *British Capitalism, the Curriculum and School Organisation*

Despite the post-war changes in education, strong elements of continuity exist in the curriculum, the organisation of educational institutions, the 'sorting' function of grading and examinations, and the pedagogic principles governing the relations of teachers and learners.

One major determinant of the curriculum has been the ideal of the educated Christian gentleman, which was developed in the reformed public schools in the last century. The subjects studied reflected the preferences of an aristocratically-inclined ruling class which saw itself as the custodian of a traditional 'high' culture and which directed its male children towards the empire, the City, the traditional professions, and to leading positions in the state, rather than into manufacture. The emphasis on classics, the humanities and pure science, and the exclusion of most kinds of engineering and technology, reflected the traditional curriculum of the universities as well as a distaste for knowledge directly subordinated to the requirements of profitable business. The intellectual culture of the dominant class, as indicated by the subjects studied by its children, still remains influenced by these patterns.

As secondary education for the working class developed in the twentieth century, it adopted a modified version of this curriculum. However, the pursuit of a minimal competence in basic skills of literacy and numeracy, combined with a strong emphasis on moral training, has existed alongside the partly opposed desire to expose the working class to a version of the full range of traditional culture. This conflict reflects a division between the proponents of liberal education, and the proponents of minimal training. Changes have taken place in the curriculum, particularly in primary education, where a rather broader programme of studies has become the norm. Additional subjects have also become available at secondary level, particularly because of the growth of new disciplines within the universities. However, secondary education for those leaving school at the minimum age has changed less and still reflects a combination of liberal education and minimal training.

The curriculum has little connection with work skills. Schools have not taken on an occupational training function and neither, in the main, have universities, although polytechnics and technical colleges have. Education has, however, played a major role in moral training. The formal requirement to promote religion in schools testifies to this. Other subjects, such as history and geography, have entered the curriculum of working-class schools in a form highly amenable to the inculcation of an uncritical and often laudatory view of existing social organisation, the ruling class, the state and, in the past, Britain's imperial role.

A key feature of any system of schooling is its impact on the experience of the pupils. State schooling is compulsory and legal sanctions have always been available to suppress non-attendance, emphasising the custodial role of the school. The emphasis on punctuality, subordination to hierarchical discipline, and the absence of formal democratic procedures within the school habituate children to a particular form of authority that was initially based explicitly on that of the factory. The ways in which schools vary the education provided for different children also follows long-established principles. Pupils are distinguished on the basis of age and sex, some subjects are confined to certain age-groups, and boys and girls are not provided with a common syllabus. Pupils are also classified and graded on the basis of a variety of tests and examinations, which separate out an elite of high achievers whose education will be prolonged.

8.2.5 Inequality and Education: Class, Sex and Race

The development of schooling in the twentieth century has established and lengthened full-time compulsory education for all children. Real expenditure per pupil has increased, staff/student ratios have improved and post-compulsory education has grown. Some of the impetus for expansion was due to a desire to reduce inequalities in educational achievement, but examination passes and the usage of the education system at the post-compulsory stage still strongly reflect major divisions in society based on class, sex and race.

Class origin as measured by occupational status affects the education which a person receives. The relative difference in the rates of university entrance has remained remarkably constant (see Table 8.1). The overall level of educational achievement is also closely related to the occupational class of the child's family (see

Table 8.1: Percentage University Attendance by Class and Period of Birth in Great Britain, Men

Father's occupational class	Child born in			
	1913–22	1923–32	1933–42	1943–52
Professionals/managers	7.2	15.9	23.7	26.4
Other non-manual/supervisory	1.9	4.0	4.1	8.0
Manual workers	0.9	1.2	2.3	3.1

Source: Adapted from A. H. Halsey, A. F. Heath and J. M. Ridge, *Origins and Destinations* (Clarendon Press, 1980), Table 10.8.

Table 8.2: Highest Qualification-level Attained by Occupational Class of Father in Great Britain, 1981–2

Qualification	Occupational class of father							
	Professional/employers and managers (%)		Other non-manual (%)		Manual workers and own account non-professional (%)		Total (%)	
	M	F	M	F	M	F	M	F
Degree or other higher education qualification	38	27	35	24	16	8	21	13
A Level	12	8	12	6	9	3	9	4
O Level	19	25	17	22	14	15	15	18
CSE/Other	11	16	13	19	17	14	15	15
None	20	24	22	29	52	60	40	50
	100	100	99	100	98	100	100	100

Source: Calculated from OPCS, *General Household Survey* (HMSO, 1984), Table 7.5(a), p. 138.

Table 8.2). So, for example, 24 per cent of daughters from professional families have no qualifications, compared to 60 per cent of daughters from manual workers' families. The level of qualifications a person achieves has a major impact on his or her future earning-power and chance of obtaining paid employment.

Class inequalities in education also involve substantial differences in state expenditure. Higher classes benefit disproportionately, because they receive a longer education *and* because the extra education they receive is more expensive to provide. These effects are intensified by spatial differences. LEAs with a relatively well-off population spend *more* on education, and middle-class suburban areas often have newer and better-equipped schools than inner-city working-class areas.

State expenditure on education also benefits those who are educated in independent schools. These children are overwhelmingly from well-off, and often upper-class families. A wide range of subsidies and tax reliefs is available to parents of these children and to the schools themselves. The 'assisted-places' scheme, like free places in direct-grant schools which it replaces, mainly benefits middle-class children. Various schemes exist whereby parents or grandparents can avoid paying tax on funds used to finance private education. Some occupational groups such as army officers and diplomats receive subsidies for their children to obtain private education. The schools themselves benefit from charitable status, which exempts them from income, corporation and capital gains taxes. They also obtain teachers trained at public expense in the state system.

Table 8.2 illustrates major sex differences in education. Boys achieve more qualifications than girls and receive a longer education. The difference increases the further one moves up the hierarchy of qualifications. From the beginning of state education, girls have studied subjects related to domestic labour or relevant to work that was considered suitable for women, and they have been encouraged to adopt specifically 'feminine' attributes. Though in a modified and reduced form, nevertheless these differences remain today and have been justified in major reports on education produced in the post-war period. Some sexual inequalities, however, have been reduced. There is no longer a sex difference in the proportions leaving at the minimum school-leaving age. Inequality in access to higher education has been reduced, but major differences remain in the subjects studied, reproducing the sexual division of labour. Women are under-represented in engineering and technology, architecture, medicine and science, and over-represented in the arts and education. The post-war reduction in the differences between the education of girls and boys was related to the increasing labour-market participation of women throughout the long boom. This provided favourable conditions for viewing women's 'under-achievement' as wasteful and for attempting to improve women's educational performance.

The education received by ethnic minorities also shows a number of distinctive features and has been the subject of special policy measures. Particularly in the 1960s, attempts were made to 'assimilate' members of ethnic minorities by special language training and through the use of 'bussing'. However, the general approach has now moved towards 'cultural pluralism'. A survey carried out in six LEAs with a high concentration of ethnic minorities demonstrated the relatively low educational achievement of West Indians (see Table 8.3). All ethnic minorities had a lower chance of taking up university education, even where the qualifications for it existed. The differences between Asians and West Indians reflect the different class composition of these two minorities, although racism and low-quality schooling in inner-city areas are also important. The material benefits of education achievement are also lower for members of ethnic minorities. Of those with degrees, a far higher proportion of blacks than whites are in manual jobs, due to discrimination and marginal status in the labour market.

Inequalities in education and the unequal distribution of access to formal and elaborated knowledge which this involves closely reflect the inequalities in income and wealth created by the CMP. In the

Table 8.3: Education and Ethnic Minorities, 1978–9

	No A levels (%)	One or more A levels (%)	University (%)	Other FE or HE (%)
Asians	87	13	3	18
West Indians	98	2	1	16
All LEA school-leavers	87	13	5	14

Source: Adapted from V. George and P. Wilding, *The Impact of Social Policy* (Routledge and Kegan Paul, 1984), Table 3.5.

present century, access to post-compulsory education has depended both on ability to pay and on the principle that those who find it most easy to learn should receive the most education. Education can be viewed as a process for selecting a minority to undergo intensive teaching and study, whilst making minimal provision for the rest. As long as educational credentials remain a commodity that is used to enhance the value of labour power, this is likely to continue.

8.2.6 Education and the Capitalist System

The final issue to be raised in this section concerns the effects of education on the workings of the capitalist system. The effect on accumulation is complex and contradictory. Its major effects are on labour efficiency. Education helps to prepare people, especially women, for subordinate and poorly paid employment. The widely held view that mass education functions to provide a highly skilled workforce for the era of advanced technology is a myth. Given widespread deskilling and the nature of the curriculum, little effect on productivity through improved work skills is likely as a result of schooling, although further education does perform this function, while higher education provides some highly trained workers and increases the stock of exploitable knowledge. However, the general effect of schooling on labour efficiency is more related to the habituation to routine and authority which schools undertake. Finally, the existence of full-time education socialises some of the costs of reproduction as well as facilitating the participation of parents in the labour force. Full-time compulsory education confers benefits on capital, but the cultivation of skills and values consistent with capitalist wage labour has not dominated every aspect of education. The system identifies a pool of able children and confers a prolonged education on them, but it channels many into the professions and the state, although this may have substantial indirect benefits for capital as a whole.

So far as legitimation is concerned, the curriculum helps to generate 'misrecognition' of the nature of class relations, and the system of grading and examinations helps legitimate the inequality of material rewards. Working-class access to higher education contributes to legitimation by underpinning the imagery of meritocracy. Education can also undermine legitimacy, however. The student movement of the 1960s provided evidence of a degree of hegemonic breakdown. The radical tradition in the social sciences, the humanities and even in natural science is also significant.

The contribution made to internal security by education mainly results from the custodial function of schools, which constrains opportunities for disorderly juvenile behaviour. So far as external security is concerned, schooling has always been an important medium for the propagation of patriotic and chauvinist imagery and sentiments, which can be activated for the purposes of military mass mobilisation.

This account of the effects of education on capitalism demonstrates the extent to which the nature of cultural reproduction through state schooling diverges from the model of bourgeois culture outlined at the start of the chapter. This has occurred because of the distinctive nature of the British ruling class with its strong aristocratic element, and because of the influence of progressive educational thought amongst many of those involved in education, especially in the post-war period. The past and prospective significance of this is substantial. The education system harbours reformist and radical currents in a labour force that is by no means solidly attached to the existing order. The breakdown of the long boom also appears to be creating growing difficulties for the schooling of older working-class boys, who clearly perceive its irrelevance as a preparation for work in a period of mass unemployment. The nature of the education provided for working-class girls continues to reflect the unresolved contradiction between the demands of paid work and those of domestic labour. In these circumstances, the re-emergence of education as a major political issue makes the critical reassessment of existing patterns of provision all the more important.

8.3 Capitalism and Scientific Knowledge

The sciences were characterised at the beginning of this chapter as those systematically elaborated forms of knowledge that have resulted from the application of the positivist methods of enquiry first developed in the natural sciences. The term is taken to include social science, where this is based on positivist methods. Defining science in this way involves the inclusion of technology, where this is developed by the use of these methods. However, a great deal of technology in the form of craft skills and traditions has grown up through practical experience, not systematic enquiry.

8.3.1 The Development of State Science

A key feature of the culture of capitalism is the continuous growth of scientific knowledge and its application to more and more areas of life. Within the central tradition of Marxism, science and technology have not been a major issue, although the Frankfurt school has developed a wide-ranging critique of modern science. The reason for this relative lack of interest lies mainly in the legacy of classical Marxism, which viewed science as an unambiguously progressive force growing according to its own logic. From this viewpoint, the main issue to be raised was the way capitalism impeded its free development. In contrast, the view taken here is that capitalism determines the overall pattern of scientific development largely in accord with the contribution this can make to the capitalist system. It is therefore not the logic of science, but the logic of capitalism that determines the development of science and its application. The rest of this subsection will contain a brief account of the growth of state involvement in science and of the distinctive features of the production of modern scientific knowledge. The impact of science on accumulation, legitimation and security will then be considered in subsection 8.3.2.

The foundations of modern science were laid in the seventeenth century in a period of expanding commercial and colonial capitalism. Although most of the advances were made by private individuals, an extensive system of scientific intercommunication grew up with a degree of state sponsorship. Important early steps were the establishment of the Royal Society in 1662 and the Royal Observatory, under the control of the Admiralty, in 1675. The orientation of enquiry towards the scientific problems of an emerging capitalist world power, especially those of shipping, mining and the armed forces, was evident. However, little direct state involvement in the organisation of science occurred in the next two hundred years, due, in the main, to the largely unimpeded development of commercial and then industrial capitalism in Britain.

Many of the major technological developments up to about 1850 were based on inspired craftsmanship, and the extension of traditional techniques, stimulated by direct economic pressure, rather than the pursuit of new scientific knowledge for its own sake. The major exception was the development of chemical processes, which relied heavily on trained scientists, who in the UK were often graduates of Scottish universities, where, unlike in England, a good scientific education was available. Government intervention in science remained limited. In the 1850s, the three Royal Technical Schools that later became Imperial College were established. However, in contrast to France and Germany, science was not strongly promoted. Indeed, considerable resistance to scientific knowledge as such existed, as the bitter controversy in the 1860s over Darwin's work on evolution illustrated. By the end of the last century, despite the growing importance of the application of science to industry (for example, in steel, aluminium, electricity generation and dyestuffs), there was no major state-backed scientific effort in Britain.

It was not until the First World War that science as a whole became an object of public policy. The capital-intensive nature of modern warfare and the role of science in weapons development led to the establishment of the Department of Scientific and Industrial Research (DSIR) in 1916, with the aim of co-ordinating civilian and military research. After the war, the model provided by the Medical Research Council (founded 1920) and the Agricultural Research Council (founded 1931), each of which ran their own research establishments, was not applied to other industries. So far as basic research was concerned, there was little money to finance university research.

The Second World War had a profound effect on science policy. Substantial state-backed advances took place in physics, particularly electronics and nuclear physics. The pace and complexity of scientific discovery led to the increasing industrialisation and bureaucratisation of scientific research. The application of science to warfare and war production also led to the growth of control techniques such as linear programming and operations research. The Manhattan Project for the construction of the atomic bomb exemplified the most advanced form of organisation for the production of scientific knowledge.

A major feature of the modern organisation of science is its scale and complexity. The traditional community of individual scientists has been replaced by the large-scale specialised laboratory, the research and development organisation or the project team. The research effort of individuals is now mainly determined by the requirements of the employing organisation, and scientists have largely been transformed into scientific workers. Important remnants of the traditional organisation of science exists in the universities, but university research financed through the Research Councils only accounts for about 15 per cent of state scientific expenditure, and increasingly this is being subject to the principles of the market through the use of the customer-contractor relationship recommended by the Rothschild Report of 1972. The expansion of science has been enormous. In 1930, there were about 2,000 scientists who were mainly employed in the universities. By 1980, although scientists in the universities and the state-run laboratories had increased in number to about 20,000, there were also about 330,000 scientific workers employed in research and development in the private sector of industry.

The utilisation of science as a solution to Britain's relative economic backwardness was a major theme in Labour's modernisation programme of 1964, which led to the establishment of a Ministry of Technology, although curiously 'science' was located in the DES. However, the expansion of state-financed or controlled science was already well underway by this time in the major fields of defence, aerospace and nuclear power. In 1980, defence took over 55 per cent of government spending on research and development, with nearly half of this going to private industry.

8.3.2 Science in a Capitalist Society

The impact of science policy on accumulation, legitimation and security raises many complex issues. Scientific advance and the development of capitalism are closely related. 'Long waves' of economic development are associated with the appearance of major technological advances, while growth depends in part on technological advance. However, recent science policy in Britain has involved massive expenditure on defence, aerospace and nuclear power, which mainly serve to benefit the supplying industries, while working to the detriment of capital as a whole by absorbing much of the surplus available for investment as well as most of the scientific manpower. Science and technology have played a major role in increasing labour efficiency, through allowing employers to replace skilled by unskilled or semi-skilled labour, thus reducing labour costs and exerting greater control over the workforce. The tendency to restrict scientific knowledge of the labour process to the management has gone hand in hand with the exclusion of the majority of the working class from effective scientific education.

Scientifically-based advances in housing and household equipment have expanded the labour force through the virtual disappearance of household servants, and led to improvements in health and thus in labour efficiency. Science has also been employed to justify sexist and racist beliefs and practices that reinforce divisions in the working class to the benefit of capital, including intelligence testing and the 'new' science of sociobiology, which portrays a male-dominated competitive organisation of society as based on biological imperatives.

Science has played a major role in legitimation through the development of the technology of mass communication. Science also reinforces the view that all problems have a technical solution. This forms the basis for the 'technocratic' legitimation of authority, which in Britain exists in uneasy alliance with a more deferential respect for a traditional ruling class. The role of science in providing surveillance and communications equipment, as well as weapons for use in internal security, is briefly discussed in section 9.4.2 below. The use of anti-depressants, tranquillisers and even psychosurgery to suppress the effects of stress individualises personal problems and directs attention from their social origins. Finally, the armed forces rely heavily on scientific enquiry for the manufacture of equipment of all kinds, as well as for the design of organisations, training, interrogation and other procedures.

The nature of science and science policy in Britain can be understood in terms of the usual forms taken by science under capitalism, in combination with the peculiar characteristics of British development. There is centralised control of scientific activity, and research is largely undertaken for profit or to increase the security of the state. This pattern of scientific development is portrayed as inevitable. The maintenance of this reified view of science is facilitated by the enormous inequalities which exist in access to, and understanding of, scientific knowledge, which this form of scientific organisation creates. In addition, due to the failure to establish an effective system of scientific education and industrial science in the formative stages of modern large-scale industry, in many older industries scientific knowledge is not fully utilised. This situation coexists with the over-development of those areas of science that have been subject to considerable funding in the post-war period. A further problem arises from the loss of scientific manpower to more dynamic sectors of the world capitalist economy, through the 'brain drain'.

8.4 The State Information System

In this section of the chapter the relationship between capitalism and the state information system is examined. A major part of the state information system is mass communication, insofar as it is under state control and regulation. Mass communication refers to the production and distribution of cultural materials in a way that allows their simultaneous reception by a mass audience. This includes written publications for mass consumption, films, radio and television. The state information system also includes other means through which the state produces and distributes cultural material, such as the statistical services and the various means employed to provide information for the mass media. In addition, the state influences the availability of cultural material through public libraries, museums, and subsidies to the arts. More symbolic forms of communication are undertaken through the organisation of state ceremonials. The development of the state information system and the main features of its organisation are first outlined. This is followed by a consideration of the factors governing its content, in subsection 8.4.2. Finally, the impact on accumulation, legitimation and security is briefly examined in subsection 8.4.3.

8.4.1 *The State and the Development of Mass Media*

Although a variety of legal and extra-legal devices have been used to discourage particular kinds of written material, there has been no direct system of state control since the non-renewal of the Printing Act in 1695. From the eighteenth to the mid-nineteenth century, the state attempted to stifle the growing radical press through laws designed to undermine its finances, such as stamp duties, duties on press advertisements, a tax on paper and, after 1819, by a system of registration involving a cash bond. During the period of crisis following the end of the Napoleonic war in 1815, the state also resorted to the widespread use of the laws on seditious and blasphemous libel, although the publicity this produced was counter-productive and by the 1830s the practice was largely discontinued. The failure to suppress the radical 'unstamped' press in the first half of the nineteenth century, as literacy and the working-class movement grew, led to a major debate with the ruling class over whether to abandon restrictions. This closely paralleled that taking place over the provision of education for the working class. The removal of the restrictions eventually took place over a relatively short period as advertising duty (1853), stamp duty (1855), paper duty (1861) and registration (1869) were abolished. Paradoxically, this created the conditions for the virtual destruction of the radical press. Improvements in printing technology, and consequent increases in investment costs, a reduction in newspaper prices, the increase in the level of circulation needed to ensure viability, and the increased dependence on advertising revenue all operated against the establishment and success of papers with a minority appeal.

The growth of the popular capitalist press from the late nineteenth century established a pattern that has largely continued to the present. Newspapers are distributed on a national basis and range from the high-circulation dailies designed for a working-class readership, to the 'quality' papers which survive on a lower, but better-off readership by virtue of the higher advertising revenues they are able to command. The overall political complexion of the national press has always been right-wing, although moderate Labour opinion has also been presented.

The state has not developed its own papers or undertaken major continuous regulation of the press. A strong attachment exists to a 'free' press, and even during the Second World War the state did not make extensive use of the powers given in the Defence of the Realm Act to ban publications, apart from the closure of the *Daily Worker* and *The Week* in 1941. The consistent policy of the state towards the press has been to leave it to the market. In the post-war period there have been three Royal Commissions on the press – in 1949, 1962 and 1977. In practice, few changes have resulted; newspaper mergers have continued, although some of these have to be reviewed by the Monopolies Commission, and a Press Council was set up in 1953. The latest Commission expanded the traditional view of press freedom as based on the proprietors' rights of ownership to a view that it consists in the absence of controls on proprietors, editors and journalists, by the state, or by trade unions through the closed shop.

The state has played a major role, however, in the development and control of broadcasting. The BBC was set up in 1922 and put under public ownership in 1926, in which year it demonstrated its support for the existing order during the General Strike. The income of the BBC comes from a licence fee determined by the government. The values propagated by the BBC, and embodied in its first Director General, were those of a patrician liberal elite, emphasising high culture and attempting to elevate the level of public taste. BBC sound broadcasting was considerably expanded during the Second World War, and took on the form of Third, Home and Light Programme, a division that echoed the tripartism recommended for secondary schooling at this time. The ethos of sound broadcasting was transferred to BBC television, as this gained a mass audience in the 1950s. It was only with the establishment of commercial television in 1956 that significant changes in approach began to take place.

Commercial television was introduced in a form subject to stringent state control. Nothing comparable to freedom of publication for the press was permitted. A state-appointed body, the IBA, distributed franchises giving each television company a local broadcasting monopoly. As finance comes from the sale of advertising, the companies are basically in business to assemble audiences to sell to advertisers. In the search for greater audiences, the commercial television firms moved away from the paternalistic approach of the BBC. The BBC has followed these changes, and success in the competitive struggle for audiences has become a major objective for both systems. The BBC gained a second channel in 1964 and ITV in 1982. Both of these were designed to cater more for minority interests. Commercial radio broadcasting has also been established, with the first local stations opening in 1973.

8.4.2 Information Control and the State

The major organs of mass communication in terms of audience size are the national press, which is owned by private capital, the system of state-regulated commercial broadcasting, and the BBC. The most general form of control exercised over these institutions is through the law, such as the provisions concerning contempt of court, breach of confidence, and even blasphemous libel. However, the importance of these legal barriers should not be overstated; material can be published in defiance of the law. More significant is the role played by the state in regulating the information made available through and about its own operations.

The mass media are the main source of information about the activities of the state for most members of society. Obviously the kind of information obtained will depend on the level of interest, the extent of exposure to coverage, and the nature of the coverage itself. Since the state is the source of much of the information on which media coverage of political issues is based, the ways in which it processes and transmits this information is of considerable importance. Government departments normally have a press office. Meetings with ministers also take place, in which information is given to trusted journalists on a non-attributable basis. This method is also used for the 'lobby', in which a select group of journalists are given special permission to attend Parliament, and receive regular briefings from the party leaders and their press staff. Given the lack of other sources of information due to the secrecy in which the core institutions of the state operate, journalists are forced to rely for copy on sources that can be withdrawn, if the resultant reporting finds disfavour.

Large quantities of documentary and statistical material are also made available by the state. However, access to official records is subject to a 'thirty-year' rule and these are 'weeded' to remove sensitive material before being made available. The data collected and tabulated by the various arms of the Government Statistical Service are also an important source of information about the state and about social and economic conditions. However, far from being an 'objective' and neutral record of facts, these statistics are often collected, collated and presented in a way that encourages a relatively uncritical interpretation of society, whereas figures that might form the basis for a more unfavourable evaluation may sometimes be concealed.

The state plays a much more direct role in relation to broadcasting than to the press. The elite social composition of the boards of the BBC and the IBA is very similar, as is their sensitivity about programmes that imply a degree of political criticism beyond the range of the current consensus. The IBA and the BBC seek to secure 'balanced programming' and 'due impartiality', which is broadly interpreted as reflecting the range of views implied by the parliamentary strength of the major parties.

The state also influences the mass media in less formal ways. A 'voluntary' system of censorship operated with the co-operation of the media exists in the form of the 'D'-notice system. In addition, ministers have often attempted to exert an influence on broadcasting through the threat of financial and other sanctions. Wide reserve powers exist to take over broadcasting organisations. In times of crisis the scope of state involvement may widen, as with the establishment of a Ministry of Information during the Second World War or the close control of the media during the Falklands conflict. Finally, governments may organise covert and sometimes illegal operations to influence the mass media.

The content communicated and its effects differ between press and broadcasting. The press deals mostly in news and has a mainly right-wing editorial policy; broadcasting deals mainly in entertainment and strives to achieve 'balance' in its news and current affairs coverage. So far as television news coverage is concerned, however, although it is subject to a degree of state regulation, it mainly reflects the influence of the press. The 'news values', which define the characteristics of events and which constitute them as newsworthy, were developed in the press. The press presents as particularly newsworthy those events that can be portrayed to the discredit of radical opinions, and emphasises stories that reflect credit on the ruling bloc and the capitalist system. The procedures and assumptions that determine the presentation of events on TV news are also taken from the press. These include the language used, and the implicit and explicit evaluation of events which the coverage contains, such as the frequent description of the end of an industrial dispute, regardless of the terms, as 'better news on the industrial front'. Official spokespeople are used to establish the orthodox interpretation of events whenever a challenge to this is reported. The coverage of any form of deviant behaviour is based on the assumption of a wide and well-established consensus in society, which it is seen to threaten. Social and political issues are personalised and often trivialised, and sensational, but atypical events are portrayed by implication as normal. Every newspaper has a 'social personality' in the sense that it concentrates on certain kinds of stories and reports them in a particular way. The same can be said of television news and current affairs, although its social personality has changed since the advent of commercial television, as it has moved from a patrician to a more populist style. The existence of a critical perspective is most evident in documentary broadcasts, and the BBC and IBA boards have often intervened to amend or withdraw particular programmes.

8.4.3 The State Information System and British Capitalism

The impact of the state information system on accumulation, legitimation and security can only be assessed in broad outline. The process of accumulation may be furthered by the production of information relevant to business, as well as the dissemination of information affecting patterns of consumption. The existing technology of broadcasting also provides a basis for the growth of new markets in new technologies such as viewdata or cable TV. So far as legitimation is concerned, existing economic, family-household and state forms are not subject to sustained critical treatment. Indeed, the image which is presented of many aspects of society is systematically distorted. The media undoubtedly have the power to influence

Table 8.4: The Impact of State-sector Cultural Production on the CMP (positive '+' and negative '—')

		Accumulation		Legitimation		Security
Education	−	Surplus diverted by tax used for finance	+	Encouragement of mis-recognition of social relations	+	Custodial function for working-class youth
	+	Labour force habituated to subordination	+	Legitimation of pattern of distributional inequality	+	Reproduction of attachment to national values and symbols
	+	Sexual division of labour reinforced	−	Maintenance of anti-capitalist cultural products		
	+	Selection of educational elite				
	+	Partial socialisation of costs of reproduction				
	+	Reinforcement of family-household forms				
Science	+	Development of forces of production	+	Basis for mass communication	+	Techniques for regulation of deviant behaviour
	−	Surplus diverted to unprofitable uses	+	Generation of technocratic form of legitimation	+	New forms of surveillance
	+	Deskilling of labour force	+	Scientific basis for racism and sexism	+	New means of coercion

	Accumulation	Legitimation	Security
State information system +	+ Reduction of reproduction costs	− Provision of technical and organisational basis for non-capitalist economy	− Development of anti-capitalist scientific knowledge
	+ Increase in size of labour force	+ Selection of material on basis of support for existing economic, political and social arrangements	+ Support for existing foreign and defence policy
	+ Production of information useful to capital	+ Deflection of criticism away from capitalism	+ Direct control by government in emergencies
	+ Basis for new markets through technological innovation	+ Encouragement of mis-recognition of social relations	
	− Surplus diverted through taxation for finance	− Communication of critical material	

opinion. The continuous and uncritical repetition of particular themes in the form of media campaigns can provide a basis for popular public opinion, whether the subject is 'mugging', mods and rockers, strikes or the causes of inflation. So far as internal security is concerned, the media play a major role in structuring perceptions of the nature of the threat to it. In relation to external security, the mass media were used during the Second World War to mobilise support for, and participation in, the war effort. More generally, the media present a very partial view of the world, strongly linked to orthodox foreign policy concerns. In addition, the external services of the BBC are used for foreign policy purposes.

The account of the state information system given in this section has emphasised the influence of private capital on the structure and output of those parts of the mass media in state ownership. Control of the state sector of the media is highly centralised and not subject to any direct form of democratic regulation. However, a degree of autonomy for programme-makers is unavoidable, and radical currents exist within many media organisations, whether in the state sector or not. A wide-ranging critique of the media has been raised in demands for a 'new information order'. This has arisen from a recognition that the Western media constitute an information system that is oriented primarily to the requirements of the capitalist mode of production and the capitalist states. A growing internationalisation of the media has occurred as a result of the interlinking of state information systems through co-productions, satellite transmissions, and the increasing role of the media multinational corporations. Other changes in media organisation and technology, such as viewdata systems like 'Prestel' and 'Ceefax', and the introduction of cable TV, highlight the continuing and expanding role of the state information system.

8.5 Cultural Production and the Capitalist System

The cultural institutions of the state share a number of common characteristics. First, they all tend to maintain inequalities in access to knowledge in its systematically developed forms. As a result, working-class people are largely excluded from understanding and experience of much of the available pool of systematic knowledge. Second, the institutions which dominate cultural production are not subject to democratic control by either the recipients of their output or their employees. Third, the content of cultural production tends to create conditions favourable to the CMP. In the cases of education, science and the state information system, the patterns established during the initial period of large-scale state involvement have continued to exert a major influence. However, the overall impact of cultural production on accumulation, legitimation and security illustrates the complex and contradictory effects of state policy. These are summarised in Table 8.4

It is clear that culture diverges from both capitalist rationalism and competitive individualism. This is partly due to resistance to the complete penetration of capitalist values, by non-capitalist elements in the ruling bloc, within parts of the apparatus of the state, and in the liberal professions. The Labour Party, the trade unions, and a range of organised groups such as the alternative press and the women's movement also provide cultural alternatives.

Competitive individualism has not become a dominant theme of working-class culture, which has developed through the traditions arising from the directly encountered experience of work, community, and the labour movement. To the extent that the working-class movement in the post-war period has been enveloped within a hegemonic culture, it has been mainly through the attachment to moderate labourism, rather than to directly capitalist values. The end of the post-war boom, which sustained this moderate labourism, has created the conditions in which existing culture and the organisation of the institutions that produce it have begun to be widely opposed, even within institutions themselves. It remains to be seen, however, what forms will emerge from the restructuring of culture and consciousness that is at present under way.

Further Reading

General

Barrett, M., Corrigan, P., Kuhn, A. and Wolff, J. (1979) *Ideology and Cultural Production*, Croom Helm
Williams, R. (1981) *Culture*, Fontana

8.1

Centre for Contemporary Cultural Studies (1978) *On Ideology*, Hutchinson
Femia, J. (1975) 'Hegemony and Consciousness in the Thought of Antonio Gramsci', *Political Studies*, vol. 23

Marcuse, H. (1964) *One-Dimensional Man*, Routledge and Kegan Paul
Sharp, R. (1980) *Knowledge, Ideology and the Politics of Schooling*, Routledge and
	Kegan Paul

8.2.1

Bernbaum, G. (1967) *Social Change and the Schools 1918–1944*, Routledge and
	Kegan Paul
David, M. E. (1980) *The State, the Family and Education*, Routledge and Kegan Paul
Simon, B. (1974) *The Two Nations and Educational Structure*, Lawrence and Wishart

8.2.2–8.2.3

Centre for Contemporary Cultural Studies (1981) *Unpopular Education*, Hutchinson
Finch, J. (1984) *Education as Social Policy*, Longman

8.2.4

Williams, R. (1965) *The Long Revolution*, Penguin, pt II, ch. 1

8.2.5

Deem, R. (1978) *Women and Schooling*, Routledge and Kegan Paul
LeGrand, J. (1982) *The Strategy of Equality: Redistribution and the Social Services*,
	George Allen and Unwin

8.3

Rose, H. and Rose, S. (1970) *Science and Society*, Penguin
Rose, H. and Rose, S. (1976) *The Political Economy of Science: Ideology in the
	Natural Sciences*, Macmillan
Rose, H. and Rose, S. (eds.) (1976) *The Radicalisation of Science*, Macmillan

8.4

Curran, J. and Seaton, J. (1985) *Power without Responsibility*, 2nd edn, Fontana
Curran, J., Gurevitch, M. and Woollacott, J. (eds.) (1977) *Mass Communication and
	Society*, Edward Arnold
May, A. and Rowan, K. (eds.) (1982) *Inside Information: British Government and the
	Media*, Constable

8.5

Albury, D. and Schwartz, J. (1982) *Partial Progress: The Politics of Science and
	Technology*, Pluto
George, V. and Wilding, P. (1984) *The Impact of Social Policy*, Routledge and Kegan
	Paul

LAW AND ORDER POLICY

9.1 The Marxist Approach to Law

This chapter examines the role played by the law and by the operation of the legal system in relation to capitalism in the UK. The basic Marxist approach sees the law, first, as a means by which the coercive power of the state is wielded in the interests of the capitalist class. A second theme involves the legal 'needs' of the CMP, including provision for the enforcement of contracts and for capitalist enterprises to act as 'legal personalities'. A third theme stresses the democratic constitutional state as the 'normal' form associated with the CMP. These three themes focus on different ways in which the legal framework relates to the needs of the CMP. The historical formation of the capitalist state is seen as involving the establishment of a constitutional-bureaucratic form during the early phase of capitalist development. Democratisation occurs with the establishment of industrial capitalism and the associated process of class formation. The capitalist class seeks political influence through a parliamentary regime within which the varying interests can be reconciled and the dominant class from the previous mode of production displaced. Democratisation also results from working-class pressure.

Since the patterns described in this simple model do not develop in an unproblematic fashion, an adequate Marxist approach must also focus on divergencies from this 'normal' form due to barriers to accumulation, historical influences, gender divisions, international factors and the impact of class relations. In reality, the CMP may be accommodated within a variety of legal frameworks so long as basic features such as contract are available. The capitalist state itself may vary substantially from the constitutional democratic form. Capitalism is also compatible with a variety of systems of criminal law enforcement. The basic approach also fails to recognise adequately the contradictory nature of legal institutions: how they may both reinforce some elements of the capitalist system and act to undermine others. It neglects the fact that many of the characteristic institutions of the legal system predate the appearance of industrial capitalism and have thus been shaped by forces unconnected with capitalist interests. Class conflict has had a substantial impact on the law itself and the operation of the legal system during the capitalist era. Constraints on the unfettered pursuit of private profit, on the dominance of the capitalist class, and on the exploitation of workers have been instituted. The legal system as it actually exists and operates is therefore a product of complex historical processes.

This chapter is organised on a topic basis as follows. The development of the legal system and its relation to the CMP are examined in the next section. In section 9.3, the legal foundations of the state are examined, while section 9.4 explains how the law is used to protect the state and maintain public order. Policing is discussed in section 9.5, and in section 9.6 the system of criminal justice is considered. Individual rights are examined in section 9.7. Finally, in section 9.8 the overall impact of the law on British capitalism is discussed.

9.2 The Development of Law in the UK

9.2.1 Law and the Control of the Legal System

Law in the UK does not derive from a single legal code; it is based on the historical accumulation of a mass of disparate legislation (*statute law*) and court decisions (*common law*). There is, however, no written constitution which defines the structure of the state and the rights of citizens. As well as British laws, the courts also enforce some laws enacted by external organisations such as the EEC and the European Human Rights Convention. There are different categories of law. *Public law* governs the structure and operation of the state sector. *Civil law* deals with the adjudication of private disputes involving individuals or organisations, where one party seeks damages and/or to control the behaviour of the other. *Criminal law* deals with offences where the state, through the police or some other body, brings a prosecution. All cases are decided by a court procedure in which adversaries are allowed to present evidence and challenge the evidence provided by the other side.

Overall state control of the legal system is centred in the Home Office, which was set up in 1782. In the early decades of its operation, the main function was the organisation of a network of informers reporting on radical dissent. The Home Office gradually acquired new functions as the control of crime and public order was put on a more formal basis with the expansion of the prison system and the development of a full-time police force. Today the main exclusive responsibilities of the Home Office are crime, public order, prisons, immigration and citizenship, although it also plays a major role in the internal security system. The Home Office also has some influence over the administration of justice, though judges are appointed by the Lord Chancellor.

The police, the security services, and the courts, in varying degrees, are not subject to direct control by the Home Office. In the case of the police, this is due to the absence of a single national police force. The security services have obtained a degree of independence of direct central bureaucratic or political control. The courts are generally allowed to operate without direct political intervention in their everyday operations, although judicial appointments are centrally controlled.

9.2.2 *Legal Requirements of the CMP and the Common Law*

The long-term pursuit of profit through capitalist enterprise requires a consistent application of existing law so that legal obligations are always clearly known. In Britain, this is achieved by the existence of a system of precedent, whereby the principles determining decisions made by higher courts are binding on lower courts and subsequent cases. The historical development of the law in the UK has both reflected and reinforced the growth of capitalism. The common law developed a number of substantive features amenable to capitalist production. Economic transactions were given a legal basis very early on with the development of the key notion of contract, while the common law also developed a system that defined legal wrongs in terms of their impact on the economic status of the wronged party, which the imposition of damages would then restore. Other common law doctrines, such as those that made behaviour 'in restraint of trade' actionable, also facilitated the development of capitalist economic relations. During the eighteenth century, judicial decisions removed many ancient and customary rights, enabling both labour and land to be treated as commodities to be bought and sold at the going rate. By the early nineteenth century the law itself approximated to a set of general abstract rules facilitating the free purchase and sale of commodities including labour, but criminalising threats to persons, property and the existing political order.

The common law assumptions built into legal concepts such as contract, negligence, property and individual responsibility were based on a society of independent commodity producers associating freely on the basis of purely personal considerations. The existence of systematic inequalities of power and opportunity between employers and employees, firms and consumers, landlords and tenants means that the form of a free contract between equal parties now masks the exploitation of one group by another.

9.3 Legal Foundations of the State: Constitutionalism, Territoriality and Citizenship

The modern form of the British state dates from the 1688 settlement that provided the basis for parliamentary rule, a constitutional monarchy, a state administration established on the basis of legal enactment, and an independent judiciary. Legislative power was placed jointly in the hands of the monarch and the two Houses of Parliament, the Commons and the Lords. In the formative period of the modern state, a restricted franchise allowed the propertied classes to monopolise high political office. The Reform Acts of 1832, 1867 and 1884 gradually reduced the extent of the property qualification for male voters, but women did not receive the vote until 1918 and not on the same basis as men until 1929. While the monarchy had ceded effective legislative power to the Houses of Parliament by the late eighteenth century, it was not until 1911 that a Parliament Act finally placed restrictions on the legislative power of the Lords.

The relatively late establishment of a democratic electoral system, the continued legislative power of the aristocracy, and the political role of the monarchy illustrate ways in which the core state institutions in the UK diverge from the model of the 'normal' democratic constitutional state. In addition, the absence of a written constitution and of judicial review of legislation, and the attribution of sovereignty to Parliament rather than 'the people', means that parliamentary government, elections and any other political or civil rights can be, and sometimes have been, abandoned through the normal legislative process.

Although central government has enjoyed, with the exception of the Cromwellian period, centuries of uninterrupted political dominance in England, the territorial extent of the rest of the Kingdom has been subject to a number of changes involving the relations with the other nations in the British Isles. The subjugation of Ireland in the sixteenth century, the later settlement of its northern counties, the resurgence of Irish nationalism in the nineteenth century, and finally the Government of Ireland Act 1920, which retained the six counties as part of the UK, but with special constitutional status including its own parliament, formed the background to the present conflicts over the future constitutional position of Northern Ireland. The abolition of the Stormont parliament in 1971, the imposition of direct rule, the continuous attempts to devise new and more stable constitutional arrangements, the existence of a distinctive system of policing and of a locally based part-time military force designed for internal operations (the Ulster Defence Regiment) all indicate the failure to incorporate Northern Ireland within the normal jurisdiction of the British state. Indeed, under the Northern Ireland Act 1949, the province has a legal right of incorporation into the Irish republic on a vote of a majority of its electorate.

Scotland was once a fully fledged and independent state. Although the crowns of England and Scotland were united in 1603, Scotland retained its own parliament until the Act of the Union 1707, when it abolished itself and accepted the sovereignty of Westminster, in what has been described as 'a bargain between two ruling classes'. Scotland, however, still retains its own legal system, Established Church and educational system and, with Northern Ireland, and to a much lesser extent Wales, a special legislative and administrative status. Legislation passed at Westminster does not necessarily apply to Scotland and there is a Scottish Office that deals with specifically Scottish matters.

The multinational character of the jurisdiction of the UK state means that nationalism remains as a basis of political organisation. While nationalism always has a historical and cultural aspect, it is also associated with the impact of uneven development, insofar as this leads to national inequalities within the UK and to variations in the forms of class structure and conflict associated with differences in the pattern and pace of capital accumulation. National differences complicate the patterns of conflict within society, especially in terms of how they relate to class divisions. The multinational nature of the state in the UK highlights the importance and complexity of nationalism, even under conditions of advanced industrial capitalism.

The final aspect of the legal basis of the state involves rights of citizenship. The legal basis for contract, involving rights possessed by individuals and enforceable through the courts, formed the framework which was adopted for other rights which were established in the course of the long struggle for parliamentary supremacy and democracy. The civil freedoms of assembly, of speech and of freedom from arbitrary arrest, far from being a legal expression of the interests of the capitalist class, have formed a focus of working-class radicalism from the earliest period of its emergence. The extension of these rights to all members of society has been a factor in changing the form of class conflict. However, these rights are not always effectively enforced, particularly in the case of women and ethnic minorities, as is recognised by the existence of legislation dealing with sex and race discrimination. Laws also govern the qualifications necessary to obtain citizenship rights in the UK. Mental illness, imprisonment and youth are all used as criteria for exclusion from rights. The major form of legal regulation of citizenship, however, involves immigration.

Right of residence in the UK does not necessarily confer full citizenship rights. The open-door policy of Victorian England involved only a right of entry. Restrictions on this right were first established by the Aliens Act 1905, which followed the Jewish immigrations of the late nineteenth century and the growth and exploitation of racism. The British Nationality Act 1948 in effect conferred citizenship rights on all members of the British Commonwealth and allowed free right of entry. As a result of successive Commonwealth Immigrants Acts in 1962, 1968 and 1971, rights of entry are now confined to 'patrials', this is those with parents or grandparents who were born, registered or naturalised in Britain. The 1971 Act also allows detention without trial and deportation without judicial appeal in cases of suspected illegal immigration. In 1980, the numbers detained or removed totalled 1,577.

Citizenship is now defined by the British Nationality Act 1981, which removes the right of Commonwealth citizens settled in the UK to register as citizens. Aliens may apply for naturalisation after five years' residence, but in these cases, as well as those of applications for registration by Commonwealth citizens, the decision is made by the Home Secretary without right of appeal. Regulations under this Act maintain a long-standing sexist practice in that, although men can transmit their British citizenship to a spouse on marriage, women cannot, so that the foreign husbands of female British citizens have no automatic rights either to entry or citizenship.

The failure to incorporate democratic principles to the full, the continued existence of a nationalist challenge to Westminster control, and the existence of racist and sexist laws regulating entry and citizenship are problematic features of the legal structure of the British state. They generate political conflict, which lies outside the immediate capital-labour relation, although in many respects it is conditioned by the economic crisis and its uneven impact throughout British society.

9.4 State Security: Subversion, Public Disorder and Emergencies

9.4.1 The Protection of the State Apparatus and Counter-Subversion

The protection of the machinery of state and the maintenance of the effectiveness and loyalty of key personnel and organisations within it is required. The bureaucratic organisation of the civil service with its career structure, security of employment and pension scheme is designed to maintain a commitment to the service. Recruitment operates to ensure a supply of upper-middle-class entrants with moderate views, while long-standing departmental policies also ensure that advice from civil servants remains within the prevailing consensus. In addition, the tradition of secrecy operates to insulate the state bureaucracy from popular pressure.

The loyalty of the police and the armed forces is particularly important to the survival of the state. The Police Act 1919, which followed the police strikes of that and the previous year, made it an offence to attempt to cause disaffection in the police, forbade police membership of trade unions, and set up the Police Federation as a representative body. The separation of the police from the public is reinforced by segregated housing for many police officers and cadets, and the separation of most police training from the normal education system. Similar forms of isolation are imposed on the armed forces through military housing policies, the Queen's Regulations, the Incitement to Mutiny Act 1797 and the Incitement to Disaffection Act 1934, which makes the possession of any document which *might* cause disaffection an offence. The absence of 'citizens in uniform' since the end of conscription also reinforces the separation of the armed forces from civilian life.

The task of protecting the state from subversive activities is concentrated in the hands of the Special Branch and MI5. The Special Branch was founded in 1883. In 1984 the total number of police in the Special Branch in the UK was about 1,800, compared with about 250 in 1960. Its current duties include guarding VIPs, surveillance of entrants into the country, embassy security, monitoring of aliens and the enforcement of Official Secrets Acts, as well as surveillance of subversive individuals and organisations. It keeps files on a wide range of possible 'subversives', obtaining information from publications, court records, surveillance of demonstrations, petitions, employers, educational institutions, members of the public and informers. Other methods, such as opening mail, telephone tapping and bugging, are also used to an unknown extent.

MI5 (also known as DI5 or the Security Service) carries out counter-espionage activity, but in the course of this also deals with anti-subversion. It was founded in 1909 and employs about 2,000 people. Little official information is available on its history, budget and staffing levels, and it does not operate under explicit statutory authority. Its routine duties include 'positive vetting', or security clearance, of those in positions of state authority, and security in firms undertaking defence contracts. It liaises with the Special Branch, which normally carries out its prosecutions. It is believed to hold files on about half a million people including active trade unionists, members of the peace movement, radical journalists, lawyers and teachers, as well as members of far left and sometimes far right groups.

A feature of the practice of both the Special Branch and MI5 is that the very broad definition of subversion they employ includes all manner of perfectly legal, political and industrial activity. Radical movements of the left have been a prime target for these organisations throughout the present century, along with the activities of Irish nationalists.

9.4.2 Public Disorder and Major Strikes: The Police and the Armed Forces

The security of the state also involves public order, that is the control of public meetings, demonstrations and processions. Breakdowns in public order face the authorities with a dilemma; failure to restore order rapidly may be interpreted as weakness, whereas the use of an excessive level of force may focus resentment on the authorities themselves. Since the Peterloo massacre of 1819, the authorities have attempted to use the army for public-order policing only as a last resort. Consequently, the police have gained extensive experience of crowd control. Until 1936 no general legal regulation of public assemblies existed except through the Riot Acts, and the common law offences of riot, affray, unlawful assembly, breach of the peace and obstruction. The Public Order Act 1936 was a response to the disorders associated with the fascist Blackshirts. It banned uniforms, drilling and military training, and allowed the police to re-route marches and to ban processions. Additional powers exist in London to control the route of marches in the vicinity of Parliament.

The use of reinforcements from other police forces has long been a feature of public-order policing, but in recent years it has been put on a more systematic basis. Most police forces now provide riot training and equipment for officers, who are then assigned to Police Support Units (PSUs) to be used as reinforcements where necessary. In the miners' strike of 1984/5 about 14,000 police were deployed in this way; they were co-ordinated by a 'National Reporting Centre', run by the President of the Association of Chief Police Officers. This strike also involved tactics not previously employed in Britain in the post-war period in an industrial dispute: for example, snatch squads; checkpoints on roads, at which pickets and others are refused entry to an area; and turning back pickets some 200 miles from their destination. The use of massive concentrations of police has been accompanied by a number of judicial measures, including special sittings of courts, the use of serious charges such as riot and affray, and restrictive bail conditions.

Threats to public order have also arisen through rioting. The most intense and widespread post-war riots occurred in 1981, especially in Brixton, Southall, Liverpool and Manchester. The most obvious immediate and focused grievance of many of the rioters was the pattern of policing. The Scarman Report into the Brixton riots subsequently made numerous recommendations for changes in police practice. More generally, lack of jobs, poor housing, falling living standards, lack of political incorporation, and a population made up of groups mainly located in the reserve army of labour are key factors in causing this form of urban violence.

A feature of public-order policing of all kinds since the 1960s has been the use of new kinds of protective equipment and weapons. These have been deployed in response to the growing social disorders associated with the intensification of the economic crisis. Riot shields were first used in Great Britain in 1977, while CS gas was first used in 1981. Other weapons have been introduced in Northern Ireland, including water cannon (1968), rubber bullets (1970) and plastic bullets (1975). These weapons are now available on the mainland, although not all forces are eager to obtain them.

In recent years, the army has once more begun to play a prominent internal role in the UK. In the aftermath of the 1972 miners' strike, provision for police-army co-operation was expanded. Since the mid-nineteenth century the army has had the right to come to the aid of the 'civil power' on the written request of a magistrate. From 1973, however, the police themselves may request military aid and the decision rests with the Home Secretary. The army can also be used for disaster aid and for maintaining essential services cut off by strikes.

Closely related to the question of public order has been the concern with the threat posed by industrial conflict. The police have always been used in industrial disputes to support the interests of employers, or of workers acting in opposition to strikes. In addition, governments have made detailed contingency plans for dealing with major strikes and have often attempted to use state power to destroy the solidarity and effectiveness of militant unions. Recent governments have made frequent use of the Emergency Powers Act 1920, which allows a declaration of a state of emergency when it appears that 'the essential services of the country are threatened'. The willingness to employ troops in industrial disputes has recently been demonstrated in the Glasgow dustmen's strike of 1975, the firemen's strike in 1978, and the ambulance drivers' dispute in 1979.

Police-army co-operation has also been extended in dealing with political violence, most obviously in Northern Ireland. The current conflict has seen the major involvement of the army in a policing role, especially in areas where the RUC could not operate, as well as the widespread use of house-to-house searches by the army in the early 1970s. The use of emergency legislation, the emphasis on the collection of 'low-grade intelligence', the employment of psychological warfare ('psyops'), particularly through the management of news, and the close co-ordination of police, army and civil administration are in line with current military planning on internal subversion. So far as the rest of the UK is concerned, military involvement is more restricted, although planning for 'civil defence' in the event of war envisages a major increase in military regulation of civilian life.

9.5 Policing in the UK

9.5.1 The Development of Policing and the Centralisation of State Control

A full-time uniformed police force was first established by the

Metropolitan Police Act 1829. Prior to this, the normal mode of law enforcement was organised through JPs using constables and watchmen. The establishment of a nationwide system of policing was not completed until 1890, and at times it encountered considerable resistance. The avowed ethos of the founders of the Metropolitan police stressed crime prevention, the duty to protect and help the public, and the desirability of an unarmed force. In the late nineteenth century, however, more emphasis was put on criminal detection, through the establishment of the first CID in London in 1878, the growth of criminal records and the use of fingerprints.

Boroughs controlled their forces through 'Watch Committees', although different arrangements existed in the counties and in Scotland. Administrative uniformity was not finally established until 1929. The role of Chief Constable had been enhanced by the reduction in the number of forces from 239 in 1857 to 52 by 1981. The present system of control dates from the Police Act 1964, which abolished Watch Committees and set up local Police Authorities to ensure the 'maintenance of an adequate and efficient police force'. In England and Wales, Police Authorities are made up of two-thirds local councillors and one-third magistrates; in Scotland, the forces are responsible to regional councils; and in Northern Ireland, since 1970, the Home Secretary appoints the Police Authority. The Home Secretary himself is the Police Authority for the Metropolitan Police.

Police Authorities select Chief Constables, although the Home Secretary can veto the appointment; they receive an Annual Report though there are no legal stipulations as to its contents; and they can call for special reports on particular problems, though only a minority of authorities do so. Local authorities may refuse to provide finance — they pay 50 per cent and the Home Office provides the rest — but the police may still spend any money required by regulations, such as wages, which make up over 70 per cent of total costs. Chief Constables argue that they alone are responsible for 'operational' decisions and strongly resist attempts by Police Authorities to define guidelines on forms of policing and priorities in law enforcement.

Considerable control over policing is now exercised by the Home Office Police Department and Inspectorate through the threat of withholding finance, the veto on senior appointments, the making of regulations, the issuing of circulars, and the power to appoint inquiries and to call for special reports. The Home Office also provides central services for the various forces such as the Police

National Computer, the Police Scientific Development Branch and the Police College. The control exercised by the Home Office is not subject to detailed parliamentary scrutiny, because of the fiction that the various police forces are independent.

9.5.2 Policing and the End of the Long Boom

From 1961 to 1981, the police force grew from 88,000 to 140,000 and civilian back-up rose from 12,000 to over 40,000. The police can also call on over 20,000 unpaid members of the Special Constabulary. The cost of policing and other expenditure involved in law enforcement has increased, due both to increases in numbers and in pay. The proportion of public spending on law and order has risen from 3.7 per cent in 1978 to 4.5 per cent in 1983–4.

Considerable changes in the organisation and practice of policing have taken place in recent years. New forms of centralisation and specialisation have occurred with the formation of Regional Crime Squads (1964), the Drugs Intelligence Unit and the National Immigration Intelligence Unit (both 1973). Record-keeping has been reorganised with the development of the Criminal Records Office, which contains some 3.5 million files. Many forces now use computers for maintaining records, collating information and monitoring the disposition of police resources through 'Command and Control' systems. These decrease the time taken to respond to incidents and increase information available to those on the spot. The use of personal radios and of motorised patrols has also become standard.

Another significant trend in modern policing has been the growth of specialised units, exemplified by the Special Patrol Group (SPG) in the Metropolitan Police. This was originally established for anti-crime work in 1965, based on the model of the New York Tactical Force. Following a decision by the government in 1972 not to set up a 'third force' between the police and the army to deal with serious threats to public order, the SPG, and similar units in other forces, were encouraged to take on this role. These units are used for public-order policing, anti-terrorism and to provide reinforcements for 'saturation policing'.

Ordinary uniformed policing has also changed. Preventive foot patrols ('the beat') have, in many cases, been replaced by motorised police, who undertake 'reactive' or 'fire brigade' policing. 'Policing by consent', to the extent that it ever existed, has broken down. In particular, 'saturation policing', whereby large numbers of police are deployed for a period in a given area, has created antagonism. The practice of 'stop and search' has also been viewed as a form of police aggression. Evidence of racism in policing and in the enforcement of immigration laws exists. The procedure for dealing with complaints against the police has also caused controversy.

The response of the state to these challenges to the pattern of policing is most clearly articulated in the Scarman Report, which makes a range of proposals, many of which have been taken up in varying degrees. In particular, increased emphasis on 'community relations' and 'liaison' schemes, along with some changes in training, have taken place. At the same time, however, the police are continuing to employ specialist units and to make greater use of weapons and protective equipment, so that in effect a two-stage pattern of policing is developing with a combination of 'community policing' at street level, when conditions are relatively peaceful, and a rapid and substantial deployment of specialist units, when any collective threat to order or security arises.

A final feature of policing during the present economic crisis has been growing political intervention and politicisation of the police. The Association of Chief Police Officers and the Police Federation have made considerable efforts to promote a 'law and order' ideology, while individual Chief Constables have used public platforms to promote their (usually) right-wing views on law and order and other subjects. In particular, they have publicly opposed attempts to secure greater dramatic control of police forces by elected representatives on Police Authorities.

9.6 Crime, Capitalism and Inequality

9.6.1 *Crime, Victims and Criminals under Capitalism*

The body of criminal law provides the broad policy framework for the policing of crime. The law not only defines the activities which are to be criminalised, it also regulates the sentences for particular offences. The major classes of offence are violence, sexual offences, property offences and motoring offences. The system of criminal justice involving the reporting of offences, and the apprehension and trial of offenders, is a complex process. First, offences have to be reported to the police or other relevant authority for investigation. Frequently offences are not reported because there is no victim, or the victim does not wish to complain. The gap between recorded and unrecorded crime varies with the offence. For example, the proportion of various offences actually recorded in the crime figures is 8 per cent for vandalism, 11 per cent for robbery, 26 per cent for sexual offences and 33 per cent for thefts from a dwelling. The zeal with which particular laws are enforced and cautions or charges are administered is subject to policy decisions made by Chief Constables and, for some offences, by the Director of Public Prosecutions. Drives against particular crimes can result in a dramatic increase in the number of offences recorded and offenders prosecuted. Vague offences such as obstruction, and 'sus' (until its abolition in 1981), can be enforced with varying degrees of rigour, while laws that have fallen out of use can be reactivated. Criminal statistics therefore need to be treated with care, although they do show a considerable increase in almost all types of crime in the present century, particularly in recent years. The total number of recorded indictable offences rose by nearly 300 per cent in the period 1960–79, although over 80 per cent concerned relatively minor non-violent property offences. Clear-up rates also vary substantially between different categories of crime, from about 75 per cent for violence and sexual offences to below 30 per cent for malicious or criminal damage.

The pattern of crime in society is strongly influenced by the social impact of the process of accumulation, by the class structure, and by ethnic and gender differences. Class structure influences the kinds of offence that individuals are likely to commit, both through a resort to certain traditional kinds of crime and because the opportunities for criminal behaviour differ for members of different classes. Members of the working class are particularly prone to criminal behaviour of a kind which normally attracts the attention of the police, since it involves individual victims who are likely to complain. Working-class offences also constitute what are usually considered 'real' crimes, rather than technical violations. For example, employees have often sought to supplement their income by petty theft and various 'fiddles', whereas forms of street crime have a long association with working-class areas that lack stable employment opportunities. Working-class youths are particularly likely to engage sporadically and sometimes impulsively in various forms of petty crime, as are members of ethnic minorities, especially where they suffer exclusion from employment. About 30 per cent of all recorded indictable offences are committed by juveniles, and they account for a disproportionate number of thefts, burglaries and acts of criminal damage.

The crimes of the middle and upper classes are rather different. Minor theft from employers is common amongst white-collar employees, particularly in the form of 'fiddled' expenses. Major crimes for gain are of two kinds. A small number of 'professional' criminals undertake organised, systematic and continuous criminal activities in a variety of forms, such as robbery, burglary, fraud and handling stolen goods. Whereas these criminals come mainly from working-class backgrounds, the class background of those engaged in large-scale fraud and, to a lesser extent, handling stolen goods, is likely to be middle or upper class. Organisations also systematically violate laws, usually on the basis of cost calculations that indicate a profit greater than the size or risk of penalty.

A major factor in understanding the pattern of crime is gender. Overall, the conviction rate of women for indictable offences is only 17.8 per cent of that for men. The only offence for which the female rate in any way approaches that of men is shop-lifting (80.2 per cent). The reasons are complex and not fully understood. Girls are more subject to the control of the family-household than boys; they therefore have fewer opportunities for crime. Women generally are less likely to meet others engaged in criminal behaviour and they are also excluded from crime by men. Over the post-war period, the proportion of women convicted for indictable offences against property, though not for violence, has risen. This *may* reflect women's greater role in wage labour and their exposure to the values of the market.

An important influence on the pattern of property crime is the process of accumulation. This increases the available surplus and thus the opportunities for illegal acquisition of property. The mass consumption of valuable, durable and portable consumer goods has been important in creating the motive and the opportunity for crime. The development of the forces of production is also significant. The technologies employed by criminals and by those guarding property exert a reciprocal influence on one another. A huge private industry has grown up to protect valuable property, while criminal techniques and organisation have been adapted to meet the problems this poses.

Except in cases where people are caught in the act or are known to the victim, the apprehension of criminals and the accumulation of sufficient evidence to secure a conviction poses enormous difficulties. Criminal detection, which is largely the work of the CID, tends to be concentrated on what are seen as serious offences. Most detection involves the use of informants, and the CID develops extensive personal links with those involved with criminal activities. Although this is an effective technique, it also creates the opportunity for corrupt practices involving bribes, shares in the proceeds of rewards and police involvement in the planning and execution of crime.

The likelihood of being a victim of crime is influenced by a variety of factors, which relate closely to the pattern of inequality produced by the CMP. Residents of inner-city areas and those who live in flats are more likely to be burgled than others. Working-class people are also more likely to live in areas where criminal damage and minor street disturbances are relatively common. Members of ethnic minorities, particularly if they live in inner-city areas, are particularly subject to unprovoked violence. The fear of crime is also differentially distributed. This is greatest amongst women, and for both sexes it increases with age. The experienced seriousness of being a victim of crime also varies, with the highest impact being found amongst women, especially those living alone.

The middle and upper classes tend to be subject to a different pattern of crime. Middle and upper-class residential areas have less street crime and less casual burglary, although they may be more subject to organised or professional criminal attempts to acquire their property, since they have more valuable possessions. To some degree, they are less likely to suffer permanent material damage, because they are more likely to hold effective insurance. The same is true of firms and other organisations which may be victims of large-scale and organised crimes.

The pattern of victimisation and the distribution of fear of crime are also affected by the pattern of policing. Those crimes that create most distress amongst their victims fall heavily upon members of the working class. These crimes are most likely to increase during periods of economic crisis, which decreases the opportunity for continuous access to wage labour. They are also crimes that tend to be given a low priority in policing policies.

9.6.2 *Police Powers, Court Procedure and Sentencing*

The system of criminal justice involves the procedures for dealing with offenders. The pre-trial process covers a series of powers possessed by the police to search, arrest, detain and interrogate suspects, to gain access to premises, documents, etc., and to bring charges. Until the Police and Criminal Evidence Act 1984, a general power to stop and search only existed for those suspected of certain offences such as unauthorised possession of drugs, although in a few localities wider powers were available. Premises could be entered to prevent or stop a breach of the peace or to carry out an arrest, in which case a search could also take place. Otherwise searches required a warrant. A person could only be arrested in relation to a specified arrestable offence, and the individual had to be brought before a court 'as soon as is practicable'.

The Police and Criminal Evidence Act 1984 increased powers to stop and search and to set up road blocks in order to search vehicles and their occupants. Private homes may now be searched for evidence, even though the occupants are not suspected of any offence. Refusing to give a name and address to the police has been made an arrestable offence. With the permission of a magistrate sitting in private, suspects can be detained without charge for up to four days and access to a lawyer can be withheld for 36 hours. Some of these changes were anticipated in Scotland by the Criminal Justice (Scotland) Act 1980. Amongst other provisions, this allowed police to detain people for six hours for questioning. This provision has been used about 25,000 times each year. The Act also allowed those in custody to be refused access to a lawyer for 36 hours.

The granting or refusal of bail is an important part of the pre-trial process. Bail may be granted by the police or on an appearance before the magistrates. Although the Bail Act 1976 was intended to liberalise the granting of bail, there is little evidence since of substantial change. The Judges Rules regulate the process of interrogation, which is supposed to be conducted without violence, threat or inducement. Once a charge has been brought, further interrogation is not allowed.

Considerable abuse of the procedures regulating the pre-trial process takes place, because people are unaware of the limitations on rights to search and arrest; because the police routinely violate Judges Rules, although this does not automatically invalidate the consequent prosecution; and because it is extremely difficult to obtain convincing evidence of malpractice. In addition, not all suspects are covered by these arrangements. Changes in the law following the Birmingham pub bombings led to the Prevention of Terrorism Acts 1974 and 1976, which allow detention for up to five days, and a form of internal exile in which a British citizen living in Northern Ireland can be banned from the rest of the UK without trial or judicial appeal. In the seven years after 1974, this provision was used 272 times. Detention without a finding of guilt is also involved in the refusal of bail, and through provisions under which about 4,000 people each year are detained under the 1971 Immigration Act.

The public face of criminal justice is the criminal trial. The organisation of the court system and the trial procedure, with its archaic formalities in the higher courts, bears a strong imprint from the past. The dual system of criminal justice involving lay magistrates, who deal mainly with summary or non-indictable offences, and the higher courts, dealing with more serious offences, was established very early. The vast majority of criminal cases are dealt with in magistrates courts. During the present century the number of offences that can be dealt with in this way has been increased. Other criminal cases are dealt with in Crown Courts or, where the prosecution decides, in the central criminal courts. Juvenile courts exist for defendants aged 10–17, although in serious cases the offence is tried in a Crown Court. In Scotland, however, juveniles are now dealt with in 'children's hearings' rather than courts. A minority of those apprehended are not taken to court, but either 'cautioned' or issued with a 'fixed penalty' notice. For indictable offences, about 84 per cent of alleged offenders are charged and the remainder cautioned. For summary offences, the number cautioned is about 10 per cent. Of motoring offences, about 22 per cent involved court proceedings, with 74 per cent of the guilty receiving a 'fixed penalty notice' and the remainder a written warning.

Those charged with criminal offences are not always legally represented. Under the Poor Prisoners Defence Act 1903, a limited scheme of legal representation was first instituted. The present system of legal aid dates from the Legal Aid and Advice Act 1949. However, nearly a third of those tried in magistrates courts are unrepresented, and magistrates use their absolute discretion to deny legal aid, in some areas, to up to 75 per cent of those being tried for non-indictable offences. The quality of legal advice is also variable. In the vast majority of contested criminal trials in the higher courts, the client does not see his/her barrister until the morning of the trial, whereas defendants with sufficient funds can afford to buy better legal advice and representation.

Although trial by jury figures strongly in the symbolism of the legal system, in fact only about 2 per cent of criminal trials are decided in this way, since in most cases the defendant pleads guilty and/or is tried in a magistrates court without a jury. Very strong pressures are put on defendants to plead guilty. This process starts in the police station, where granting of bail may be used as an inducement. It continues in the process of interrogation, where the police may undertake to bring lesser charges. Immediately before or during a trial, 'plea bargaining' may also take place with consultation between prosecution and defence lawyers, sometimes with the judge also present. It is generally understood that a plea of guilty will result in a lesser sentence.

The language, procedures and ritual of the courts and the symbolic physical isolation of the defendant seem designed to baffle and overawe him or her. The defendant receives some protection from the rules of evidence and the requirement to prove the case, in criminal trials, beyond a reasonable doubt. The jury is also often an important safeguard, although the practice of 'jury vetting' is widespread. Officially this can only take place in exceptional circumstances. However, summoning officers frequently perform their own informal vetting, reducing the representation of those of low status, such as women or ethnic minorities. In addition, since 1967, majority verdicts with up to two dissenting are permitted. In Northern Ireland, under the Emergency Provision Act 1973, in the so-called 'Diplock' courts, jury trial has been abolished for 'scheduled offences', and the rules governing the admissibility of evidence have been substantially relaxed.

Apart from regulating the trial procedure, the main function of judges is to sentence those found guilty, as most offences do not carry mandatory sentences. The present century has seen a decline in the proportion of offenders imprisoned, the abolition of some forms of punishment such as whipping and hard labour, and the development of new means of dealing with offenders, such as probation (from 1908), detention centres (from 1948), suspended sentences (from 1968), and community service orders (from 1973 in England and Wales, and 1977 in Scotland). Arrangements for dealing with offenders reflect ambivalence about whether they should be seen as wicked, and punished, or as sick or misguided, and treated. The 'treatment' model has been particularly influential in juvenile crime, where as far back as the Children and Young Persons Act 1933, the 'welfare of the child' was to be taken into consideration. This tendency reached its zenith in the Children and Young Persons Act 1969, which allowed social workers, not magistrates, to decide on the fate of juvenile offenders. However, it is also influential in other areas of the penal system that employ welfare professionals, such as the probation service. Although the 'treatment model' might appear as an advance on a purely deterrent or punitive approach, it can also be used to justify sentences of indeterminate length and the use of medication to control behaviour. There is little evidence to suggest that the aims of a treatment model — to 'cure' the offender — are achieved by any of the innovations in penal policy that have taken place in the post-war period. The present government, however, has adopted a law and order rhetoric sharply critical of the treatment model, and the Home Secretary has recommended increased, or high, mandatory penalties for serious crimes of violence and firearms offences, as well as a tightening of the rules for parole.

9.6.3 The Prison System

In the Elizabethan period, local lock-ups known as Bridewells existed, and later in some areas 'houses of industry' and 'houses of correction' were established. However, the prison system developed its present form in the period in which industrial capitalism was being established in Britain. For most of the eighteenth century, transportation rather than imprisonment was the main means of excluding offenders from society. The death penalty was used for a wide range of offences ('the bloody code'), and various bodily punishments were also widely employed, such as whipping and the pillory. The use of imprisonment increased substantially after 1775, when transportation to the US had to be stopped as a result of the American War of Independence. Prisons at this time were run by private contractors for fees. Like the mental hospitals, they were the subject of a reform movement. This sought to impose an organised and systematic regime and to dispense with frequent public executions, which appeared unable to stem the rise in crime and which also often led to public disorder and attacks on the legitimacy of the legal system. The Penitentiary Act 1779 allowed for two penitentiaries to be established in London, based on daytime labour and solitary confinement at nights. These prisons were not built, but similar schemes were undertaken elsewhere. The strict regimes proved hard to sustain and in many cases degenerated. From 1818 onwards, various counties began to introduce hard-labour regimes in their prisons, using the newly invented treadwheel. Bread-and-water diets and a rule of strict silence became widely used.

Throughout the first four decades of the nineteenth century crime continued to increase, putting pressure on existing prisons. Although the Gaols Act 1823 gave the Home Office the power to advise on prison arrangements, a national pattern of imprisonment did not develop until after the opening of Pentonville in 1842. This established a harsh disciplinary system based on solitary confinement for the first eighteen months of a sentence, intense supervision, unvarying routine, silence, work and daily attendance at chapel, with punishment by confinement in darkness, or the birch or the cat, for breaches of rules. This regime was designed to reform the inmates and it was widely emulated. After 1853, when transportation was suspended, prison sentences were substantially increased in length from the previous maximum of three years, and imprisonment became in effect a punishment, although the rhetoric of rehabilitation was retained. By 1877 a centralised prison system existed, and all prisons were run by the Home Office. Transportation had ended and imprisonment had become the standard punishment for all crimes except murder. The Victorian prisons, usually built prominently open to public view in the cities from which their inmates came, symbolised the capacity of the state to enforce the law in the new conditions of industrial capitalism.

The official aims of the prison system, even today, refer to the use of 'training and treatment' to encourage the prisoner on discharge to lead a 'good and useful life'. The service is run by the Prison Department of the Home Office. In 1979, in England and Wales, there were 24 local prisons and 41 training prisons, nine of these being 'open' prisons. Prisons are run by Governors who are appointed by the Home Office; in most cases, however, the internal organisation of the prison and the treatment of inmates is largely controlled by the prison officers, who have strongly and successfully challenged the authority of Governors, particularly in the last decade. In this period, the number of prison employees has increased by 45 per cent, to reach a total of nearly 27,000 by 1981.

Committals to prison each year have been rising, due to the increasing numbers who are found guilty of offences and to the increased proportion of those committing a particular offence who receive a custodial sentence. The numbers sent to prison as a result of convictions increased by 46 per cent in the period 1971–81. There has also been a doubling of those imprisoned as a result of failure to pay fines. As a result of these changes, as well as an increase of about 50 per cent in the length of prison sentences, and because of an increase since 1961 of over 200 per cent in the numbers being held on remand, the prison population rose by 54 per cent from 1961 to 1981, to reach a figure of 50,300. In recent years, various attempts have been made to reduce the prison population, including community service orders, suspended sentences and parole. The overall impact of these schemes has been insufficient to prevent the continued rise in the prison population. However, in mid-1984 the minimum length of sentence qualifying for parole was reduced, which should increase the numbers released on parole from 4,000 to 6,000.

Most adults are held in local prisons or 'closed' training prisons. Only about 9 per cent of adults are held in 'open' prisons, although 30 per cent of borstal places are open. Prisoners are categorised according to the security risk they appear to offer, and seven prisons are now designated as high-security establishments. About 60 per cent of all prisoners have committed non-violent petty offences, and only 16 per cent have committed crimes of violence. Many have experienced prison before. In Scotland, for example, 68 per cent of prisoners have been in prison before, and about a quarter have served six or more previous sentences. At the other extreme are prisoners serving life sentences. In 1979 these numbered 1,881, including 54 women. However, most prisoners receive relatively short sentences. In 1979, 43 per cent of men received sentences of six months or less, with remission of one-third, (one-half in Northern Ireland) for good behaviour. Those convicted of serious offences are 85 per cent male, living mainly in urban areas, and are disproportion-ately young and poorly educated. About 40 per cent are unemployed and about 30 per cent are black. The Criminal Justice Act 1982 restores full powers to imprison the young and reduces the age-limit from 17 to 15. Blacks, the young and the unemployed appear increas-ingly to be viewed as a threat by the judiciary during the present crisis, and the willingness of the courts to imprison them has grown. Although the number of women in prison has increased, courts are still reluctant to imprison women because of the effect on their repro-ductive roles, and they are more likely than men to be given non-custodial sentences.

Most prisoners are held in prisons built in the nineteenth century. Conditions are poor, with overcrowding, minimal facilities for sanitation, education, exercise and work, and many prisoners spend most of their time locked in their cells. Due to overcrowding in 1980, army camps had to be used to house prisoners. The maintenance of order within prisons has become more difficult. Riots and demonst-rations have occurred and organisations like PROP have gained support amongst some prisoners. Since 1978 collective resistance to prison discipline has been countered by the use of MUFTI (minimum use of force tactical intervention) squads, who were responsible for the suppression of the 1979 riots at Hull and

Wormwood Scrubs. Individual resistance to prison discipline is dealt with by the Governor, or in more serious cases by Boards of Visitors. Although sentences can be effectively and substantially increased by the withdrawal of remission, the normal procedural rules for criminal trials do not apply. Drugs are also used to control prisoners. In recent years, the Home Office has also experimented with a punishment regime for recalcitrant prisoners including the 'cages' and the use of Control Units, though the latter have now been abandoned. Imprisonment clearly has little rehabilitative effect and indeed the entire system of criminal justice has only a minor effect on the pattern and extent of crime, which is a complex product of general social conditions.

The sequence of detection, trial and the disposal of offenders is only partly concerned with individual offences and those who commit them. Criminal justice is certainly used to impose discipline on the working class and to criminalise forms of working-class industrial and political activity, especially in periods of crisis and social breakdown. However, the impact of criminal justice is not simply to directly reinforce the maintenance of internal security; it also plays a major role in reinforcing the dominant ideology and maintaining legitimacy (see section 9.8).

9.7 Individual Rights involving the State, Personal Security, Capital and Gender

The law is extensively involved in regulating individual rights in relation to the state, to other individuals, to the operation of private business, to sex and gender, and to the family-household. These rights and obligations are enforced through the ordinary civil law process and the use of tribunals. Civil cases are usually conducted without a jury and proof has to be 'on the balance of probabilities'. Cases in tribunals are normally decided by a panel, often containing a representative of business and the trade unions, and an 'independent' chair who is often a lawyer. Procedure is relatively informal and decisions are often not bound by precedent. Only a small proportion of civil cases reach court or tribunal. Many of those wronged are unaware of possible legal redress or lack access to legal advice and the resources to risk legal action. Many cases are settled out of court.

Individual rights frequently involve the relationship people have to various parts of the state apparatus. These rights are often enforced through tribunals dealing with disputes over National Insurance, supplementary benefits, employment, rates, rent and immigration. The actions of those who work in the state sector are governed by the principle of *ultra vires*, which restricts public bodies to those actions explicitly laid down by law. Victims of maladminist-ration by the civil service, the health service and local government may pursue their complaints through three 'ombudsmen', the Parliamentary Commissioner (for maladministration), the Health Service Commissioner and the Commissioners for Local Administ-ration. In 1982, these received in total 5,052 complaints, of which 7.7 per cent were upheld. Individuals may also complain about the police. Since 1977 the reports of internal inquiries into complaints against the police have been received by the Police Complaints Board, but in only 0.2 per cent of all cases is the internal police inquiry challenged.

The law provides some redress for a person whose property, body, prospects or reputation are damaged. Most physical injury claims arise from vehicle accidents. Around 90 per cent of these are settled by insurance and only about 1 per cent reach court. Where claims do reach court, legal costs reach about 85 per cent of the value of compensation. The necessity to prove negligence means that those injured by accident have no legal redress. The Small Claims courts (now largely defunct) were set up in 1973 to provide a cheap and informal procedure for consumers. In practice, most of the cases heard in them involve firms bringing cases for non-payment of debts. Although legal aid for civil cases in the courts (but not tribunals) is available, because of the risks of legal action few individuals claim it. Claims of under £500 are now settled by the Arbitration Procedure of the County courts, for which there is no legal aid. The main work of the County courts involves complaints over economic transactions of various kinds. In 1982, out of a total of 2.12 million proceedings started, 68.3 per cent involved the sale of goods, and 18 per cent involved debt proceedings of various kinds, including hire purchase.

The law regulates the operation of business through the impos-ition of limitations on contract. In labour law, this involves the expansion of employee rights, which are mainly enforceable through tribunals. Some protection is also offered to consumers through laws concerning the quality of products, fair trading, and the regulation of monopoly and restrictive practices. The obligations of landlords and tenants have also been subject to extensive legal regulation. A noticeable feature of these laws is the reluctance of enforcement agencies to prosecute, and the tendency for judges to interpret the law in a way favourable to business and landlord interests.

The law also regulates sexual relations, gender and the family-household form. In most capitalist societies, a nuclear family structure exists along with the domestic and economic subordination of women, and the law is normally used to reinforce this pattern and to discourage alternatives. In the UK, heterosexual relations are subject to an age of consent (16 at present), while male homosexual relations are not permitted until the age of 21 — though Northern Ireland and the armed forces are excluded from this provision. The main form of legal regulation is marriage. Marriage is not a contract of the normal kind, where the partners negotiate terms, but a defined legal status which is voluntarily adopted. The strict legal regulation of marriage dates from an Act of 1753, though the present system of registration was not adopted until 1836. Marriage is easy to enter, but it is more difficult to leave, although the law governing divorce has been progressively relaxed since 1857, when it was first allowed at all without an Act of Parliament. In fact, under the Divorce Law Reform Act 1969, divorce is little more than a formality in uncontested cases where the marriage has broken down. The law associates marriage with other legal rights and obligations, including property ownership, inheritance, maintenance, taxation, welfare benefits and citizenship. Women still do not have equal rights with regard to maintenance, taxation, welfare benefits and the conferment of citizenship on a foreign-born spouse. The Domestic Violence Act 1976 and the Sexual Offences (Amendment) Act 1976 improve the legal position of women who are subject to male violence, though the reluctance of the police to intervene and the procedures adopted in the investigation of rape vitiate the effectiveness of these laws.

The legal rights of individuals are difficult to enforce where the state acts outside the law, particularly in the case of the police. Rights involving the security of the individual's person and property are difficult and expensive to enforce, particularly for those who are poor. To some extent a dual system of civil justice exists, between tribunals, dealing mainly with issues involving the working class, and the civil courts, which mainly cater for the middle and upper classes.

9.8 The Law and the Capitalist System

This final section of the chapter briefly reviews the impact of the legal system on accumulation, legitimation and security in the UK. The law has played a major role in creating the conditions necessary for accumulation through contract, legal personality, legal certainty and through commodification, while territoriality and legal uniformity have aided the creation of a secure national market.

The law has played a role in relation to particular capitals in industrial conflict, where both the police and the courts have been used to support employers. With the important exception of private security firms, law enforcement has been monopolised by the state with few opportunities for private capital, except in the supply of equipment. The impact on labour efficiency is mixed. Legal constraints on the exploitation of labour exist. However, the law reinforces labour discipline by deterring or penalising those who seek to reduce dependence on wage labour by the illegal acquisition of property. The law supports labour and generational reproduction through the legal regulation of sexuality, marriage and the family-household.

A major role in legitimation is played by the existence of a widespread belief in the positive value of obeying the law, that is, of legality. This long predates the development of industrial capitalism, and has its origins in the judicial functions of Kingship ('the just ruler') and the notion of the central power as a guarantor of justice. Support for legality rests on the belief in justice based on equality before the law. The legal regulation of the actions of the state is an important factor in the acceptance of its authority, and legal rights of citizens not only involve a form of protection by the state, they also support the notion of individualism central to the dominant ideology.

The legal system also clarifies the boundaries of legitimate behaviour. Criminal law enforcement is not only the occasion for dealing with offenders and for demonstrating the power of the state, but for publicising the limits of acceptable behaviour and for symbolically expressing the moral outrage of the law-abiding. The legal system also influences political discourse. Before the development of the mass media and the creation of a national political culture, the law and its administration was the major popular encounter with state power. The language of law has entered into political discourse in the form of disputes about rights, duties, justice, etc. The pluralist notion of the state as a neutral arbiter also owes something to legal imagery. Legal processes are also the occasion for rituals symbolising the awesome power and historical continuity of the state and its repressive apparatuses.

Finally, and pre-eminently, law and order policy plays a major role in internal security. Although all individuals and legally constituted bodies receive the protection of the law, a particularly high level of security is provided for key institutions such as the state apparatus, capitalist enterprises and those who perform the functions of capital. The degree of internal security which is achieved varies with the extent of the threat and the capacity of the state to deal with it. Threats to security are continuously generated by the operation of capitalism. The function of state policy is not to eliminate them, but to contain them at an acceptable level and to prevent the development of a situation which threatens accumulation and the continued existence of the capitalist class. The state also makes provision for the maintenance of security under those conditions where the threat to it increases rapidly in scope and intensity. The activation of various contingency plans, the use of existing 'emergency' legislation, the use of troops to 'aid the civil power', the massive expansion of the 'Special Constabulary', and internment without trial on the basis of existing security files are all likely responses in the face of an increased threat to security, especially if this takes a political form and involves widespread public disorder. In this crucial area, above all, the capacity for a massive expansion of state power with little or no possibility of democratic control is evident. In periods of crisis, the framework of law is seen by the state less as a set of rights to be guaranteed than as a series of limitations on its ability to maintain security. Under these circumstances, civil liberties and legal guarantees may be subject to widespread violation or suspension.

Further Reading

General

Fitzgerald, M., McLennan, G. and Pawson, J. (eds.) (1981) *Crime and Society*, Routledge and Kegan Paul
Hain, P. (1985) *Political Trials in Britain*, Penguin

9.1

Collins, H. (1982) *Marxism and Law*, Oxford University Press

Fine, B. (1984) *Democracy and the Rule of Law*, Pluto
Jessop, B. (1980) 'On Recent Marxist Theories of Law, the State, and Juridico-Political Ideology', *International Journal of the Sociology of Law*, no. 8

9.2

Harding, A. (1966) *A Social History of the English Law*, Penguin
Thompson, E. P. (1977) *Whigs and Hunters*, Penguin

9.3

Hewitt, O. (1982) *The Abuse of Power*, Martin Robertson
Nairn, T. (1981) *The Break-up of Britain*, 2nd edn, Verso
Poggi, G. (1978) *The Development of the Modern State*, Hutchinson

9.4

Ackroyd, C., Margolis, K., Rosenhead, J. and Shallice, T. (1980) *The Technology of Political Control*, new edn, Pluto
Bunyan, T. (1978) *The History and Practice of the Political Police in Britain*, Quartet
Cowell, D., Jones, T. and Young, J. (eds.) (1982) *Policing the Riots*, Junction

9.5

Lea, J. and Young, J. (1984) *What is to be done about Law and Order*, Penguin

9.6

Box, S. (1983) *Power, Crime and Mystification*, Tavistock
Fitzgerald, M. and Sim, J. (1982) *British Prisons*, 2nd edn, Basil Blackwell
Gordon, P. (1983) *White Law*, Pluto
Ignatieff, M. (1978) *A Just Measure of Pain*, Macmillan
Roshier, B. and Teff, H. (1980) *Law and Society in England*, Tavistock
Zander, M. (1976) *Inequalities Before the Law*, D302, Unit 14, Open University Press

9.7

Griffith, J. A. G. (1981) *The Politics of the Judiciary*, 2nd edn, Fontana, chs. 3–7
Sachs, A. and Wilson, J. H. (1978) *Sexism and the Law*, Martin Robertson

10 FOREIGN AND DEFENCE POLICIES

10.1 Capitalism and Foreign Relations

This chapter is concerned with the foreign and defence policies of the British state. The simple model of the CMP makes little direct reference to external relations, except in so far as the state is partly defined by its ability to maintain political control over a given territory and population against the threat posed by other states. However, a consideration of the historical development of the capitalist state indicates the importance of external relations. A major part in the process of the formation of European nation-states was played by the centralisation of the control of armed forces and the growth of the administrative framework required to finance their existence. The process of democratisation was also associated with the expansion of military participation and the growth of nationalism. Relations between states therefore are a major determinant of the character of a society, the state apparatus and public policy. The external policies of states are also influenced by the level of development of productive forces, which determines the potential power of a state.

The major body of Marxist writing on the relations between capitalist states grew out of the analysis of imperialist rivalries between states at a roughly equal level of development, and of the relationships between capitalist states and more backward territories. The Marxist analysis of the relations of advanced capitalist states was a critique of the view of the 'liberal world order', which saw the free movement of capital and goods as leading to an efficient allocation of resources, economic growth and peaceful ties between nations. The Marxist view suggests that the operation of the law of value results in a pursuit of economic advantage through *any* means available. In the early stages of the CMP, colonialism develops as states use military power to monopolise foreign markets in colonies. With further development, large-scale exports of capital as well as goods take place. Classically, imperialism involves the seizure of foreign territories in order to provide outlets for investment, to secure access to markets and raw materials, and to deny them to foreign competitors. The regular resort to military force and the growth of military capacity reinforces the likelihood of direct conflict between the imperialist powers. As further accumulation becomes increasingly linked to the successful exercise of state power, numbers of states undertake aggressive foreign policies. Warfare restructures the relative position of states within the state system and may be sought as a means of establishing a dominant position within it.

Marxism views imperialism and militarism as normal tendencies in the international capitalist system. Militarism refers to the readiness to use force in international relations and may also involve a strong domestic military influence and high levels of military expenditure. Imperialism refers to the use of state power to expand accumulation through improving the prospects of domestic capital operating abroad. The form and the intensity of these tendencies, however, varies from one state to another, due to historical factors, such as a tradition of foreign conquest; geographical factors, such as the existence of secure frontiers; demographic factors affecting population resources; and the nature of major barriers to accumulation, such as the non-availability of crucial natural resources and 'expensive' labour power. Additionally, uneven development will lead to shifts in the distribution of military and economic power, as the geographical location of the most rapid accumulation of capital changes. Both militarism and imperialism have a significant domestic impact. They may directly affect the CMP both by increasing the opportunities for favourable accumulation abroad and by imposing costs on domestic capital in order to finance the necessary military and diplomatic resources. They affect consciousness and class relations through the ideological impact of nationalism. Finally, they affect state policy in general through the priority given to external policy.

Classical Marxism assumed that the introduction of capitalist relations of production in the backward territories would form the eventual basis for the development of capitalism on a world scale. Modern theories of imperialism, in contrast, have usually argued that in countries subject to colonialism and imperialism, the CMP has encountered substantial barriers to its development.

Participation in the global struggle against the political opposition to capitalism has become, in the present century, a major feature of the external policy of the capitalist states, which has influenced relations between the advanced capitalist states themselves and their relations with relatively backward territories. The use of armed force against revolutionary and independence movements was an established feature of imperialism from the mid-nineteenth century. Since that time, the normal tendency of the imperialist states has been to subject revolutionary movements everywhere to direct or proxy intervention. As a result, modern imperialism above all cannot be understood simply as a consequence of state support for the economic interests of capital, narrowly defined. It is also an attempt to arrest the historical transition to socialism. The establishment of a system of socialist states—no matter how great the divisions within it — and the augmentation of its numbers, has posed a clear threat to the existence of world capitalism. This threat arises from restrictions on the expansion of the world market and from the reinforcement of anti-capitalist movements that the existence of socialist states makes possible. These factors, along with the growing internationalisation of capital, have helped to create the conditions for a degree of unity among the major capitalist powers. The global struggle against socialism also has major domestic implications for the capitalist powers. The 'Communist threat' has become a theme in the dominant ideology of many states and a weapon against indigenous socialist movements.

The external policies of the British state are viewed here as dominated by the attempt to establish and maintain the economic and political conditions for the continued existence of British capital. Policy is directed towards three main areas: other advanced capitalist states, relatively backward states, and socialist states. The economic, diplomatic and military aspects of external policy are primarily an attempt both to secure economic advantages for British capital and to advance the interests of global capital in the struggle with anti-capitalist states and movements. However, the balance of domestic and world class forces may modify the extent to which external policy is guided solely by these objectives. The treatment of external policy in the remainder of this chapter begins in section 10.2, with an account of the period up until 1945. This is followed in section 10.3 by a discussion of the post-war world and Britain's position within it. Policy relating to the armed forces is examined in section 10.4. Finally, the impact of external policy on the workings of British capitalism is discussed in section 10.5.

10.2 Industrial Capitalism and the Development of External Policy until 1945

By 1750, at the start of the era of industrial capitalism, external policy and the domestic accumulation of capital were closely linked. At this time Britain was a major maritime power with numerous colonial possessions, which were the basis for extensive foreign trade. Substantial economic benefits had accrued from the trade in goods and slaves, and from the plundering of the resources of the colonies. Foreign and defence policy were strongly orientated towards an increase in trade and colonial possessions. Various Navigation Acts since the seventeenth century had prevented colonies from producing goods that would compete with British manufactures. The same legislation also required that only British ships could be used for trading purposes. The dominant mercantilist economic theory supported the removal of internal barriers to trade, emphasised the economic role of war and conquest, and sought to encourage exports. The land-owning upper class was commercially oriented and capitalist relations of production were strongly established in agriculture, commerce and manufacture. This same class also had close links with colonial trade and with the financial services largely associated with it which were developing in the City of London. The growth of the leading sector of industrial capitalist development — cotton textiles — also depended heavily on exports to the colonies in the latter part of the eighteenth century.

The employment of military force formed a major aspect of state policy as Britain faced the challenge of revolutionary nationalism. The unsuccessful attempt to retain the American colonies which culminated in the establishment of the USA in 1776, was followed by the Napoleonic war. At the end of this war in 1815, after two decades of land and naval conflict, Britain was established as the major world military power. This military primacy corresponded with the growing dominance of British capitalism.

Throughout the nineteenth century the main thrust of policy on international economic relations was based on expanding the world market. In colonised territories, commodity production was encouraged. Weak foreign governments were also persuaded to open their economies to British imports by force. These policies were normally justified by reference to 'free trade'. Naval power was used to protect trade routes, to project military power abroad and for the defence of the British Isles. The main role of the regular army was the acquisition and defence of overseas possessions. During the period 1815–1914, the army, with the sole exception of the Crimean War, was not involved in European conflicts. It was, however, involved in numerous colonial campaigns, annexations, punitive expeditions and suppressions of uprisings. It was also used to defend overseas naval bases, and to enforce law and order in overseas possessions.

The organisation of the army was strongly influenced by its colonial role. Its continued success kept pressure for change to a minimum. Until the reforms of 1870–1, both commissions and promotion were open to purchase at fixed and high rates, and up to three-quarters of promotions were obtained this way. The officer corps was and remained dominated by members of the landed gentry and aristocracy. Military operations continued to be conducted according to traditional methods. Little effective co-ordination and integration of forces existed above regimental level, officer training was rudimentary, and little military planning took place. It was only in the Scientific Corps, which comprised the Engineers and the Artillery, that effective training and a prohibition on the purchase of commissions and promotion existed. The Engineers, in particular, played a major role in creating the colonial infrastructure, especially by building railways, that was necessary for economic penetration and political control in large overseas possessions.

Throughout the nineteenth century the armed forces also played a domestic role. During periods of social unrest, troops would be stationed in affected areas. Serving officers also played an important part in the operation of the central state apparatus. By the end of the century, some 10 per cent of MPs were officers. Military organisations also formed a model for large-scale industrial organisation, especially in the railways, where the organisation was based on that used in the Royal Navy.

In the second half of the nineteenth century, the nature of warfare changed substantially in the conflicts that broke out around the consolidation of the nation-states of the emerging capitalist powers. Technical developments in the means of destruction increased accuracy, firepower and the scale of warfare. The battles of the American Civil War (1861–5) demonstrated the importance of the level of development of productive forces as the basis of military strength, while the Franco-Prussian War (1870–1) demonstrated the military effectiveness of a general staff planning the mobilisation of troops on a hitherto unknown scale, based on the use of rail transport.

In the last two decades of the nineteenth century, the dominant position of British imperialism came under challenge from Belgium, the Netherlands, France and Germany, as much of Africa was subject to intensified imperialist penetration. During this period British military expenditure increased rapidly. Between 1870 and 1910, expenditure on the army doubled, while on the navy it quadrupled, largely due to a substantial battleship-building programme. The scale of British armed external intervention also increased due to the Boer War (1899–1902). Despite the presence of 300,000 British troops, poor organisation and archaic equipment and tactics led to severe reverses and eventually to a substantial reappraisal and reorganisation of British military capacity.

In the first decades of the twentieth century, the combination of imperialist rivalry, increasing military capacity and the growth of nationalism — which was exploited by ruling classes in many states as a means of integrating the proletariat — created the conditions which led to the First World War. This war, in which all the leading capitalist powers of the time participated, was a conflict of unprecedented scope and intensity. It had a major impact on the economic, social and political organisation of the countries involved and on the international system.

The effects of the war on the external policy of the British state arose from changes in the international system and from changes in ideology and class relations in Britain. First, Britain's economic position suffered a relative decline, due to the increased economic strength of Britain's competitors, and the liquidation of overseas assets. Second, the war accelerated the growth of nationalism in the foreign possessions. This increased the difficulty of retaining control of the more backward parts of the empire, and accelerated the trend towards self government in the Dominions. Third, the war led to a sharing out of the foreign possessions of the defeated powers through the 'Mandate' system, under which Britain gained control of Palestine, Tanganyika and South West Africa. Fourth, the outbreak of revolution in Russia and parts of Europe from 1917 led to concerted action by the victorious powers to contain and destroy these movements where possible by armed force, as in the intervention by Britain and thirteen other nations, on the side of the 'Whites', in the Russian Civil War. In the long term, the reaction to the threat of socialism was a factor in the growth of fascism and militarism in Italy, Germany and Japan, which came to pose new threats to Britain and its empire. Finally, revulsion at the scale of death and destruction caused by the war led in some nations to increased opposition to the use of force and to an attempt to create a supranational authority in the form of the League of Nations.

The main internal political effect of the war was to strengthen the position of labour as a result of the growth of trade unionism, the extension of the franchise (from 7 million to 20 million electors in 1918), and the growth of radicalism in the conditions of dislocation produced by the war and the demobilisation. This moderated the extent to which force could be used for imperialist purposes and as a means of opposing foreign anti-capitalist movements. In the period following the First World War, Britain continued to pursue traditional free-trade policies and returned to the gold standard in 1925. The demobilisation of the armed forces (around 6 million people) was undertaken, and defence expenditure fell from £766 million in 1919 to £102 million in 1932. These cuts reflected the prevailing policy on state expenditure and the assumption that no European war was likely. As a result, the army returned to its traditional imperial role. Major changes in weaponry had taken place and war was becoming more capital-intensive, thus the importance of economic strength as a basis for military power was further increased.

External policies in the 1930s in the UK began to shift in response to the domestic economic crisis and the increasing military threat abroad. A system of tariffs favouring the empire was introduced in 1932. During the mid-1930s, the use of force by Germany, Italy and Japan posed a threat both to European peace and to British overseas possessions. The foreign intervention in the Spanish Civil War reaffirmed the internationalisation of the struggle against socialism. In these circumstances, Britain adopted a policy of 'appeasement', which aimed to prevent European war, at the same time as rearming. Defence expenditure was increased substantially from 1935, conscription was introduced in 1938, and extensive plans were made for war.

The Second World War began in 1939 as a European conflict, although hostilities became worldwide following the involvement of the USSR from June 1941, and the US and Japan from December 1941. This war resulted from an increase in imperialist rivalries in conditions of economic crises, together with a growth of intense militarism in the forms of 'exceptional' state in the fascist powers. This was combined with an attempt to destroy the international socialist movement in general, and the Soviet state in particular. By the time of the victory of the Allied powers in 1945, a thorough restructuring of the world state system had taken place. The position of the US amongst the capitalist powers was for the moment unchallenged, while the USSR at enormous cost had defeated Germany and become the dominant influence over the states of Eastern Europe, in which it sought to establish its form of socialism. Britain ended the war with troops stationed around the world, a large empire in which war had again accelerated the formation of nationalist movements, and huge debts to the US, largely as a result of the provision of war materials by the US through the 'lend-lease' system.

During the twentieth century the key features of Britain's external relations were the central role played in imperialist rivalries; the involvement in two world wars, which themselves reflected the uneven development of world capitalism, and the militarist degeneration or failure of capitalist democracy in some of the new capitalist states; participation in the struggle against nationalist and anti-capitalist movements on a worldwide scale; and the continued support for a liberal world economic order, except in exceptional conditions. Throughout, policy was primarily directed to secure the strength and security of British capital, its continued external penetration, and the maintenance of foreign trading relations and investment outlets. Even in 1945, there was still a strong imperialist influence on foreign policy, despite the growing relative weakness of British industrial capital, which the war had only intensified.

10.3 External Policy in the Post-War Period

This section of the chapter first examines the pattern of the development in the world system, considering relations between leading capitalist states, between the capitalist states and the socialist states, and between the capitalist states and the emergent nations. Second, British external policy with regard to these three sets of relations is discussed.

10.3.1 The Post-War World System

At the end of the Second World War, under the 1944 Bretton Woods agreement, the US sponsored a liberal world trading order based on the removal of barriers to the free movement of trade and capital, underpinned by a system of fixed exchange rates with the dollar as the basis of the system of international payments. In 1945, the International Monetary Fund (IMF) was established to regulate exchange rates and to prevent balance of payments crises in member countries from destabilising the international monetary system. The General Agreement on Tariffs and Trade (GATT) was established in 1947, in an attempt to liberalise trade. The US was also closely involved in the economic and political reconstruction of the capitalist powers through the 'Marshall Aid' plan (officially called the European Recovery Program), through which grants totalling $17 billion were given to the participating nations. In France and Italy, these were made conditional on the non-participation of Communist parties in government. The US was also directly involved as an occupying power in the consolidation of capitalism and parliamentary democracy in Japan and the western-occupied zones of Germany.

During the 'long boom', the volume of trade and capital movements between the capitalist powers grew rapidly. However, the process of development was uneven. Accumulation in Japan, and to a lesser extent in mainland Western Europe, proceeded more rapidly than in the US or the UK. The end of the long boom, the oil crisis, the increased instability of the international monetary system as exchange rates shifted due to the changing balance of economic strength amongst the established capitalist powers, the emergence of new centres of capitalist growth in South-East Asia and South America, and the increasing political and economic cohesion of the EEC, all weakened the willingness of the other capitalist powers to accept US leadership.

Throughout the post-war period, relations between the capitalist and socialist nations have formed a major element in the international system. During the war, a considerable degree of co-operation developed amongst the Allied powers. The formation of the United Nations, in 1945, constituted an attempt to guarantee a world order for the post-war period. Within the UN, the major victorious powers — Britain, the US and the USSR — were given a special place with permanent seats on the Security Council. The Yalta and Potsdam conferences of 1945 designated 'spheres of influence', in which each side was free to install 'friendly' regimes. However, this *rapprochement* between the US and the USSR soon broke down and led to an era of permanent conflict, based in the West on resistance to the 'Soviet threat'. This involved a restriction of economic links with the socialist bloc, and an attempt at military encirclement through a worldwide system of US-sponsored military alliances.

The relative military balance between the two sides has changed over the post-war period. During the early post-war years, the US enjoyed a monopoly of nuclear weapons and the USSR did not develop a credible nuclear capability until the late 1950s. Since that time the USSR has sought parity with the US. Throughout the period, the US has also possessed a worldwide capacity for military intervention based on naval power, mobile land forces and foreign bases. During the 1970s, the USSR developed a worldwide naval capacity, though it lacks the permanent foreign bases necessary for widespread overseas deployment of troops. Direct armed intervention by the USSR, until the incursion into Afghanistan in 1979, had been restricted to Eastern Europe. Throughout the period, an arms race involving the development of nuclear weapons has taken place, with almost every significant advance in weapons technology, except in rocketry, being initiated by the US.

Direct armed conflict between the US and the USSR has been avoided, although the US has sometimes threatened to initiate a nuclear exchange, most notably during the Cuba crisis of 1962. The reciprocal deterrent threat of nuclear weapons clearly acts as an inhibition on their use, although this is periodically undermined by technological developments which appear to offer an opportunity of successfully destroying the adversary's forces before the opponent's weapons can be used. Within the framework provided by this continued armed confrontation, the degree of co-operation between the two sides has varied with phases of intense hostility alternating with phases of relaxation or 'thaw'. The latter have been associated with the agreements on arms control such as the 1962 partial test ban treaty and SALT 1 and SALT 2. The nature of the conflict between the capitalist and socialist nations has altered in recent years as a result of the weakening of American dominance over the other capitalist powers, the developing military balance between East and West, and the growth of economic links between the capitalist and socialist nations. West Germany, in particular, especially during the periods of Social Democratic government, has pursued a more relaxed policy.

The relations between the capitalist powers and the emerging nations have altered substantially over the post-war period. The colonial possessions of the European powers, with few exceptions, have achieved political independence. The process of decolonisation resulted from the growing cost of maintaining control and from the lack of US support for European imperialism. The US has been more concerned to encourage pro-capitalist regimes in the new states in order to speed their integration into the world capitalist economy. It has thus tended to support intervention against left-wing nationalist movements, but not the maintenance of colonial possessions *per se*. It has intervened throughout Latin America, the Middle East, and in the new nations of Africa and Asia in support of pro-capitalist forces in accordance with the 'Truman doctrine' of 1947 which stated that the US would intervene anywhere in the world where its vital interests were threatened. The US has also reinforced sympathetic states with military aid. This militarisation of the new states has contributed to a number of regional wars and military coups. It has also led to nuclear proliferation, on the basis of technology exported by advanced capitalist states. Some pro-capitalist states such as Israel and South Africa have been given military support in order to enhance their regional role in the struggle against socialism.

Developments in the new nations have posed a major threat to the capitalist world system. Anti-capitalist regimes have been established as a result of the Chinese revolution in 1949, the Cuban revolution in 1959, the reunification of Vietnam in 1975, and the defeat of Portuguese imperialism in Angola and Mozambique in 1975. The conflict between capitalism and socialism has, however, become fragmented, due to the Sino-Soviet split and the development of armed conflict between socialist states.

About one third of the flow of foreign capital into the emergent nations consists of aid. This can be 'bilateral', where one country provides aid to another, or 'multilateral', where some agency such as the IMF or the World Bank dispenses aid on behalf of a number of donors. Aid has a political and strategic role. The US, for example, concentrates aid on Latin America, on nations bordering the Soviet Union, and on states performing a regional 'sub-imperial' role. Aid may involve grants, technical assistance or military aid, although most aid consists of loans tied to particular projects with economic or political conditions attached to its receipt. IMF stand-by credits, for example, are normally conditional on the pursuit of monetarist policies. There is little evidence that aid is of great benefit to recipient states. Aid may lead to an unbalanced pattern of develop-ment, to technological dependence, to massive outflows of capital, and to crippling debt repayments. Its main general function is to increase the political and economic integration of the emergent states into the world capitalist system and to benefit capital in the donor state.

The uneven pace of capital accumulation in the emerging nations has produced further destabilisation of the world capitalist system. Many new states have been unable to break out of the colonial trade patterns based on exports of primary products, due to barriers to the import of manufactured goods from many of the emergent states by the use of tariffs, quotas, foreign exchange restrictions, licences and anti-dumping regulations, as well as to slow domestic accumulation. The emergent states have therefore often encouraged foreign investment to overcome these barriers, which has resulted in increased economic and technological dependence, the destruction of local industries, and capital export in the form of the repatriated profits of multinational corporations. The resultant barriers to further accumulation create the conditions for labour-repressive regimes and encourage the growth of anti-capitalist movements. Except for a minority of new states such as Taiwan, Singapore and South Korea, integration into the world capitalist market has not proved a route to rapid capital accumulation. Where industrial development has taken place, it has been largely for export markets as part of the new international division of labour under high rates of exploitation.

The overall development of the world system has increased the likelihood of violent conflict. The emergence of new centres of accumulation challenging the dominance of the established capitalist powers, growing conflict over access to resources, the appearance of revolutionary movements in those new states where substantial barriers to development exist, the increased ability of the socialist states to render aid to revolutionary movements, and the continuous worldwide growth in the capacity to deploy armed force all point to a high level of open conflict and to substantial and unpredictable shifts in the international system.

10.3.2 British Policy in the Post-War World System

Throughout the post-war era, Britain has sought to maintain a harmonious relationship with the other capitalist powers through participation in the liberal world order. External economic policies were strongly influenced by the cancellation of lend-lease at the end of the war in Europe, followed by the offer of American loans of $3,750 million, on condition of the re-establishment of a sterling exchange rate at the pre-war level of £1 = $4, along with free convertability of sterling. Britain was also required to accept, within a week, the 1944 Bretton Woods agreement establishing the IMF and the World Bank. Despite Britain's weakness and dependence, the City retained a world role in the system of international payments through the maintenance of the 'sterling area', though at considerable cost to domestic British capital, as a result of periodic reductions in domestic expansion due to exchange rate and balance of payments crises.

In the early part of the post-war period, external economic policies were directed towards the re-establishment and expansion of links with the empire/Commonwealth. This was also a source of migrant labour in the period of low unemployment in the 1950s. The effect was to keep the general level of wages down by increasing the supply of labour. In addition, this labour was obtained without state expenditure on reproduction, since the migrant workers were brought up and educated abroad. However, as unemployment increased in the 1960s, the entry of Commonwealth immigrants was progressively restricted. Commonwealth immigration is now severely restricted, although a few occupations such as medicine and nursing still recruit large numbers of Commonwealth workers, normally to the cost of the sender states, who lose the services of scarce trained staff (see section 4.4).

Britain did not participate in the early stages of the establishment of the EEC, preferring to retain links based on the traditional outlets for British capital, and cheap sources of food, in the colonies. However, a first application for EEC membership was made in 1961, though this was not achieved until 1973. The need to share in the rapid post-war expansion of the economies of continental Western Europe, the growth of trading and investment links, and the desire to substitute European influence for the collapsing imperial role were important factors in the decision to join.

The basic organisational principles of the EEC rest on support for private capital. The EEC, through its policy of freeing internal trade and capital movements, and through the development of common policies towards agriculture, industry and energy, is designed to restructure European industrial capital in order to improve its competitiveness, while retaining a measure of protection through the common external tariff. Agriculture is protected through the Common Agricultural Policy (CAP). However, British industrial capital is uncompetitive compared to most of that in the other EEC nations, and the intensification of competition and the outflow of capital produced by membership have accelerated the relative economic decline of the UK.

In recent years, there have been attempts to broaden the scope of the activities of the EEC. The Regional Fund, which provides aid to peripheral regions, has been given more emphasis, although the CAP still accounts for around 70 per cent of the EEC budget. In addition, moves have been made in the direction of greater political unity through 'direct elections' for the European Parliament. However, their main function is legitimation, and effective power still resides in the European Commission in partnership with the Council of Ministers. Some attempts have been made to co-ordinate foreign policy, and the foreign ministers of the EEC member states have on occasions issued joint statements on policy issues. It would be wrong, however, to conclude that 'Europe' is moving away from dependence on the US; if anything, the interpenetration of European and American capital is increasing, and political pressure for 'Western' unity in the face of the present economic crisis remains a strong influence on EEC member states.

The post-war period has seen a high degree of political unity amongst the capitalist powers based on opposition to socialism and to the socialist states. The UK has given strong support to this. It assisted in the restoration of capitalist relations of production in the occupied zone of Germany after the war. It also intervened with armed force on the anti-Communist side in the Greek civil war. In the crises of the early cold war period, including the Berlin blockade of 1948–9, the UK joined concerted action by the capitalist powers. It participated in the formation of NATO (North Atlantic Treaty Organisation) in 1949, along with the major nations of Western Europe, apart from Germany and Italy. The UK also sent troops to fight in Korea in 1950, in the American-controlled intervention undertaken under UN auspices. The decision to join the intervention in Korea was taken by the Labour government, which cut its social programme to finance the increase in military expenditure required by the war.

The general policy pursued by the Labour government in the period 1945–51 was to secure an American military commitment to the defence of the capitalist powers of Western Europe, and support for US policy has subsequently been designed in part to reinforce this. It has involved acquiescence in American domination of NATO, the extensive provision of military bases for American forces in the UK, and British participation in the 'containment' of the socialist states through a worldwide system of military bases and alliances, such as the South-East Asia Treaty Organisation

(SEATO), established in 1954, and the Central Treaty Organisation (CENTO), established in 1955. Britain also supported the rearmament of West Germany, and the invitation to Germany and Italy to seek membership of NATO, which precipitated the foundation of the Warsaw Treaty Organisation (WTO) in 1955, nine days after West German membership of NATO was accepted. Britain has also supported American policy on diplomatic relations with the socialist bloc, on economic relations and on arms control, and has failed to develop significant independent initiatives in any of these areas.

Relations with the emergent nations have been conducted in a more independent fashion, as a result of the existence of imperial possessions. Immediately following the war, Britain attempted to retrieve possessions in South-East Asia, which had been overrun by the Japanese, and to reinstate its presence in the Middle East, North Africa and the Mediterranean. The 1945–51 Labour government ceded independence to India and Burma and withdrew from Palestine, which had been a 'mandated' British territory. However, numerous territories in Africa, the Middle East, South-East Asia and the Caribbean were retained. These territories were involved in trade links and they provided an outlet for British capital. They were also a source of foreign exchange business for the City, since their trade and capital balances were denominated in sterling, through membership of the sterling area.

During the 1950s, it was becoming clear that the retention of colonial possessions would involve growing costs and would lead to the radicalisation of independence movements. In addition, the US supported decolonisation to break the economic links of the European imperial powers with 'their' colonies, and to provide new outlets for American capital and commodity exports. British policy shifted to a concern for the emergence of 'friendly', 'pro-Western' governments in the newly-independent states. This involved, first, vigorous opposition to those independence movements with anti-capitalist objectives, as in the Malayan 'emergency' and the opposition to Mau Mau in Kenya, and secondly, from 1957 the granting of independence where nationalist movements were pro-Western. Although the peak period of decolonisation was the decade after 1957, the process is not yet complete. The last African colony to gain independence was Zimbabwe, where full independence with majority rule was obtained in 1980, after a long civil war. Remaining colonial possessions include Hong Kong (until 1996), Gibraltar, St

Helena, Ascension Island and the Falklands/Malvinas.

The British Commonwealth has expanded, as most of the ex-colonies have joined it, and its conferences are a forum for the discussion of political, economic and cultural issues. In common with the other former colonial powers, Britain maintains a number of bilateral agreements with ex-colonies on economic and military matters. Aid policies are mainly directed towards the Commonwealth, which receives 80 per cent of the funds distributed. Aid favours countries that purchase substantial British exports or that provide Britain with important raw materials.

Overall, British external policy in the post-war period can be seen as an attempt to adjust the pursuit of the goal of the maintenance of British capitalism within the world capitalist system, to the contingencies arising from changes in the international environment. However, the unresolved dilemma between the great power tradition and a realistic adjustment to economic decline has continued to influence external policy as a whole. This can be seen particularly clearly in defence policy, which is examined in the following section.

10.4 Post-War Armed Forces Policy

Defence policy involves the provision of armed forces and their use in inter-state relations. In the post-war period, changes in the world system, in Britain's location within it, and in the nature of warfare have influenced the form of perceived external threats and the military forces deployed to meet them. The overall changes in policy can be seen in relation to the three spheres of external policy. Relations with the other capitalist states have been pacific and Britain has sought military alliances with them. The socialist states, on the other hand, have been viewed as hostile and military forces have been deployed against them. As a result of decolonisation, the capacity for military intervention in the emergent states has been substantially reduced. In complete contrast to the pre-war period, Britain now maintains a major commitment to a military alliance, NATO, and a substantial European military presence. At the same time, however, the present day armed forces retain many of the organisational forms and practices developed during the imperial era. This is reflected in the scale of Britain's military establishment and the retention of an independent nuclear capability.

This section of the chapter is arranged as follows. Membership of NATO is dealt with in the following subsection. This is followed in subsection 10.4.2 by an account of the independent deterrent, and other functions of the armed forces are discussed in subsection 10.4.3. The structure of the services is outlined in subsection 10.4.4, and is followed, in subsection 10.4.5, by an account of the making of armed forces policy.

10.4.1 Membership of NATO

The dominant feature of post-war defence policy has been commitment to NATO. Although NATO has a federal structure and is controlled by the North Atlantic Council, on which all members are equally represented, its operation is dominated by the US. The supreme commander is always an American, though Britain's leading role behind America is symbolised by British access to major command posts. Within NATO, strategic doctrines and shifts in alliance policy are normally determined by the US. The total forces available to NATO number approximately 3 million troops, and include both a conventional and a nuclear capability. Although the US dominates the alliance, it only provides 11 per cent of ground troops, 20 per cent of seapower and 25 per cent of tactical airpower. Within NATO, Britain's role consists of the maintenance of the 55,000 troops of the British Army of the Rhine (BAOR), the deployment of naval forces in the English Channel and the North Atlantic, and the provision of bases in Britain for other, usually American, NATO forces.

NATO strategy has always depended on the possession of nuclear weapons. The European capitalist powers have generally supported the expansion of the NATO nuclear arsenal as a means of 'coupling' the defence of capitalist Europe with that of the US, particularly through the deployment of low-yield, 'tactical' or 'battlefield' nuclear weapons, which have been introduced in large numbers since the mid-1950s. NATO's plans in the event of a European war with the Warsaw Treaty Organisation (WTO) are based on the questionable assumption of WTO's superiority in conventional weapons and the willingness to engage in the 'first-use' of nuclear weapons.

NATO's nuclear weapons are also designed to deter nuclear attack. The precise uses which it proposes for them in terms of targeting policy and the levels of retaliation planned for particular kinds of threat or attack are kept secret. Officially, NATO nuclear strategy was first based on a 'counter-city' strategy, involving the threat of massive retaliation and mutual assured destruction (MAD). In the 1960s, this doctrine was replaced by 'flexible response', in which the object was to deter war by acquiring the capacity to fight and win a nuclear conflict. More recently, the official doctrine has been based on the capacity to retain sufficient 'second-strike' destructive power to destroy the other side, even after it had launched a surprise 'first strike'. However, in these circumstances, the possession of super-accurate weapons to wipe out the opponent's missiles ('counter-force'), would be irrelevant, since they would already have been launched. This has given rise to the view that accurate nuclear weapons could be used themselves for a 'first strike' and that their possession makes this, as well as a pre-emptive strike against them, a dangerous possibility. The deployment by NATO of ground-launched, radar-invisible Cruise missiles and Pershing ballistic missiles in Europe adds to this possibility.

Given the enormous nuclear arsenals on both sides, and thus the problematic success of any attempted first strike, as well as the stated attachment of the USSR to a policy of massive retaliation to any nuclear attack, the strength of deterrence remains high, though it is vulnerable to destabilisation. Particularly dangerous would be the development of the capacity to launch an effective surprise attack against presently invulnerable weapons such as submarine-launched ballistic missiles. The US has plans to seek to acquire this capacity, and to protect itself from nuclear retaliation through the development of a satellite-based anti-missile system ('Star Wars').

In recent years, NATO's policy has become a subject of political controversy throughout Europe. This began in 1977, as a result of the proposal to deploy the enhanced radiation 'neutron' bomb for use against a possible large-scale attack by conventional armoured forces. The radiation would kill the tank crews, whilst producing less blast-damage than normal nuclear weapons. Opposition to it took place on the grounds that its characteristics seemed designed more to make its use acceptable than to deter attack. More recently, the decision taken in 1979 to 'modernise' NATO's 'theatre' nuclear forces by the deployment of Cruise and Pershing missiles in late 1983 has led to widespread political opposition from some member states and from the peace movement. Some states, and in particular West Germany, were eager for the introduction of these weapons as a further means of 'coupling' the US to Europe. However, their possible destabilising effect on the European nuclear balance, their damaging effect on arms-control negotiations, and the problematic issue of who was to control the decision to fire the weapons have resulted in considerable opposition to NATO's current nuclear strategy.

10.4.2 The Independent Deterrent

Britain possesses an independent nuclear force which has been assigned to NATO since 1963, although it is under British control and can be used 'independently'. Since its inception, its existence has played a key role in defence policy. Britain's involvement in nuclear weapons began with its participation in the Manhattan project, which produced the bombs dropped on Japan in 1945. Anglo-American nuclear co-operation was terminated at the end of the Second World War and Britain proceeded independently with the development of nuclear weapons, following a decision made in secret by Attlee and a few close associates in 1947. The first British atomic bomb was exploded in 1952 and the first British hydrogen bomb in 1957.

The existence of a nuclear force was a factor in the run-down of conventional forces in the late 1950s. Britain's strategic deterrent initially consisted of the V-bomber force of 180 aircraft. However, its growing vulnerability led eventually to dependence on US technology. Britain was able to retain a strategic nuclear capacity only through the purchase of the Polaris submarine system under the Nassau agreement of 1962. Since their deployment from 1969, this force of four submarines has remained the mainstay of the strategic nuclear deterrent. Although the missiles and their guidance systems were provided by the US, the hulls and the warheads were produced in Britain. In the 1970s, as a result of secret decisions taken by both Labour and Conservative governments, the 'Chevaline' programme was undertaken to fit a system of multiple warheads, some dummies, to the Polaris missiles.

At present, the future of the strategic deterrent is in doubt. The Conservative government is committed to replacing Polaris with the Trident system. Trident, however, involves an increase in dependence on the US, since not only the missiles and their guidance systems, but also targeting and communications will depend on access to American resources. Trident involves an eightfold increase in the firepower of Britain's strategic nuclear arsenal. It will also be extremely expensive, possibly reaching a total cost of about £12,000 million. The long-standing post-war consensus on the strategic nuclear force is also in jeopardy, since neither the Labour Party, nor the Liberal-SDP alliance are in favour of Trident. In addition, the Labour Party is currently opposed to Cruise missile deployment in the UK, and indeed to all US nuclear bases in Britain. British nuclear forces are by no means restricted to the strategic deterrent. Nuclear weapons of various kinds are found in each of the three services. The RAF deploys numerous 'nuclear-capable' aircraft. The Army has tactical nuclear missiles, nuclear artillery and nuclear mines. The Navy possesses helicopters armed with nuclear depth charges for anti-submarine use.

The explicit rationale for the retention of a strategic nuclear force has been variously stated. It has been argued that its existence increases the deterrent effect of Western nuclear forces, since the USSR has to reckon with a 'second centre of decision' in calculating the effect of any military move. It has also been suggested that the forces offer an insurance against a possible breakdown of NATO and a withdrawal of the American nuclear 'umbrella', although in these circumstances, given the dependence on US technology, the forces would probably have little credibility. In reality, however, the independent deterrent reflects the great power illusions that continue to exercise an influence on external policy.

10.4.3 Other Functions of the Armed Forces

Over the post-war period, the numerous conflicts in which British forces have been involved have all taken place outside NATO. British troops have been used for policing throughout the empire, in opposition to radical nationalist movements as in Malaya, Kenya and Aden, and against separatist movements within colonial territories, as in Cyprus. British forces have also been used to assist post-colonial governments faced with internal and external threats, for example, in Belize and in some Gulf states. Britain has also acted in concert with other imperialist powers, most notably in Korea and Egypt. In the Suez operation of 1956, a concerted British-French-Israeli attack on Egypt took place in an unsuccessful attempt to reassert influence in the area. The Suez operation was a turning point in US-British relations, since the US opposed the operation and employed diplomatic and economic pressure to bring it to an end. Since that time the US has become heavily involved in the Middle East, and the British military role has been subordinated to its policy. Important recent developments have been British support

for the American 'rapid deployment force' and the British participation in the multinational 'peace-keeping force' in the Lebanon.
However, the British government did not endorse the American-led
invasion of Grenada in 1983, and the completely unfettered inter-
ventionism implied by the 'Reagan doctrine' is likely to prove
embarrassing for many allies of the US.

The most recent substantial conflict involving British forces was
the Falklands war of 1982. In response to an Argentine invasion, a task
force was despatched which landed troops on the islands and defeated
the Argentine garrison forces. Although the campaign demonstrated
a continued ability to deploy effectively substantial forces at long
range, it also highlighted the vulnerability of modern weapons
systems, as well as the consequences of the modern arms trade in up-
grading the military capacity of poorer nations. In the medium term,
due to the failure to resolve the disputed political issues of sovereignty
and political control in the Falklands/Malvinas, the British government has adopted a 'fortress Falklands' policy, involving massive
investment in defensive facilities and an expensive military garrison.

The armed forces also play an important domestic role, especially
in Northern Ireland. Since 1969, when troops were sent from the
mainland to maintain order and, it was claimed, to protect the
minority Catholic population, the use of the armed forces has been
substantial. Troops have been used in co-operation with, and
sometimes as an alternative to, the police force. They have been used
to suppress disorders, to collect intelligence and to undertake covert
operations. The Northern Ireland operation has had a major impact
on the Army. Problems have arisen over providing sufficient troops,
due to the NATO commitment, and due to the fact that the 'Irish'
regiments have not been deployed in Northern Ireland. The Army
has used Northern Ireland to try out new tactical approaches to
'counter subversion', involving new weapons, new forms of intelligence gathering, and operating in close co-ordination with police
and civil authorities. The Army has also had a major influence on
policy towards Northern Ireland. For example, it was largely due to
military advice that no attempt was made to use force to defeat the
successful loyalist general strike against the Northern Ireland
assembly in 1974.

In recent years, the domestic role of the armed forces has been
given increased prominence, in line with the increased emphasis in
military doctrine in 'combating subversion', 'low-intensity operations', and 'aid to the civil power' in the case of major industrial

disputes. The armed forces are also involved in contingency plans that envisage what is, in effect, a form of military government organised on a regional basis, in the event of nuclear war.

10.4.4 The Structure of the Armed Forces

The structure of the armed forces has undergone considerable alteration in the post-war period. There have been major changes in defence commitments, continuing increases in the costs of major weapons, substantial developments in military technology, and a major shift towards full-time 'professional' armed services.

Changes in defence commitments have paralleled Britain's transformation from a world power to a medium-range European power attempting to maintain a major role in NATO and a close attachment to US external policy. In 1957, the defence White Paper proposed that the numbers in the services should be cut, that air defence should be based on missiles rather than aircraft, and that substantial reliance should be placed on the defensive shield provided by the nuclear deterrent. In the period 1953–9, real expenditure on defence fell. Service manpower was reduced, and conscription was ended in 1962.

A major shift in policy occurred in 1966–7, in the context of the growing economic crisis. In 1965, the TSR2 aircraft project had been cancelled and in 1966 defence commitments 'East of Suez' were substantially reduced, orders for the American F-111 aircraft were cancelled, and cuts were made in the fleet, although plans to phase out and not replace the existing aircraft carriers were not carried through. Although these changes did remove some expensive commitments, rising equipment costs and the intensifying economic crisis created pressure for more cuts. The Labour government elected in 1974 at first planned to reduce defence expenditure, mainly by withdrawing from the Mediterranean, but following the 1977 NATO decision, it agreed to increase real expenditure by 3 per cent per annum, although this was not to start until 1979. In 1981, a further series of cuts was announced and, since there were few remaining imperial commitments which could be liquidated, the cuts fell heavily on the equipment programme. In particular, amidst considerable controversy, the size of the fleet and the naval dockyard capacity was to be substantially reduced, while submarines and aircraft were to be emphasised at the expense of surface ships.

The major influence on defence costs has been expenditure on equipment, which increased from 31 per cent of the defence budget in 1974 to 46 per cent in 1983. This trend to capital-intensiveness will be accelerated by the Trident programme. If this is continued and the 3 per cent per annum real increase in expenditure is maintained, whilst growth rates in the economy in the 1980s average about 1 per cent per annum, then the proportion of GDP spent on defence will rise from 4.6 per cent in 1980 to 7.2 per cent in 1990. A particularly unpredictable element in Trident costs is the development of warheads, which are likely to overrun initial cost estimates. The Chevaline warhead programme, for example, initially costed at £200 million, eventually required about £1,000 million.

The main cause of the equipment increases has been the cost of major weapons systems such as combat aircraft, warships and tanks (see Table 10.1(b)). Each weapons system consists of weapons, a mobile 'platform' on which they are carried, and a system of communications. Their development has involved the application of scientific knowledge to improve speed, range, firepower and accuracy, on the 'worst-case' assumption that any feasible technical improvement must be pursued, since an enemy could also have acquired it. However, critics have claimed that the technology has become 'baroque', i.e. over-elaborate. Investment in research to improve performance has yielded diminishing returns. Some aspects of 'improved' performance may be irrelevant. Reliability has decreased and maintenance costs have increased, while the supply of spare parts poses major logistical problems. Because of their complexity, it is difficult to train those who are to operate them.

In order to reduce the cost of defence, two methods have been used: the production of 'all-purpose' weapons systems that will perform several roles, and engagement in inter-state collaboration in weapons system development. However, multi-role weapons systems tend to be particularly over-elaborate and often fail to perform well, because they incorporate a set of contradictory performance characteristics. International collaboration, although it shares the capital costs, is wasteful, due to high assembly costs and design co-ordination problems. The effectiveness of weapons systems is also under challenge, due to the development of 'precision guided munitions' (PGMs), which have increased their vulnerability. PGMs are relatively cheap, so that they can be economically deployed in large numbers. These weapons may change the nature of conventional warfare, since fighting surface ships, and armoured land forces with air support, will no longer be as effective as before.

The pattern of organisation and control in the armed forces has not

Table 10.1:   Armed Forces in the UK: Numbers and Equipment

(a) Personnel

	Army	Navy	Air Force	Totals
Regular forces	163,100	73,100	91,700	327,900
Regular reserves	139,600	28,000	29,500	197,100
Voluntary reserves, TA, etc.	70,200	6,400	600	77,200

(b) Equipment

Army		Navy		Air Force	
Armoured vehicles		Ships		Aircraft[a]	
Heavy tanks	960	Submarines (inc. 4 Polaris)	31	Strike/attack	164
Light tanks	271	Carriers	3	Ground support	68
Armoured cars	243	Destroyers	12	Maritime patrol	28
Artillery		Frigates	44	Reconnaissance	44
155 mm	296	Patrol craft	21	Air defence	111
175 mm	31	Sweepers/ Hunters	34	Airborne early warning	6
203 mm	16			Transport (planes,	56
				helicopters)	70
Aircraft		Aircraft			
Helicopters	252	Combat planes	15	Tankers	16
		Helicopters	102	Search and Rescue (helicopters)	32

Note: [a]Excludes 105 aircraft used for training, etc.

Source: Adapted from Alternative Defence Commission, *Defence without the Bomb* (Taylor and Francis, 1983), Appendix 1; International Institute for Strategic Studies, *The Military Balance* (IISS, 1982), pp. 30–2.

been radically changed in the post-war period. The three services have retained their separate identities, and a policy of 'balanced' forces, involving the allocation of broadly equal resources to each service, has been followed, at least until 1981, when severe cuts were imposed on the Navy. The reduction in numbers of servicemen and women has particularly affected the Army, and some long-established regiments have been disbanded or merged. However, the regimental structure has been maintained and the high proportion of upper-class officer recruits into elite regiments such as the guards or hussars remains.

Both the strategic and tactical approach to conventional warfare in Europe remains within the traditional mould. A possible attack by WTO armoured forces is to be countered by the same kinds of forces, though with upgraded weapons, as were employed in the Second World War; nuclear weapons will be used by NATO, however, if the WTO advance cannot be halted. The main area of innovation has been in the internal use of armed forces as exemplified by Northern Ireland and by anti-terrorist operations in mainland Britain. There has been an increased emphasis on specialised technical skills, both in the officer corps and the ranks, in all three services, though to a lesser extent in the Army than the Navy and the RAF. The rigid, hierarchical form of organisation of the forces seems strongly resistant to change. Basic training still emphasises unquestioning subordination and employs traditional methods of habituation to command.

The decision to rely on a full-time 'professional' army was partly justified by the heavy training programme required in a conscript army, and the large numbers of inexperienced and often uncommitted personnel that this policy produces. The absence of conscripts, segregated housing, and the practice of encouraging recruitment at a very early age facilitates a high degree of separation of the armed forces from civilian life. The separateness of the military is also apparent in the reserve and auxiliary forces, which are made up entirely of former service people and volunteers. One effect of this segregation is to reduce the problems associated with the use of forces for internal purposes.

Finally, the system of military planning and control remains highly centralised, at least in part, because of the danger of decentralising authority to local commanders when tactical nuclear weapons are widely deployed. Recruitment to senior posts in the armed forces, with the partial exception of the RAF, which is more 'meritocratic', also continues to follow long-standing patterns. Most senior officers come from upper-class backgrounds, many from service families, and in the Army they have generally worked in an elite infantry or cavalry regiment, rather than pursued a scientific or technological service career.

10.4.5 The Determinants of Armed Forces Policy

The armed forces constitute one of the core institutions of the state. Their effective functioning is a precondition for the survival of the state, and the retention of control over them, in effect, is a precondition for the exercise of political power. Consequently, the ruling bloc is likely to support a strong military capability and to foster military support for the existing order. Many features of the armed forces and their operation were established prior to the advent of parliamentary democracy, at a time when upper-class interests could be directly incorporated into key aspects of their structure, including methods of appointment and promotion, the nature of military discipline, and the form and extent of political control. These aspects of structure, which continually reproduce the historic form of class control in the armed forces, are now seen as beyond controversy and even as inescapable features of any effective military force. Consequently, the armed forces are not particularly amenable to democratic political control.

An outstanding feature of armed forces' policy-making is secrecy. Secret treaties have often been used to conceal military commitments. Secrecy, due to the Official Secrets Acts and the Queen's Regulations, also restricts information on the activities of the services, members of which, at every level, are forbidden to reveal details of their work. Consequently, journalists rely on official spokespeople through the lobby system, and information is made public through 'leaks', often in an attempt to manipulate public opinion.

Another important feature of armed forces' policy-making is the role played by senior officers. Many of the senior posts in the Ministry of Defence are held by serving officers. In addition, the Chiefs of Staff have the right to demand access to the Cabinet. This right is normally exercised when Cabinet policy is viewed as threatening what the military see as their vital interests.

Defence policy is also constrained by powerful external influences. For much of the post-war period, British defence policy has been subject both to direct American influence, and to influence by NATO, as in the case of the 3 per cent real expenditure increase agreed in 1977. In addition, the integrated multinational command structure of NATO puts British forces outside the exclusive control of the British government. The existence of numerous American bases in the UK also has substantial defence implications, since attacks could be launched by the US from these bases without any control by the British government.

In the long term, the major determinants of shifts in defence policy are changes in the world system, and in Britain's position within it. The restructuring of international relations, brought about by each of the world wars, had a major impact on subsequent defence policy. In the years since 1945, the main pattern has involved attempts to adjust defence commitments and expenditure in a period when economic and military strength were in relative decline. As the economic crisis intensified in the 1960s and 1970s, a succession of defence reviews failed to provide a sustainable defence posture at stable expenditure levels. Most recently, defence expenditure has been increased, although whether this can be sustained remains to be seen.

None of the determinants of defence policy discussed so far fit the classic pluralist model of policy being made after open and informed public debate. Numerous examples exist of crucial defence decisions, especially in the area of nuclear weapons policy, being made without Cabinet knowledge, let alone parliamentary approval. Parliamentary debates on defence policy, apart from the routine approval of the estimates, are rare. The debate in January 1980 on the nuclear force was the first for fifteen years.

10.5 External Policy and British Capitalism

In this final section of the chapter, the impact of external policy on accumulation, legitimation and security is discussed. The impact of external policy on accumulation has changed fundamentally since the industrial revolution. The use of armed forces for the acquisition and control of colonial territories was closely associated with the expansion of British trade and investment, and the growth of the world market. However, although the liberal trading order sponsored by Britain initially worked to the advantage of all sections of British capital, the appearance of other industrial capitalist states exposed British manufacturing to strong competition. Although this liberal trading order partly broke down in the 1930s, it has been re-established in the post-war period. Britain's endorsement of this order has not been beneficial to British capital as a whole, although many British-based multinational companies and financial capital have benefited.

The major change in external economic policy in the post-war period has been membership of the EEC. The effect on accumulation has been generally unfavourable, as domestic industrial capital has further been weakened through increasing competition. Membership has also involved a substantial unfavourable balance in the funds paid to and received from the EEC. However, there has been an expansion of the role of the City in the Eurodollar market and in servicing European trade.

The present crisis of world capitalism has had a particularly intense impact on British domestic manufacturing capital, due to the high level of integration of the UK into the world economy through trade and capital movements. Historically, the threat to domestic industrial capital has led to opposition to the liberal trading order, for example, in the tariff reform movement in the early part of the century, the support for protectionism during the 1930s, and at present with the 'alternative economic strategy'. However, an external policy not based on an open economy has been opposed by major class fractions such as financial capital and, more recently, international capital. The absence of an effective administrative apparatus for controlling external economic relations is linked to the strength of this opposition. The diplomatic service is deficient in economic expertise. Its organisational structure arose in the diplomatic pursuit of the political objectives of a world power, rather than in the detailed supervision of economic relations. The Bank of England is opposed to restrictions on trade or on international financial operations, and although the Department of Industry has entered into agreements, sometimes with the EEC, to regulate trade in some commodities, this has not formed part of a consistent policy for the protection and expansion of domestic industry. The post-war policy of decolonisation, in contrast, has had a favourable effect on accumulation. Colonial military expenditure has been reduced, and trade and investment links with what are mostly now Commonwealth countries have been increased.

The impact of defence expenditure on accumulation is a matter of controversy. Until quite recently, Marxist analysis of defence expenditure was based on an 'under-consumptionist thesis', which viewed it as making a major contribution to employment, technological advance and economic growth. However, there are indications that growth rates are lower in those capitalist states where defence expenditure is high, probably because a substantial proportion of investment in these states goes into defence industries, which employ a disproportionate number of scientists and engineers and thus deprive other sectors of capital of their services. Although some technological spin-offs occur that benefit capital in general, most of the effort goes into 'product' rather than 'process' improvements, and the products normally do not have a civilian application. In addition, defence contractors tend to be insulated from market pressures by 'cost-plus' contracts and lack of effective competition; consequently productivity tends to be low.

The amount of employment resulting from defence expenditure is substantial. In addition to over 300,000 employed in the armed services, the Ministry of Defence (MoD) has 224,000 civilian staff. The number employed in defence industries supplying equipment for British forces has been estimated at 560,000 and, in addition, a further 140,000 are employed in the production of defence equipment for export. The value of arms exports in 1981–2 was about £1,500 million. Industries with a major stake in defence have been subject to considerable restructuring, involving either nationalisation, and a consequent reduction in capacity, or state-aided mergers. Both shipping (40 per cent to MoD) and aerospace (50 per cent to MoD) were nationalised in the 1970s, following years of state involvement.

In Britain, defence expenditure affects capital in general through its impact on the balance of payments. For much of the post-war period financial crises, linked to deficits in the balance of payments, led to policies to reduce aggregate demand, which had a strong adverse effect on much of domestic capital. Defence expenditure contributed to these crises, because of the high foreign-exchange costs of defence. These amounted to the equivalent of about two-thirds of the total balance of payments deficit in the period 1958–81. The main beneficiaries of defence expenditure are contractors, who profit at the expense of the rest of domestic capital and of labour. Defence policy has also had an impact on accumulation, through its effect on labour and generational reproduction. At times of external threat, when concern about the health and strength of possible military recruits increases, the role of women (as mothers) to men (as soldiers) is emphasised. State support for the reproductive role of families can thus indirectly aid accumulation by improving the material conditions of the family-household.

The influence of external policy on legitimation is wide-ranging. Militarism, and an emphasis on martial attributes such as strength and courage, has been an element in the definition of gender roles and a support for male domination. Military values such as obedience, hierarchy and discipline have also been portrayed as desirable features of various aspects of social organisation, such as the labour process. More broadly, the military values of order, efficiency, clear definition of objectives and the mobilisation of resources to achieve them have strongly influenced many areas of thought, such as management science and educational theory. Military imagery, at a less explicit level, is used in the great rituals of the state to renew memories of national power and imperial dominance.

External policy also affects legitimation through its impact on national identity. Mobilisation against external threat and war itself require a general willingness to subordinate personal interests to the collective good, and this has often been achieved through the creation and intensification of patriotic and nationalist sentiments. In the decades preceding the First World War, the ideological under-pinnings of imperialism penetrated widely throughout society, combining the 'civilising mission' of Britain with a belief in its military greatness. The acquisition of colonies and the subjugation of their populations provided a basis for sentiments of national superiority and racism. Rivalries between the imperialist powers, culminating in the First World War, further reinforced militarist sentiments, though the ensuing slaughter somewhat reduced their appeal. In the present century, an additional ideological 'layer' has been added to national sentiment through the struggle against socialism, particularly during the period of cold war. The external struggle against socialism has been closely linked to the domestic political offensive against the left, which has been pursued with particular vigour during periods of intense external conflict. Military success itself has a major legitimating effect. The avoidance of defeat and invasion have been powerful factors in the continued dominance of the British upper class and the survival of the state apparatus. This has been most recently exemplified by the Falklands/Malvinas war of 1982, which itself has formed the basis for new ideological motifs in the class struggle.

The significance of external policy for internal security mainly concerns the uses that can be made of the armed forces for internal purposes. These are briefly discussed in subsection 9.4.2 above. In addition, however, it is possible to envisage circumstances where membership of NATO has implications for internal security, perhaps in the case of a campaign against foreign bases and weapons in the UK, or in conditions of intense internal disorder if a British government called for assistance from NATO allies. With regard to the impact of foreign and defence policy on external security, Britain occupied a prominent position in the world order that produced ten years of world war in the first half of this century. Since the Second World War, the major capitalist powers have enjoyed a sustained period of peaceful economic competition and advance, in the course of which the growing internationalisation of capital and the process of decolonisation have reduced the opportunity and the impetus for the use of military solutions in conflicts between them. However, the end of the long boom may lead to a resurgence of economic nationalism and the re-emergence of violent inter-state rivalries.

A more immediate threat to security arises from the form taken by the relations of the capitalist and socialist powers. Although the consequences of war with an adversary armed with nuclear weapons is a powerful deterrent, its strength is being continuously under-mined by the development of weapons with a first-strike capacity. Added to this are the unavoidable dangers of war starting by accident or miscalculation. The prospects of preventing all-out war after an accidental nuclear detonation are problematic, in part because a state facing an opponent armed with first-strike weapons has an incentive to launch its own at the first indication of an attack. Given the short flight time of some 'forward-based' weapons, a 'launch-on-warning' response is likely.

The risks of nuclear war are also raised by the increasing spread of the conflict of capitalism and socialism to the emerging nations, and by the possibility of regional wars involving these states getting out of control. Indeed US threats to use nuclear weapons have all taken place in conflicts involving these countries. The growing number of nuclear-capable states adds to the risk of nuclear war. Proliferation, the miniaturisation of nuclear weapons, the possibility of nuclear weapons coming into the possession of irregular forces, and the possibility of anonymous nuclear attacks (against which there is no deterrent effect) all increase the general risks of war. Thus whether or not Britain's possession of nuclear weapons increases its security is highly open to question.

A notable feature of the existing consensus on external policy is that opinion is paralysed by a failure to face up to the dilemmas posed by the inability to reconcile the great power tradition with the economic, diplomatic and military capabilities of a weak and declining power. It is undoubtably true, however, that *any* shift away from the external economic, diplomatic and defence postures of the post-war period would involve considerable difficulties, since British policy is thoroughly enmeshed in the US-sponsored international, economic and military framework of post-war Western capitalism.

Further Reading

General

Kaldor, M. and Smith, D. (eds.) (1982) *Disarming Europe*, Merlin
New Left Review (1982) *Exterminism and the Cold War*, Verso
Shaw, M. (ed.) (1984) *War, State and Society*, Macmillan

10.1

Brewer, A. (1980) *Marxist Theories of Imperialism*, Routledge and Kegan Paul

10.2

Gamble, A. (1981) *Britain in Decline*, Macmillan
Harries-Jenkins, G. (1977) *The Army in Victorian Society*, Routledge and Kegan Paul
Hobsbawm, E. J. (1969) *Industry and Empire*, Pelican

10.3

Armstrong, P., Glyn, A. and Harrison, J. (1984) *Capitalism Since World War II*, Fontana
Halliday, F. (1983) *The Making of the Second Cold War*, Verso
Horowitz, D. (1967) *From Yalta to Vietnam*, Penguin
Spero, J. E. (1982) *The Politics of International Economic Relations*, 2nd edn, George Allen and Unwin

10.4

Alternative Defence Commission (1983) *Defence without the Bomb*, Taylor and Francis
Freedman, L. (1980) *Britain and Nuclear Weapons*, Macmillan
Ministry of Defence (1983) *Statement on the Defence Estimates*, vols. 1 and 2, Cmnd 8951, HMSO
Smith, D. (1980) *The Defence of the Realm in the '80s*, Croom Helm
Thompson, E. P. and Smith, D. (eds.) (1980) *Protest and Survive*, Penguin

10.5

Smith, D. and Smith, R. (1983) *The Economics of Militarism*, Pluto

INDEX

This index is designed to enable the reader to obtain relatively easy access to individual topics covered in the book. A guide to the location of more general topics/themes in the book can be found at the end of chapter 1, pages 14–16.

For Product Safety Concerns and Information please contact our EU
representative GPSR@taylorandfrancis.com
Taylor & Francis Verlag GmbH, Kaufingerstraße 24, 80331 München, Germany

www.ingramcontent.com/pod-product-compliance
Ingram Content Group UK Ltd.
Pitfield, Milton Keynes, MK11 3LW, UK
UKHW021831240425
457818UK00006B/160